Francis Russell

A Short History of the East India Company

Exhibiting a State of their Affairs, Abroad and at Home, Political and Commercial

Francis Russell

A Short History of the East India Company
Exhibiting a State of their Affairs, Abroad and at Home, Political and Commercial

ISBN/EAN: 9783337419820

Printed in Europe, USA, Canada, Australia, Japan

Cover: Foto ©ninafisch / pixelio.de

More available books at **www.hansebooks.com**

A

SHORT HISTORY
OF THE
EAST INDIA COMPANY:

EXHIBITING

A STATE OF THEIR AFFAIRS, ABROAD AND AT HOME,
POLITICAL AND COMMERCIAL;

The NATURE and MAGNITUDE of their COMMERCE,

AND ITS RELATIVE CONNECTION

WITH

THE GOVERNMENT AND REVENUES OF INDIA;

AND A

Difcuffion on the Queftion of Right to the Conquered Territories in India;

ALSO

Remarks on the Danger and Impolicy of Innovation,

AND THE

Practical Means of enfuring all the good Effects of a Free Trade to the
Manufacturers of Great Britain and Ireland,

BY

MATTER OF REGULATION, WITHOUT DISTURBING
THE ESTABLISHED SYSTEM.

THE SECOND EDITION, WITH SOME ADDITIONS.

TO WHICH IS ADDED,

AN ABRIDGMENT OF THE NEW ACT.

F. R.

LONDON:
PRINTED FOR JOHN SEWELL, CORNHILL, AND JOHN DEBRETT, PICCADILLY,
1793.

CONTENTS.

INTRODUCTION. — — — — p. 1

CHAPTER I.

The Origin of the Old and New Companies, with their Union. — 3

CHAPTER II.

The Origin of the 3 per Cent. Annuities transferrable at the India House, and the Funds chargeable with the Payment of them. — 7

CHAPTER III.

Of the Forts, Factories, and Territories in India, distinguishing those which are the Property of the Company by Purchase, *from those acquired by* Conquest. — — — — 9

CHAPTER IV.

Expences incurred by the Company in the Indian Conquests. — 13

CHAPTER V.

The Rights permanent and temporary of the India Company. — 15

CONTENTS.

CHAPTER VI.

How far the Appellation of a Chartered Monopoly is applicable to the East India Trade. — — — — p. 17

CHAPTER VII.

Plans formerly recommended for varying the Mode of conducting the Trade to the East Indies. — — — 20

CHAPTER VIII.

The present State of the Trade of Foreign Countries with India and China. — — — — — 21

CHAPTER IX.

The Returns of the Company's Trade anterior to their acquiring the Territories Abroad; the Effect produced by the Acquisition on their Exports and Imports; the present Amount of their Debts, and their Claims upon the Public for an Indemnification of their Expences incurred in acquiring and preserving the conquered Provinces. 23

CHAPTER X.

The Nature and Extent of the Trade of the Company to India and China, with an Account of the Shipping employed in it. 26

CHAPTER XI.

Respecting of the Profits derived by the Company from their Trade. 32

CONTENTS.

CHAPTER XII.

A concise View of the Company's Affairs in their distinct Capacities of Sovereigns and Merchants. — — — p. 35

CHAPTER XIII.

Recapitulation of the present State of our Trade with India and China, and the Rights of the East India Company. The Nature and Grounds of the various Objections expected to be made in Parliament, to the Continuation of the Trade on its present System. Reflections on the Effects of Innovation. — — 37

CHAPTER XIV.

Practical Means of securing to the Private Merchant and the Public, the ultimate Benefits of Trade within the Company's present exclusive Limits, without endangering the Chain of our political Connection with India, or materially disturbing the present System. 47

POSTSCRIPT. — — — — 51

ADDITIONAL CHAP. XV.

The Manner of obtaining Part of the Territories, and a Discussion of the Question at Law between the Crown and the Company, in relation to their respective Claims thereto. — — 53

Account of the Imports, from the East Indies and China, sold at the Company's Sales in the last Four Years, the Duties and Customs paid on the same; together with the Amount exported in each Year, and of the Drawbacks allowed on Exportation. — 73

Abridgment of the Act for settling the Government and Trade of India, and for the Appropriation of the Territorial Revenues and Profits of Trade. — — — — — 75

INTRODUCTION.

AMONGST the many superior advantages derived to the community from a Government conſtituted like that of Great Britain, the means which it affords, through the Liberty of the Preſs, for a free diſcuſſion and communication of ſentiment on every national concern, and more particularly ſuch as in their nature muſt paſs the Ordeal of Parliament, is one of the firſt in utility and eminence. It is by communications of this nature alone, that practical knowledge and experience can be conveyed to the uninformed, and their benefits diſſeminated and ſecured to future generations. Hence the Senator is furniſhed with information the moſt to be relied on, becauſe the moſt expoſed to ſcrutiny and expoſition; and, by comparing and weighing in his cloſet all facts, arguments, and opinions thus ſubmitted to public view, with what he may collect from private quarters, he is enabled to form an impartial judgment, and to decide upon juſt principles and intrinſic merits; and thus topics otherwiſe abſtruſe and difficult become eaſy and familiar. Under the influence of this impreſſion, the Editor of theſe ſheets, whoſe particular ſituation and line of life has, he conceives, afforded him the means of ſetting in their true lights the Nature and State of our India and China Trade, in a way that may be uſeful, at a juncture when that very important and valuable branch of our Commerce is at the eve of undergoing the moſt ſerious inveſtigation, would have thought himſelf remiſs in his duty as a good citizen, had he remained ſilent.

As the main object of this Treatise is to furnish useful information relating to the Asiatic Trade, to such, as either by their avocations, or the want of better means, have been prevented from obtaining it elsewhere, rather than with a desire to enter the lists with those already conversant on the subject, and who may be disposed to become disputants with respect to the best means for conducting it, we have thought it right to give a connected, but very brief, account of the Origin and Progress of the Trade, and the History of the Companies erected for carrying it on, previous to our entering into the consideration of the state of it, as at present circumstanced.

The favorable Reception of this Tract by the Public, under the former Edition, has induced the Editor to permit this second Edition to be printed. The Justice of the opinion he had ventured to obtrude in the 3d Chapter, relative to the Claim of the Company to the exclusive Property and Revenue of the five Northern Circars, having been in some degree questioned by respectable Characters, in high official Situations, he has added a Section on that Subject, to shew the Grounds on which that Opinion was formed. If it be a wrong one, he is open to Conviction, and will not hesitate to acknowledge his Error. The Facts he has stated may at least lead to a further Elucidation of several particulars which, however important, are at present little known to the Community.

CHAPTER

CHAPTER I.

The Origin of the Old and New East India Companies, with their Union.

THE passage by Sea to the Peninsula of India, and the Eastward part of the Continent of Asia, the present seats of our Asiatic trade, was not discovered till about the latter end of the 15th Century; and of the various attempts made from hence by individuals to open a Trade thither, none proved successful, until * Queen Elizabeth established the first Incorporated Company by the Name of *The London East India Company*. After a long series of Disasters and Losses this Company obtained from *the Country Powers*, at a great expence, the Privilege of a limited Trade in certain parts of India and Persia, and of making small Settlements or Houses of Trade called *Factories*, for the residence of their Factors and Servants. In those early times the † Charters of the Crown, and the Powers which they conveyed, were not thought to require Parliamentary Sanction; nor was it until after the Restoration of Charles II. that the Rights or Authorities derived under them, though resting on Prerogative alone, were first called in question.

The Science of Navigation, and the true Principles of Foreign Trade, during the existence of those Charters, were but beginning to dawn upon us. At the time of their cessation, we could be said to be only in a state of Commercial Infancy. We are therefore not to be surprized at finding, that by the interruptions of speculative Adventurers, called *Interlopers*, who had begun to resist the exclusive Claims of the Old Company, derived by their Charters, on the ground of their wanting the Sanction of Parliamentary Authority, and by occasional failures of investments of goods from abroad, and the not unfrequent losses of ships in their passage, the Commerce of the Company was often chequered with disasters and disappointments.

Notwithstanding these vicissitudes and discouragements, the Company, with many hard struggles and heavy expences, formed by degrees various ‡ Factories and Houses of Trade both in *India* and *Persia*; and at length becoming more

---
* The Charter was dated the 31st December, 1600. Printed Acts and Charters, Part 2, Page 3.
† See Anderson's History of Commerce.
‡ *Forts*: Mazagom, Mahim, Syon, Syere, Warlee, Carwar, Angengo, Tellicherry, Calicutt, Fort St. George, Fort St. David, Vizagapatam, York Fort or Fort Malbro', Fort William, Bombay, and St. Helena.
Factories: Surat, Swally, Broach, Amadavad, Agra, Lucknow, Gombron, Shyraz, Ispahaun, Chingu, Orixa, Cuddalore, Porto Novo, Pettipolee, Metchlepatam, Madnpollam, Indrapour, Tryamong, Sillebar, Tonqueen, Bellafore, Coffimbuzar, Dacca, Houghley, Malda, Rajamaul, and Patna, with the Customs of Trade, and a Rent of 3333*l.* 6*s.* 8*d.* granted by the Sophy of Persia.

successful, their prosperity began to excite that sort of envy in Individuals, which is too apt to result from the beneficial Commerce of Great Bodies. Various attempts were in consequence made to induce the Crown, and even Parliament itself, to interpose and revoke the Charters of the Company; some on pretext that every man had an equal Right to trade in the *East* as well as the *West Indies*, whilst others hoped to effect it on proposals of Terms of Advantage in point of Publick Finance, that they might themselves be erected into an exclusive Company, to the downfall of that which existed.

Such was the state of things in 1693, when the Company, by an accidental Failure in the Payment of a paltry Duty which had been imposed on their capital Stock, gave an opening to Government to determine their Charters: For, by the * Act which imposed that duty, any default in payment, within the time therein limited, rendered their Charters *void:* And though, in the same year, the Crown, to obviate all doubts, revived their Powers and exclusive Privileges by a new Charter, the Company were obliged to submit to a condition that their Capacity and Trading should in future be *determinable on Three Years Notice*. The legal obstacle to the erecting a new Company being thus removed, an † Act was passed in 1698 for borrowing *Two Millions* on a Loan at 8 per Cent. towards carrying on the War; and as an encouragement to Subscribers, it was declared, that they should be incorporated by a Charter from the King into *a General Society*, with liberty for each individual Member to trade to India and the other Limits of the Old Company's exclusive Charter; so that the value of his Exports exceeded not his Share of this Loan or Capital; and that such of the Subscribers as should choose to convert their Subscriptions *into a joint Stock*, should be at liberty to do so, and be incorporated *by a separate Charter* by the name of "*The English East India Company*," with the privilege of trading with and to the amount of such *joint Stock*. All persons but those incorporated, and such as they should license, were prohibited from this Trade, except the Old Company, who had time given them to wind up their Commercial Affairs. The Act reserved a power to determine the Charters both of the General Society and the New Company after September 1711, *on Repayment of the Loan, and Three Years Notice.*

The bulk of the Subscribers having agreed to trade as a separate Company with a joint Stock, the Old Company, in whose prejudice the two New Corporations were to be erected, found means to become Members *for a very large proportion* of the Loan of Two Millions. With an interest thus acquired, they joined with the English Company, and with the superior Knowledge of the Trade, which they had gained by experience over the other members, and possessed as they were of Shipping, Stores, and Stock at home, and of the Settlements and Factories necessary to the Trade abroad, they obtained a decided influence in the general Courts of the New Company, and thus paved

---

* Act 4 and 5 Will. and Mary, ch. 15. s. 10 and 12.
† Act 9 and 10 Will. III. ch 44.

the

(5)

the way to that Union which afterwards took place in 1702, and which, under the auspices of *Lord Treasurer Godolphin*, in 1708, was confirmed by Parliament. By the terms of this Union, the Warehouses at home, and Shipping, and also *all the Settlements and Factories* of the Old Company in the *East Indies, Persia, and China*, including *the Islands of Bombay and St. Helena*, with their Dependencies, and all their Rights and Privileges, however derived, became vested in the United Company, except their *Body Politic*, which they surrendered to the Queen.

The curious Reader will wish to learn what became of the *general Society*, whose Members were individually authorized to trade, as far as the value of their Subscriptions in Goods, exported from hence. All we can discover of them is, that though they were actually *incorporated* by the King's Charter, and were therefore legally authorized to send ships to India or China, it does not with certainty appear that any one ship was ever fitted out by them : and that the superior advantages of being concerned in the Trade to be carried on *with a joint Stock* were so evident, that at the time of the Union of the Two Companies, out of the whole Loan of Two Millions[*], only £. 7,000 then remained the property of *The separate Traders of the General Society*, and that this sum also was soon absorbed in the United Company, whose capital or trading *Stock*, by which their Dividend of Profits was to be governed, thereupon became fixed at *Two Millions*.

Having thus briefly traced the general History of the two Companies to their perfect Union, we shall refer our Readers to the [†] Collection of Statutes, Charters, and Bye-laws of the India Company, lately printed and published, for any further particulars they may desire on that part of the subject, and close this Chapter, with a short recital of the Acts of Parliament, by which the United Company have been continued in the exclusive Trade to the present time, and of what were the conditions of the compacts made with the Public on those occasions.

The first enlargement of their term took place in 1708 [‡], when the United Company bargained with the Public to advance £. 1,200,000 as a loan, but without any interest, (or, which operated as the same thing, at a reduced interest of 5 per cent. on the two loans conjointly), for an extension of their term in the exclusive Trade of fifteen years, and thus *their nominal trading capital*, on which the dividend was made, became advanced to £. 3,200,000.

In 1712 ‖ the Company petitioned Parliament, on the ground that the term which remained unexpired in their trade was too short to admit their risking

[*] Act of 6 Anne, ch. 17. f. 7.
[†] By FRANCIS RUSSELL, Esq. of the India Board, and printed by EYRE and STRAHAN, His Majesty's Printers.
[‡] Act 6 Anne, ch. 17.
‖ Commons Journals.

the

the further necessary expences of regaining and securing the *Pepper Trade*, which had been engrossed by the *Dutch*, that their corporate capacity might be continued, tho' the debt due to them from the Public should be redeemed. In consequence of this petition †, an act passed for repealing all former provisoes and powers of determining their trade or incorporation, but with power for the Public to redeem the debt at any time after September 1733; and thus the United Company were supposed to have obtained *a perpetuity* as well in the *exclusive trade*, as in all their *chartered rights and capacities*. They however submitted themselves in that respect to the pleasure of Parliament in 1730, when an act ‡ was passed for continuing to them their exclusive trade 'till 1766, for which they gave the Public a premium of £.200,000 without any return of either principal or interest, and also agreed to a reduction of the rate of interest to £.4 per cent. on the debt of £.3,200,000, and to accept of payment of the principal by instalments of £.500,000 at a time.

In 1744 ‖ they contracted for, and obtained a further addition of fourteen years in the exclusive Trade, for which they lent to the Public *one million* at 3 per cent.; and in 1750 § they agreed to a further reduction of the rate of interest on the former debt to 3 per cent.

Thus grew the present debt of £.4,200,000 from the Public to the United Company, carrying with it an annuity of £.126,000. But the Company's capital or nominal sum, by which their dividends were governed, continued as before at £.3,200,000, *the million* last lent having been raised by their bonds, and therefore not added to their former capital.

The *last renewal* was made by contract with the Public in 1781 *, when a further Term determinable in 1794 was granted in the exclusive Trade, on payment of £.400,000 in discharge of all claims on the Company by the Public, previous to 1st March, 1781. But it was provided by Parliament, That after payment of a yearly dividend of £.8 per cent. to the holders of India stock, the surplus of all the net proceeds of their trade and revenues should be applied, *three fourths* to the use of the *Public*, and *the remaining fourth* to the use of the *Company*.

The debts incurred by the Company in the wars subsisting in India at and after that period, have hitherto prevented any such surplus from arising, and therefore no participation of revenue hath taken place under this act. On the contrary, the pressure of those debts, and the compulsory clauses of an act of 1784, by which the Company are obliged to keep a stock of teas always in their warehouses sufficient for one year's consumption, have rendered it necessary for them to enlarge their actual trading capital, by new subscriptions, to *five millions*, for which they had the sanction of Parliament granted them by two acts of the years 1786 and 1789.

† Act 10 Ann. ch. 28.   ‡ 3 G. 2. ch. 14.   ‖ Act 17 G. 2. ch. 17.
§ Act 23 G. 2. ch. 22.   * Act 21 G. 3. ch. 65. s. 9.

In order to determine the exclusive Trade, it is necessary that the Public should first make provision for the debt of £.4,200,000 which is still due, partly to the Company and partly to the Annuitants. The nature of their respective interests in this debt we will endeavour to shew in the succeeding Chapter.

CHAPTER II.

The Origin of the 3 per Cent. Annuities transferrable at the India House, and the Funds chargeable with the Payment of them.

WE have shewn in the preceding chapter, the origin and progress of the Debt of £.4,200,000 incurred by the Public to the East India Company, and that in 1750 *the interest or annuity* payable on it was reduced to the rate of 3 per cent. or £.126,000 per annum.

The securities pledged by the Public for the payment of the annuities were these: Certain *Salt Duties* and *Stamp Duties* were, in the first instance, made chargeable for the interest of £.160,000 on the two first loans of £.3,200,000, and when in 1730, the interest was reduced to £.128,000, it was made a specific charge *on the Aggregate Fund*.

The £.30,000 per annum for the interest of the *One Million Loan* was charged on certain *Duties upon Spirits*, and upon the *Sinking Fund*.

The terms upon which the Company agreed, in 1750, to reduce the rate of their annuity to 3 per cent. were (as is specified in the act for that purpose) that they should be permitted to raise £.4,200,000 *by sale of annuities* at the same rate of interest which the Public were to pay to the Company; and it was declared that the annuities so sold should be paid half-yearly at the *India House* (where the *transfer books* were to be kept and managed) *out of the same duties and revenues* as stood chargeable with the payment of the interest of the debt due by the Public to the Company, subject nevertheless to the like proviso of *redemption* by the *Public* as the said loans were subject or liable to.

Under this power the Company sold* annuities to the amount of £.2,992,440 : 5 s. carrying an interest or dividend of 3 per cent. per ann. amounting to £.89,773 : 4 s. which sums constitute what are called *East India Annuities*, the half-yearly payments of which are regularly made at the India House, out of the annuity of £.126,000 received by the Company at *the Exchequer*, the remainder being still the property of the Company.

Some doubt having been entertained whether the Company's power to sell *the remainder* of these annuities continued in force under the act of 1750, they were

* Act 26 G. 3. ch. 62.

again

again impowered to sell it by an act of the year 1786, in which it was provided, that the purchasers thereof should hold their annuities upon the like terms as the former purchasers; and that what should be so sold should be consolidated with the annuities formerly sold, and that the debt of £.4,200,000, due by the Public to the Company, should be a collateral security to the holders thereof, but subject to redemption.

The Company however have not availed themselves of their power to alienate the remaining part of this annuity, amounting to £.1,207,550 : 15 s. producing £.36,226 : 16 s. per ann. but still retain it in property; and over and besides that income, they also receive from the *Exchequer*, by virtue of an act * of 1751, £.1687 per ann. for the *receiving, paying,* and *managing,* the amount formerly sold to the annuitants, being in proportion to the allowances made to the *Bank* for the management of Bank Annuities.

The India annuities are therefore part of the *National Debt*, charged upon *public revenues alone*, and *redeemable* only by the *Public*; and being so, provision is made by the act of 1786 " *for reduction of the national debt*," that when and as the annuities shall be purchased or paid off by the *Commissioners*, the Directors of the *East India Company* shall permit *Transfers* thereof to be made in their books into the names of the *Commissioners*, similar to what is done at the *Bank* and *South Sea House*, and the Bank are impowered to receive the *annual dividends* thereof for the use of the Public.

By the Consolidation Act † of 1787 the Annuity of £.126,000 per ann. payable by the Public to the Company, (and out of which they pay the Annuitants) is charged upon the Consolidated Fund.

The *India Annuity* has been for several years at a price *inferior* to the annuities of an equal rate transferable at the *Bank*. This difference has been probably occasioned by the distance of the place of its transfer from the *Stock Exchange*, and its *small annual amount*, preventing that frequency of its being brought to market, which is necessary to a quick demand, and where the magnitude of *other redeemable annuities* renders *this* of but little consideration. The consequence has been, that not a *single purchase* has been made of the *India Annuity* by the *Commissioners* for the reduction of the *National Debt*, though, when brought in small sums (as it usually is) to market, it has been generally sold at the rate of from 3 to 4 per cent. *less* than the *Bank reduced Annuities*, and perhaps the general knowledge that the *Commissioners* have made no purchase in it, may have operated as an additional cause in depressing its price.

It would be better if this annuity were consolidated with the Bank Annuities. The allowance of £.1687 per ann. might be saved to the Public; the value of the annuity would be improved in the hands of the Proprietors, and the

* Act 24 G. 2. ch. 56.   † 27 G. 3. ch. 13. f. 54.

Public

(9)

Public in no respect injured, while the Company, if they choose to part with their share of it, would find it more marketable, and obtain a higher price.

CHAPTER III.

Of the Forts, Factories, and Territories in India, distinguishing those which are the Property of the Company by Purchase, *from those acquired* by Conquest.

PREVIOUS to suggesting any regulations for the future Trade from Great Britain to the East Indies, it appears necessary, on account of the relative connection that subsists between the Revenues of our Asiatic Possessions and the * *Investments* of India Goods for China, as well as for Europe, to ascertain what *Fortresses, Ports,* or *other Places* of Importance *to the Trade of India* do of right belong to the Company *in perpetuity*, free from the claims of the Public, to examine what those possessions are, and to distinguish such as were acquired by actual Conquest or influence of arms, and to which *the Nation have made their claim*, from such as were *the Property of the Company* before the making of any conquests, *by purchase* from the Native Powers.

The result of this investigation is, that *Fort St. George, Madras,* and *Vizagapatam,* and every other valuable sea port possessed at this time by the Company on the *Coast of Coromandel,* and visited by their ships from hence, together with their Settlements of *Fort William* and *Calcutta* on the Ganges, *Fort Marlbro'* or *York-Fort* at *Bencoolen,* and the *Islands of Bombay* and *St. Helena*, were purchased by the Old East India Company †, and conveyed by them to the present Company, in full right *for ever*. In this description Masulipatam alone is meant to be excepted.

At these *Ports,* and above all at *Calcutta, Madras* and *Bombay,* the Company are equally intitled to *Port Duties* and *Customs* on *Imports* and *Exports*, as they are to the places themselves, and have been in the constant exercise and enjoyment thereof at all times. The *Towns of Madras and Calcutta* as well as the *two Forts*, are built chiefly, if not entirely, upon the lands of the Company, under annual *Ground Rents*. By Grants obtained from the Native Powers, they are also

---
* Though the provision of Investments is generally aided by the Revenue, in the first instance, it has frequently happened in time of war, that Bills of Exchange, to a greater amount than the prime cost of the goods, have been drawn upon the Company to reimburse the Treasuries abroad, for the money advanced from the revenues.
† Fort St. George was made a Settlement by the Old Company in 1620; St. Helena in 1651; Calcutta and Fort William in 1689; and Bombay in 1668.

B possessed

possessed of, and intitled in perpetuity to * *the Five Northern Circars*, the *Purgunnahs* and *Jaghire Lands*, and sundry valuable Factories and Houses of Trade on different parts of the Continent of *Asia*, and in the *Asiatic Islands*. To these therefore the *Public* have no Claim whatever.

But with regard to the *Provinces* (or Kingdoms as they are called) of *Bengal*, *Bahar*, and *Orissa*, the Country of *Benares*, and the Country newly acquired from *Tippoo Sultaun*, the right of property to them stands on a very different ground, and were it not for those *equitable* Claims which the Company and their *Creditors* seem to have, to be first *repaid* or *indemnified* for the expences and debts unavoidably incurred in the Conquest of those countries, and in their subsequent defence and protection, little doubt could be entertained in respect to them; for the right, subject to those claims, is indisputably in the *Public*; nor have we been able to discover from what source the doubt, which has been by some persons entertained regarding it, has arisen. As far as our researches have gone, neither the Court of Proprietors nor the Court of Directors, nor any of their Committees, ever laid claim to the property of these *conquered Territories*, either by any formal *Resolutions*, or by any of their *Petitions* to Parliament, although the *appropriation* of the revenues of those territories, underwent full and serious discussions both there, and at the *General Courts* on many occasions, and particularly in 1766, 1767, 1769, 1773, 1779, 1780, 1781, and 1784; and the Company having for a series of time agreed to become *participants* of the territorial revenues with the *Public*, and having also paid annually to the *Exchequer* ‡, for the use of the Public, their stipulated share of £.400,000 per ann. until prevented by the pressure of new debts incurred by the expences of supporting wars in *India*, it would be superfluous to create a doubt on the right of the Public at this day.

We are aware, that in the temporary Act of 1779, as well as in the Acts of 1780 and 1781, a clause was inserted declaring that the appropriation of this revenue made by these Acts should not *prejudice the Rights either of the Public or the Company:* but, if we mistake not, there was no such *saving clause* offered, much less inserted, in either of the former Acts of Appropriation.

Lest, however, any person should, for want of being better informed, hesitate to pronounce the right to these extensive and valuable territories to be in the *Public*, (subject, however, to the equitable and just claims *for indemnity*

---

* The Circars being held merely as a Farm under Nizam Ally, at a yearly rent of seven lacs of rupees, or about £.70,000 per ann. Sterling, with an exception of the Diamond Mines, and under other special conditions, we apprehend, but with submission to better judges, that the Circars stand on a similar footing with the Jaghire Lands. See Chapter XV for the History of some of these acquisitions, and particularly Masulipatam and the Northern Circars.

‡ These payments, between 1766 and 1782, amounted to upwards of Two Millions Sterling.

both

both of the *Company* and their *Creditors*), we shall briefly state what we conceive sufficient to obviate every doubt.

It will be remembered, that our conquests in *India* immediately followed that memorable and ever to be lamented act of barbarity, committed on the Company's servants in the *Black Hole of Calcutta*, by the then Nabob of Bengal. This happened in 1756, and the Company, after having directed their servants abroad to take the most speedy and vigorous measures for recompensing themselves, preferred their * Petition to the King, stating the doubt " whether the
" *lands, plunder*, and *booty* which might be conquered or taken by their forces
" upon any occasion, *would not belong to His Majesty*; and praying that in con-
" sideration of their expences and losses, the King would grant them the *plunder*
" *and booty*, and that the Company might be permitted to hold and enjoy to
" them and their successors, subject to His Majesty's right of Sovereignty
" therein, all such *Fortresses, Districts, and Territories*, as they had already ac-
" quired, or might acquire from any *Nation, State, or People, by treaty, grant,*
" *or conquest*, with power to restore, give up, and dispose of the same, as they
" might see occasion, subject to His Majesty's disposition as to lands acquired
" by conquest from the subjects of any *European* Power."

The Petition being referred to the consideration of the Attorney and Solicitor General, (the present *Lord Camden*, and the late Chancellor *Mr. Charles Yorke*), they made their report dated the 24th December, 1757, of which the following is a literal extract:

" In respect to such places as have been, or shall be acquired by Treaty or
" Grant from the Mogul, or any of the Indian Princes, or Governments, Your
" Majesty's Letters Patent are not necessary; the property of the soil vesting
" in the Company by the Indian Grants, subject only to Your Majesty's right
" of Sovereignty over the Settlements, as English Settlements, and over the
" Inhabitants, as English Subjects, who carry with them Your Majesty's Laws
" wherever they form Colonies, and receive Your Majesty's protection, by
" virtue of Your Royal Charters. In respect to such places as have lately been
" acquired or shall hereafter be acquired by conquest, the property, as well
" as the dominion, vests in Your Majesty, by virtue of Your known Prero-
" gative; and consequently the Company can only derive a right to them,
" through Your Majesty's Grant. But we submit our humble opinion to Your
" Majesty, that it is not warranted by precedent, nor agreeable to sound po-
" licy, nor to the tenor of the Charters, which have been laid before us, to
" make such a general grant, not only of part, but of future contingent con-
" quests, made upon any Power, European or Indian, to a Trading Company.
" Many objections occur to it, more material to be weighed than explained.
" If at any time the East India Company, in the prosecution of their just rights,
" shall chance to conquer a Fortress or District, which may be convenient for

* Vide Appendix to 1st vol. Bolt's History, for this Petition and Report.

" carrying

" carrying on their trade, and is afterwards either ceded to them by treaty,
" or proper to be maintained by force, it is time enough to resort to Your
" Majesty for Your Royal Grant, whenever the case arises. At the same time
" we must do justice to the honourable intentions of those who preferred this
" Petition to Your Majesty, in saying, That as soon as the objections were
" intimated, they readily acquiesced, and expressed themselves much more
" anxious for the sake of obtaining a clear rule for the direction of their officers
" in India, to have their doubts explained, as to their powers of restoring or
" surrendering places conquered; and to know whether the Company is ena-
" bled, by any of their present Charters, to yield up conquests made on the
" Indian Princes or Governments by treaty, without Your Majesty's Licence
" in every instance; the procuring of which might be attended with great
" delay in pressing exigencies. In answer to this doubt so stated, we are
" humbly of opinion, that the Royal Charters, granted to the Company,
" having repeatedly given them the Powers of making Peace, as well as War,
" with the Indian Princes or Governments, it is incident to the Power of
" making Peace to be enabled to restore conquests, or things taken in war,
" otherwise they would have the Power to make Peace, without the means
" of obtaining it. But to remove all possible doubts, we think it will not be
" improper (if it shall be Your Majesty's pleasure) to explain their Powers
" of making Peace, by a clause to be inserted in the Letters Patent proposed,
" enabling them to make cessions of new Conquests, acquired from any of
" the Indian Princes or States, during the late troubles between the East India
" Company and the Nabob of Bengal, or which shall be acquired in time
" coming; with an express exception, agreeably to the Prayer of their Pe-
" tition, of any Settlements or Territories conquered from the Subjects of
" any European Power, leaving the same open to be disposed of in all cases,
" according to your Royal Wisdom."

Upon this Report, the King granted all *plunder and booty* to the Company, under certain restrictions; and also licensed " the Company and their Servants,
" by any Treaty of Peace with any *Indian Princes or Governors*, to cede, restore,
" or dispose of any *Fortresses* or *Territories* acquired, or thereafter to be acquired
" by *conquest*, except Settlements conquered from any *European Power*, which
" they were not to dispose of without His Majesty's Permission *." Which Licence, thus restricted, was accepted by the Company. To add to all this, the House of Commons in 1773 (which was Nine Years after the Company's possession had been established by a Grant from the Mogul in the Dewanneeship of Bengal) came to a decisive Resolution, " *That all acquisitions made under the
" influence of a Military Force, or by Treaty with Foreign Princes, do of right belong
" to the State.*"

* Coll. of Statutes and Charters, 2d Part, p. xliv.

CHAP-

CHAPTER IV.

Expences incurred by the Company in the Indian Conquests.

HAVING mentioned the Expences of the Company incurred in the conquest and subsequent defence of the territories in India, it will be expected that a fuller explanation should be given on that head.

It has been asserted, with more Confidence, perhaps, than truth, that the *Territorial Revenues* have been so blended in India with the *Commercial Funds* of the Company, as to render every attempt to discover the amount of the expences sustained in the acquisition and protection of those Territories, beyond the net revenues they have yielded, fruitless and nugatory: And that no injustice will be done by setting the Receipts against the Payments, and thus closing the account for ever.

Were the Revenues to be continued under the collection of the Company until their debts abroad and at home were discharged, and the value of their commercial assets become sufficient to cover their Capital Stock, there probably would be no difficulty in acceding to the final adjustment of the Account in the manner proposed. But burthened as the Company are with debts, and after having so recently advanced large sums by new subscriptions to their Capital Stock, it behoves them, in Justice to their Creditors and to themselves, as well as for the support of their honour and character, to shew that the *Revenues of India* have *fallen short* of reimbursing *the excess of their disbursements* in respect of the territories, by the full amount of the debts owing abroad and at home, the current debts incident to their commerce excepted. And though it may be true, that the Land Revenues and the Commercial Funds have been in some respect mixed together, so as to render it a fruitless attempt to separate them at this day, yet as the Company are well known to have received no other remittances from abroad, than by the medium of their investments, we may venture to assert, that if an account were taken at home, after the following method, the out turn of it would be sufficiently correct for every useful purpose, and afford all the satisfaction the nature of the case seems to require.

1st. Let an account be taken of the *prime cost, outfit, freight, and charges of merchandize, of all bullion, goods, and stores exported by the Company to India,* for any given time; and add thereto the *profits* derived by their *sales there* (those being considered as the exclusive right of the Company). To this, add also the expences of the commercial establishments, and other charges of merchandize in India, and the *amount of bills of exchange*, and the expences of *forces and recruits* paid by the Company *in London*, and the money paid into the *Exchequer* for the
use

use of the Public.—The *aggregate* of thefe will fhew what India may be *debited* to the Company.

2nd. In contraft with that *debit* fhould be placed the amount, at their *prime coft in India*, of all *inveftments* fhipped there both for Europe and China, and all remittances from India to China within the fame period.

If the aggregate of the Payments at home have exceeded the receipts by remittances from India to China, and by the inveftments *from* India to China and Europe at their prime coft, then will the Company have a right to place the difference *as a debt* againft the *territories in India*; but if their receipts by thofe remittances and inveftments fhall be found to exceed *their payments at home*, then will the Company be indebted to that amount to the *territorial revenues*.

There will however remain another fmall account to be adjufted, to bring the intended ftatement to a nearer degree of accuracy. We have already obferved, that the Company had *forts and factories in India* before the *conqueft* of *Bengal*; and doubtlefs thefe were attended with fome, but it is prefumed not much, expence to the Company, beyond what were properly included under the head of their *mercantile eftablifhments*. We have alfo fhewn that the Company had *Land-rents, port-duties*, and *cuftoms*. Neither of thefe articles are included in them anner above recommended for taking the foregoing account. But as the Company's receipts by *rents, duties*, and *cuftoms* in *India* were very confiderable, even at an early period, as will appear by the Reports of the *Select Committee* of the Houfe of Commons of the year 1773, and as the extra expences of the *forts* are fuppofed to have been but trivial, antecedent to the war of 1756, there feems reafon to expect, that this part of the computation might ultimately terminate in the Company's favor.

It is well known, that in 1780, an account on the foregoing *datum*, or fomething very near it, was taken with very great precifion by a worthy and intelligent member of the Company, then and ftill a Director. It was printed and diftributed under the title of " *Remarks on the Eaft India Company's Balances in England from their Trade and their revenues*," and the refult of it was, that the Company had actually paid on the account of the Territories, more than had been returned from thofe Territories, by the fum of £.3,622,969, exclufive of intereft; and if that account, accurately continued to the prefent time, were laid before the Public, it would fhew that the balance above ftated, has been confiderably increafed, befides the debts ftill due for the expences of the two laft wars. The arguments and obfervations annexed to the account here referred to, are highly worthy the ftudy and attention of every one who wifhes to be informed of the particulars of this part of the Company's concerns.

CHAP.

CHAPTER V.

The Rights permanent or temporary of the India Company.

TO undeceive such as have fallen into the prevailing error, that the Company's *chartered Rights*, their *Corporate Capacity*, and their *Liberty* of trading with a *joint Stock*, are one and all determinable in 1794 (unless their Charter be previously renewed), as well as to evince how far the existing Rights of the Company, over the principal Seats of Trade, and other Settlements abroad, may stand in the way of laying the trade open to individuals with a prospect of success, it becomes necessary to bring into a collected point of view, what those *Rights* are, and to distinguish such as are only of a *temporary* nature and require renewal, if proper to be renewed, from such as are lawfully vested in them *in perpetuity*.

Their *temporary* Rights consist, *First*, of the sole and exclusive Trade with India and * other Ports within the Limits described in their Charter, so that none other of the King's subjects can go thither or trade there, except it be *by Leave* of the Company.

And *Secondly*, they have the Administration of the *Government* and *Revenues* of the *Territories in India* acquired by their Conquests during their Term in the Exclusive Trade, subject nevertheless to the various Cheques and Restrictions contained in the several Acts of Parliament which vest that Administration in them. These several *temporary* Rights are determinable by Parliament in 1794, under the Notice given *by Order of the House of Commons*, in the Year 1791.

The Rights which they possess *in Perpetuity* are,

To be a Body † *Corporate and Politic*, with *perpetual Succession*.

To purchase ‡, acquire, and dispose at will of lands and tenements in *Great Britain*.

---

* " In, to, and from the East Indies, in the Countries and Parts of Asia and Africa, and in, " to, and from the Islands, Ports, Havens, Cities, Creeks, Towns, and Places of Asia, Africa, " and America, or any of them, beyond the Cape of Good Hope to the Straights of Magellan, " where any trade or traffick of merchandize is or may be used or had, and to and from every of " them."

† By the Statutes 3 Geo. II. ch. 14.—17 Geo. II. ch. 17.—and 21 Geo. III. ch. 65.

‡ In their Charter of 10 William III. the value in Great Britain was not restricted, but by Act of 3 Geo. II. the value therein is not to exceed £. 10,000 per annum.

To

(16)

"To make * Settlements *to any Extent* within the Limits of their Exclusive Trade, build *Ports* and *Fortifications*, appoint *Governors*, erect *Courts of Judicature*, coin *Money*, raise, train, and muster *Forces* † at Sea and Land, repel wrongs and injuries, make reprizals on the invaders or disturbers of their peace, and continue to trade within the same limits, *with a joint Stock for ever*, although their Exclusive Right of trading shall be ‡ *determined* by Parliament.

Possessed, therefore, as the Company is, of *all the sea ports and places of Trade* in the East Indies in *perpetuity* acquired by *grants* from their former owners, *the Native States of India*, and held by the *best of titles*, namely, upon Rights and Powers granted upon formal *compacts* for *full and valuable considerations* paid to the *Public*, and ratified and established by sundry *acts of Parliament*, it seems evident, that although the *exclusive Trade* of the Company were to be determined, yet that no private merchant of this or any other country could justify *entering* any of those *ports or places* for the purpose of *Traffick*, but by the Company's permission, unless the Ports and Factories, as well as the Trade, were to be thrown open. This would, however, be an innovation on private rights and private property, of which the records of Parliament afford no instance, except in cases merely *municipal*, and where their extreme urgency for effecting some great and approved design manifestly tending to secure or promote the general interests of the empire, have impelled the Legislature to the exercise of *so extraordinary* a stretch of their authority. On such occasions, however urgent or important they may have been, the greatest circumspection has been always used, and care taken, as far as the nature of the case would admit, to affect the private property of the individual, be his condition what it might, as little as possible; and in no case have the applications for such like purposes proved successful, where every party was not consenting, but on the fullest proof and conviction, that the interests of the country required the sacrifice, nor without strict provision being made for giving *ample compensation* to the owners of the property to be affected, and which it has been the practice to apportion, not merely to its intrinsic worth, but according to that degree of profit which, under all existing circumstances, its exclusive possession afforded, or might in reason *be in prospect to afford*, to its former proprietors. This salutary principle is so consistent with justice, and the common rights of mankind, and is become so rooted and interwoven by practice into our Constitution, that we may with confidence affirm, it will never be shaken nor departed from by the *Parliament* of Great Britain. On the other hand, circumstanced as the case is with respect to the importance of the Company's *exclusive Right* to the *Ports and Places of Trade in India*, whereby to secure the peculiar advantages they will afford to the Company *trading with a joint stock*, after the trade of individuals shall be brought in competition and rivalship with them; and when it is considered how vast is the number of persons, *Members*

* By the Charter of King William.
† By Acts of Parliament, 27 Geo. II. ch. 9.—1 Geo. III. ch. 14.—and 21 Geo. III. ch. 65.
‡ By the Three Statutes mentioned in Note (†) in the preceding page.

or

(17)

or *Creditors* of the India Company, whose property is embarked in, or collaterally dependant upon the future success of their Commerce; and that many other descriptions of persons are also individually interested in whatever relates to the seats of Trade established with so much expence, and so necessary for conducting it in future, it appears no easy matter to devise any practicable means by which a proper compensation for the privileges to be wrested from the Company, in opposition to their wishes, and so apparently to their injury, can be adjusted or computed; or in what manner, if the *quantum* were fixed, it can be properly paid or raised.

CHAPTER VI.

How far the Appellation of a Chartered Monopoly is applicable to the East India Trade.

THE appellation of *a chartered Monopoly*, given on various occasions to the East India Company's exclusive Trade, can be meant only to excite popular odium, and bring it into general disrepute. We have, in a former chapter, shewn the origin of the two East India Companies, and that the former held their exclusive trade by the voluntary grant of the Crown, founded solely on its prerogative, while the latter, or present Company, derive their rights by actual purchases from the Public, upon solemn compacts authorized and confirmed by acts of Parliament. True it is, that King William granted a Charter of Incorporation to the present Company : but it was a Charter conceived in the very terms of the agreement previously made with, and ratified by Parliament, and can therefore be considered in no other light, than *as an instrument of investiture,* issued under the Great Seal of Great Britain, in compliance with the letter of the act, in order to perpetuate the agreement, by inrollment (as all *Charters* are, though *Acts of Parliament* are not) upon the public archives of the kingdom, kept in the High Court of Chancery, whereby to establish, more firmly, if it were possible, the tenor of the bargain, the origin of the incorporation, the extent of the rights and privileges meant to be conveyed, and the restrictions with which they were accompanied. In these important respects, did this Charter differ from all others, that it was not only the first ever granted by similar authority, but was free from every legal question which had attached on others, *because it sprung from an act of the British Parliament, and was made in all things to correspond with it.* How far the learned * gentleman, who, in 1783, made so light of Charters, and of this Charter in particular, by describing it as of no other value or virtue, than so much " parchment with a bit of wax dang-
" ling at its tail," had informed himself of these particulars, or whether he really considered (as from the very high opinion we entertain of his virtue and

---
* In a debate in the House of Commons on the famous India Bill of Mr. Fox.

C integrity,-

integrity, we hope, and believe he did), that the Charter from King William had been a mere gratuitous business, flowing, like many others, from royal bounty, and dependent on the authority of prerogative alone, we shall not pretend to determine; but we may boldly affirm, that the East India Company derive no rights, whatever, under their Charter, other than what they fairly purchased, nor any but such as are sanctioned to them in the most clear and distinct manner by the act of Parliament under which the Charter was made, and those subsequent acts by which the exclusive Trade has been continued to them, upon new bargains with the Public, to this day. And when it is recollected, that the continuance of their exclusive Trade is *not dependent on any Charter* (for they have had none for their trade since 1698), but on † Acts of Parliament only, we cannot but be forcibly struck with the impropriety of this appellation "The Chartered Trade," as generally applied to the existing exclusive Trade of the Company.

A monopoly, according to its literal, as well as enlarged sense, undoubtedly means the ingrossing and getting into the power of any individual, or of two or more persons combined for the purpose, any particular commodity, whereby to command the time and manner of its sale, and to with-hold it from the market, or deal it out at pleasure, at an arbitrary or extravagant price.

Though the spirit of our laws, at all ‡ periods, declared that trade should be free, and forbad all monopolies; yet such was the influence of prerogative, and the submission of the people to it in early times, that it was not until the 21st James I. that all grants of monopolies by the Crown, were declared null and void by statute. And in that act is contained * a provision that it should not extend " to Companies or Societies of Merchants erected for the maintenance, " encouragement, or ordering of any trade of merchandize."

What, therefore, constitutes the spirit and essence of a monopoly is, the having the sole command and power over some necessary article or commodity, in the mode of its sale and disposal, by which to enhance the value, and impose on the consumers an arbitrary price. Surely no one will gravely pronounce this sort of monopoly to apply to the Trade of the India Company, either in theory or practice: for so far were the Company from purchasing from the Public, and the Public from granting or legalizing any thing approaching to a monopoly of this kind, that it has, in the most positive terms, enjoined that the sales of goods by the Company should be made openly and publicly by Inch of Candle, or by way of Auction, within twelve months after the importation thereof §. The practice at the Company's sales has ever been strictly consonant to the law; and so far from the Company, or any of the individual members of it, having

---

† 3 G. 2. ch. 14. f. 10. 17 G. 2. ch. 17. f. 12. 21 G. 3. ch. 65. f. 4.
‡ See Statutes, 9 H. 3. ch. 30. 25 E. 3. ch. 2. 2 R. 2. ch. 1. 11 R. 2. ch. 21.
* 21 J. 1. ch. 3. f 4.
§ The Charter limits the lots to £.1,000 in value; they rarely exceed £.300; and abundance of lots are made very small to accommodate Individuals. A further latitude in respect to the time of sale, after importation, was given by an Act of 7 Geo. 1. st. 1. ch. 21. f. 10 and 11.

been

been monopolizers of India goods to their own aggrandizement, it will be found upon a strict scrutiny of the profit divided amongst them for *fourscore years past*, that their *dividends*, taken for the average of any reasonable period, have been sometimes *less* than, and *seldom exceeded the legal current rate of interest of money*, computed by the value or market price of their Stock; a fact, which alone affords an unequivocal proof, that what might otherwise have constituted a mercantile profit on the India Trade (beyond the common interest of the capital employed) in the hands of individuals, has been sunk in the reduced prices of Asiatic merchandize, and become a saving to the consumer; and thus have the Public reaped the real profits of the India commerce, whilst all the risque has been sustained by the Company.

There is also some advantage derived from the peculiar nature of the *constitution* of the East India Company, beyond what would result were the Trade in the hands of private merchants. The books are at all times open " for the " admission of every description of persons who may desire to become mem- " bers, and have money to adventure." It knows no distinction of professions, religions, or even sexes, and in the General Courts there is the most perfect equality: every one present has the same right with another to speak his sentiments, and give his advice. A difference is made only in voting, which, when taken by the holding up of hands, requires £.500 stock, and when by ballot £.1,000 stock, for a single vote; £.3,000 for two votes; £.6,000 for three votes; and £.10,000 for four votes; which is the largest number of votes any member is allowed to possess; whilst £.2,000 stock qualifies any member to become a candidate for the office of a Director, or Chairman. Hence any person without being bred to commerce, who has Money, and chuses to adventure it in this Trade, has the power of doing so.

It is admitted, that the Old East India Company might properly be termed *Monopolists*: for they were under no *parliamentary* restrictions, and in the year 1684, their trade was declared, upon a trial with Mr. Sands, an interloper, to partake of an unlawful monopoly. But it is material to observe, how widely different the state of that Company was from the present. They held their exclusive Trade solely by a *gratuitous Charter* from the Crown. The present Company hold it by *purchase* from the *Public*. The Trade of the Old Company was managed by a small Committee, and the major part of the profits were divided amongst ‡ about forty persons. The Trade is now managed by twenty-four Directors, and the number of registered Proprietors, partaking of the trading capital, is upwards of *two thousand seven hundred*, and the private, or privileged Traders, make at least *three thousand more*, besides those who trade illicitly or clandestinely, and whose number is very considerable, but whose conduct is not often scrutinized, because it might discourage the Trade in Exports, of which illicit adventures chiefly consist: so that we may fairly compute on *six thousand persons* who partake of the direct benefit of the export, and of *the first*

‡ Anderson's History of Commerce, 2d Vol. p. 171.

returns

returns of the import Trade from India and China. Besides, the Old Company could hold back their goods from the market, and sell them privately, just as suited their own purposes: The present Company can sell only to the best bidder, and were never known to keep back any goods, when a bidder could be found for them; their sales are constant and uniform; and, above all, the magnitude of the Trade, and the appropriation of its produce, amongst so great a number of persons, must ever secure the Public from every apprehension of its being converted to any of those base purposes, which, by their combination alone, can create the essence of a monopoly.

CHAPTER VII.

Plans formerly recommended for varying the Mode of conducting the Trade to the East Indies.

AMONGST the schemes devised in preference to that of a Joint Stock Company, for securing a beneficial Trade with India, we do not find any one to have been gravely proposed for throwing it wholly open to chance. The only plans that seem to have been thought worthy of serious deliberation, were such as had in view (though perhaps not all on the same model) a Regulated Open Company. Such was *the first Company* established in the year 1600, and such was the *general Society*, both of which we have seen to have grown into Joint Stock Companies. The difference consists in this: In a regulated Company, every merchant qualified according to the Rules prescribed, and conforming to them, may become a member, and may trade with his own separate capital; whereas, in a Joint Stock Company, the whole capital is thrown into one common mass. In the former case, the number of members, and the extent of the trade, are indefinite; in the latter, though the number be not, the extent of the trade is limited by the amount of the joint stock employed in it.

Although no general plan for throwing the Trade open has been suggested, history furnishes us with various instances of attempts made by individuals to trade on their own capitals, with India and China, as well before the institution of the first India Company, as since; but such attempts seem one and all, to have been attended with little better than ruin to the adventurers: and, indeed, when the distance from India, the nature of the intercourse with the natives, and the want of ports and settlements, are considered, our surprize cannot but be excited at the rashness of those who made the trial. The most flattering prospect to adventurers of this description was held out in the time of the Usurpation, when Oliver Cromwell suspended the Trade of the Company, to give to

all

all perfons a fair opportunity of trying the effect of an Open Trade. The experiment ended, as might be expected, in ruin; and, after an interval of four or five years, the Company were reftored, and the unfuccefsful adventurers were amongft the firft of thofe, who applied to the Protector for liberty to trade with a Joint Stock. Many other inftances might be adduced of failures by private adventurers, but none have come within our obfervation, that were attended with fuccefs. A remarkable inftance of the inconveniences with which experiments of this fort have been attended, happened in the reign of Charles II. Many private fhips had ventured to trade in India in defiance of the Company, and if fome of them found their account in it, a contrary fate attended the majority. Their loffes were, however, the leaft of the inconvenience; the officers and men conducted themfelves with fo much arrogance and impropriety, and created fuch difturbances, as at length to excite the general indignation of the Natives, and draw upon the Englifh in general, the refentment of the Mogul, and other native powers; who, making no diftinction betwixt the interlopers and the agents of the Company, waged war and feized on the Company's factories, and were on the brink of totally extirpating them from India, to the utter lofs of the interefts of the Englifh nation there: And it was only by the interpofition of Government, who fent a fhip of war to feize on the interlopers, with a Proclamation to compel them to repair to the Company's factories, and fubmit to their jurifdiction, that after an interruption of five years, and the incurment of a heavy expence by the Company, the Country Powers were pacified, and order reftored.

CHAPTER VIII.

The Prefent State of the Trade of foreign Countries with India and China.

THE *Portuguefe*, the *Spaniards*, the *French*, the *Danes*, and the *Dutch*, have all, in their turn, participated in the benefits of the Eaft India Commerce, each of them having obtained from the Country Powers the privilege of a Free Trade, and of making Settlements and Factories on the Peninfula of India, and the Iflands contiguous, for the carrying it on. The Trade of the three laft named has, for the moft part, been conducted by a regular Trading Company nearly fimilar to our own; that of the Portuguefe by Houfes of Trade, or private Companies, and fometimes by rich Individuals, fingly on their own Capitals. That of Spain has fo dwindled, that of late we have fcarcely heard of it. *Sweden* alfo has her India Company, fo called; but we know of no Settlements poffeffed by her on the Afiatic Continent, and her Trade of late times has been chiefly, if not wholly confined to China and other parts to the Eaftward of the Ganges.

For

(22)

For some years previous to and until the passing of the Commutation Act in 1784, and for some time afterwards, several of these Foreign Companies partook of the profits derived by the smuggling of teas into this Kingdom, by supplying it either direct from China to Ostend, Dunkirk, and other convenient places, or by selling it to others for that purpose. In consequence of the Commutation Act, and of lowering the Duties on Tea, the India Company were enabled to undersel the smuggler, and in a great degree to put an end to his traffick in that article. Our own regular imports in tea have since become more than doubled in quantity, to the diminution of the Carrying Trade of the *Swedes*, *Danes*, and the India Company of *Embden*, insomuch as almost to annihilate those Companies. That of *Embden*, if not wholly discontinued, is said to be on the eve of becoming so, and another India Company in the Low Countries, called the Trieste Company, has, after very great aids afforded her to support her sinking credit, and after losing or spending her whole capital, intirely stopped trading.

The *Dutch Company* possess not only valuable and convenient Factories, and considerable possessions in India and other parts of Asia, but also the whole of the spice trade, pepper excepted, and were for a long time the envy of their mercantile neighbours. At the commencement of the American war, the Dutch Company were rich, prosperous, and flourishing; but in the rupture of that nation with England the superior power of the latter enabled them to seize their Settlements in India, and interrupt their Commerce, which brought their affairs into such distress, that they must have been utterly ruined, if they had not been supported by loans from the States General to a very large amount, and from that period doubts have been entertained of their ever being able, with all the aid of their Spice monopoly and land revenues in Asia and Africa, to discharge their Debts and restore their Credit.

The failures of successive India Companies in *France* are too notorious to require any particular detail, notwithstanding the advantageous Settlements of *Pondicherry*, the *Mauritius*, and *other parts*. Their present Company, by confining their whole attention to Trade alone, and by taking part of their supplies for the consumption of France, by purchase of the English Company, have hitherto maintained their ground; but a war must inevitably throw them on the mercy of England.

Besides the Trade carried on by these several Companies (for they were not always in the exclusion of the private merchant), there have been ships fitted out by private Adventurers from *Sweden*, *Denmark*, *Ostend*, *France*, *Portugal*, and *America*. Some amongst them may probably have been gainers; but we know the greater part have been great sufferers, and upon the whole afford an useful lesson to such mercantile speculators if they were wise enough to benefit by the experience or misfortune of others, who have wildly engaged in the distant and hazardous commerce of Asia on small capitals. As to *America*, if we may be allowed to judge by her present slackness in the prosecution of her commerce

with

with India and China, or by the purchafes fhe has been of late in the habit of making in Europe of Afiatic goods, and the loffes fhe is known to have fuftained by her cargoes of tea from Canton of the year 1789, there feems little probability of her carrying her commercial intercourfe with thofe remote regions, at prefent, to any confiderable extent.

CHAPTER IX.

The Returns of the Company's Trade anterior to their acquiring the Territories Abroad; the Effect produced by the Acquifition on their Exports and Imports; the prefent Amount of their Debts, and their Claims upon the Public for an Indemnification of their Expences incurred in acquiring and preferving the conquered Provinces.

ANTECEDENT to the year 1757, the fale amount of the Company's Imports had rarely, if at any time, exceeded two millions in any one year. Their foreign inveftments were provided for by fales or barter of their exported goods and bullion, and by money lent them by their fervants in India on bills payable in London, which was the old method of remittance of money acquired in the Company's fervice. Thus we find the annual fales of the imports by the Company for fixteen years next preceding 1757, amounted to about £.2,055,000 on the average; and that, for the fame period, their exported goods and ftores amounted annually, at their prime coft, to £.238,000, and bullion, £.690,000; and that they paid in difcharge of bills of exchange, £.190,000. If during that period the prime coft of the goods imported exceeded the amount of thofe three fums, the difference muft have been paid by the profit on the fales of the goods exported, and by land rents and cuftoms arifing at their principal fettlements. During the fucceeding ten years, it fhould feem that the revenues of the new acquifitions afforded no profit to the Company; for though the produce of the fales of imports became increafed to the amount of £.2,150,000 annually on the average, and though the quantity of bullion exported was reduced to about £.120,000 per ann. yet we find that the exports in goods and ftores, and the money raifed upon bills of exchange, were increafed in a greater ratio, compared with the returns from abroad, the annual amount of each being as high as £.430,000. From 1767 to 1777, the exports of bullion were about £.110,000; of goods £.490,000, and the fums raifed on bills £.458,000 per annum; and by the aid afforded from the revenues, the inveftments became fo increafed as to produce about £.3,330,000 annually. From 1777 to 1784, the average fales of imports, notwithftanding the war, fell off in the proportion only of about £.200,000 annually; the export in bullion was for that period very trifling; but the goods and ftores exported were increafed to about half a million, and the money raifed upon bills to about £.761,000 yearly. For

the

(24)

the last eight years, the sale amount of imports has been £.4,763,242 [*] annually on the medium; the amount paid for bullion £.560,223, for goods and stores exported £.753,976 [†], and for bills of exchange £.1,258,870 per annum. During the last 3 years the Sales have amounted to £.5,094,535; the sums paid for bullion £.464,046, for goods and stores £.952,027, and for bills £.737,465 per annum on the average.

The comparative profits of the Company's Trade were certainly more considerable before they made their conquests, in proportion to the amount of the capital employed, and the aggregate of the Sales of Imports, than at any time since. While their cargoes were less they were purchased at more moderate prices abroad, and came to a more profitable market at home. But, by doubling the Investments in India, as in fact they have been, their prime cost, by the increased demand, became enhanced, while their sale prices at home, by the increased quantity brought into the market, became reduced. The Company had however no choice; the surplus revenue in India could no otherwise be realized at home than through the medium of commerce; and although, on a strict scrutiny, it may probably be found, that many articles from Bengal have not produced in England the amount of their invoice prices and other charges upon them, so that in the hands of a private merchant, a loss would have been sustained, yet viewing the transaction as affecting the community, it will be found that whatever investments were produced from the territorial revenue, were a clear gain. With respect to the Coast Goods, and those from China, they have been chiefly purchased or bartered for as in former times; and by the influx of teas since the Commutation act, through the medium of fair trade, a larger profit has been derived.

The Territorial Revenue, including subsidies and the income of the Company's own property possessed antecedently to the year 1756, may be reckoned at *nearly seven million of Pounds Sterling per ann.* But as the countries can only be governed and maintained, and the revenues collected, by keeping up a large standing military force, and sundry civil establishments; and as experience has proved it to be the best œconomy to allow liberal stipends to the principal officers and servants, to place them beyond the reach of temptation to do amiss; the net surplus, after providing for all civil and military charges, and paying the annual interest of the subsisting debt, does not exceed, according to a computation laid before the House of Commons by the Court of Directors, the annual sum of £.1,200,000. Be its amount what it may, the Reader may be assured that the specie of India has been so exhausted, that no part of the surplus, whatever may be its amount, can be

---

[*] Exclusive of sales of privileged and private trade, which on the same average amounted to £.755,757 per ann. besides what has been smuggled. For the present state of the trade, in other particulars, see chap. 10.

[†] Exclusive of private trade carried out in thirty ships, which at £.25,000 each, make £.750,000 a year, besides illicit and clandestine trade by other ships.

brought

brought in specie, nor can it be realized in England otherwise than through the medium of cargoes provided for the China or European markets.

With respect to the debts of the Company, their amount in India appears to be about *nine millions sterling*, and there being *available assets* in India equal to the discharge of something more than *two millions*, there remains about *seven millions* as a charge on the other assets and future revenues. This debt was incurred by war, and stands wholly unconnected with the Company's commerce.

Their debts at home, beyond the value of assets applicable to their immediate discharge, amount to upwards of *four millions*, of which £.3,200,000 is their standing bonded debt, authorized by Acts of Parliament.

We have already taken occasion to observe, that the claim of the Public to the territories in India acquired by conquest, is subject not only to the outstanding demands of the Company's creditors, but also to an equitable claim by the Company themselves. The justice of that of the creditors manifests itself too strongly to require any illustration or argument, and will doubtless obtain from a British Parliament, whenever it shall exercise its wisdom in providing any New System for the future administration of India, a suitable indemnification. The claim of the Company appears also equally intitled to the regard and support of the Legislature, since it is clear and evident, that in consequence of the unavoidable expences they have been put to by the wars in India, their Capital Stock has been twice increased by new subscriptions, as well as their Bond Debt, to enable them to carry on their Trade; at the same time their dividends have continued only at £.8 per cent.

Under such circumstances we can entertain no doubt but, from the candour and justice of Parliament, the territorial revenues of India will be so appropriated, in any new arrangement that may be made, as to provide for the existing debts abroad, and some reasonable compensation for such part of the debts at home as the Company shall be able to make appear they have disbursed in acquiring and protecting the provinces, beyond what has been produced to the Company from those revenues.

(26)

CHAPTER X.

The Nature and Extent of the Trade of the Company to India and China, with an Account of the Shipping employed in it.

EXPORTS.

WE had nearly completed the account we intended to have given of the several species, quantities, and values of the goods exported by the Company, when the House of Commons relieved us from that labour, by ordering * the three very able and satisfactory Reports, lately made on the subject to the Board of Commerce, by the Court of Directors, to be printed. These Reports have also, for their more extensive promulgation, been again printed by order of the Company. We shall therefore avail ourselves of the authentic accounts they contain, by stating a brief recital of their contents in general, but with a recommendation to our Readers to have recourse to the Reports themselves, as containing many matters, omitted by us, regarding the Trade of the Company at large, highly important to be known.

From the first of these Reports we collect these particulars:

That the Bulk of the Exports consists of,
    Camblets, cloth, and other woollens; metals (particularly tin, lead, and copper); naval and military stores; and silver in bullion.

That the Company reserve to themselves the exclusive export of cloth, woollens, copper, bullion, and military stores; and also clocks, toys, and other articles ornamented with jewels.

That other articles † exported from hence, are chiefly purchased in India by Europeans for their own consumption, and are carried abroad in what is called

* 3d January 1793.
† A List of Articles exported in Private Trade.

Anchors,	Canvas,	Copper,
Bar iron,	Cutlery,	Drugs,
Bulgia hides,	Cards,	Earthen ware,
Brandy,	Cordage,	Furs,
Beer,	Cabinet ware,	Glass ware,
Boots and shoes,	Clocks,	Gunpowder,
Braziery,	Cochineal,	Glass beads,
Buntin,	Carriages,	Ginseng,
Block tin,	Carpets,	Grapnals,
Cyder,	Cloth cuttings,	Gold thread,
Cherry brandy,	Confectionary,	Gold lace,
		Haberdashery,

called *Private Trade* *, by the Commanders and officers of the Company's ships.

That besides what are exported by the Company, and the Private Traders, regularly registered, abundance of British goods find their way to India, both by illicit Trade carried on directly from hence, and also by what is termed *Clandestine Trade*, carried on from various parts of the continent of Europe in British ships, under foreign colours.

That with a laudable zeal for the public good, by promoting the extension of exports of British manufactures, the Company have continued to export, both to India and China, large quantities, particularly of woollens, though the sale of them has not produced sufficient to repay the prime cost and all charges †: have repeatedly commanded their commercial Boards in India, *to indent* for as many as can be sold *without an actual loss*, making these commands in effect *their standing order:* have greatly enlarged the privilege of their commanders and officers, in respect to export goods, making them freight-free; and used, and continue to use, every endeavour to open new channels for the introduction of British goods in various parts beyond the peninsula of India; the result of which, as far as can be yet known, is given in these Reports: And it may be fairly inferred, that the Company's warehouses in *Bengal, Madras,* and *Bombay,* are always supplied with *more woollens* than can be sold to a profit, from the circumstance of there having been great numbers

Haberdashery,	Plate glass,	Turnery,
Hats,	Perfumery,	Tin ware,
Hosiery,	Pickles,	Pig lead,
Hardware,	Prussian blue,	Rod iron,
Ironmongery,	Prints,	Tin plates,
Lines and twine,	Quick-silver,	Wine,
Lead shot,	Rum,	Wooden toys,
Millenery,	Red lead,	Window glass,
Mathematical, and musical instruments,	Remnants of Cloths, Snuff,	Wrought plate, and White lead.
Manchester goods,	Saddlery,	
Mustard,	Steel,	And to China,
Orsidew,	Sheet lead,	
Oil,	Smalts,	Skins, and furs,
Perry,	Sword blades,	Jewellery, toys, watches, some
Painter's colours,	Stationary,	woollens, and silver.
Plated ware,	Ship-chandlery,	

* The Company may lawfully licence whom they please to trade in the East Indies. The officers and subordinates of their ships, being *Thirty* in number for every ship, are allowed the benefit of it, both in Export and Import, according to their different ranks or births. This is called *Private Trade*, and what they pay for this permission, and in lieu of freight, is called *Company's Duties*, and forms an article of the Company's profits. The servants abroad are also frequently permitted to remit home their fortunes in merchandize, for which they pay a freight to the Company. This latter Trade is distinguished from the former by the name of *Privileged Trade*.

† The loss by woollens from 1784 to 1790, exported to India, after allowing for all charges of freight, insurance, interest of money, &c. is computed £.37,790; and the loss on those exported to China at £.61,877 in the same period.

of bales of different sorts, remaining at all times in each of those warehouses, for want of purchasers, the total value of which in 1789-90 was £.167,761 †.

The Report on the India Trade, does not give the particulars of all the Exports of the Company thither, but of *woollens* and *metals*, and such part of the Private Trade as is registered. It does not give the quantity or invoice of naval and military stores, sent either as merchandize, or as supplies for the navy, army, and garrisons abroad; nor of what may be taken thither from Europe illicitly or clandestinely, beyond what is registered: it is admitted, that the excess is so different in every ship, and so fluctuating, as to baffle all computation. We are however, by other authentic documents *, enabled to state, that the prime cost or invoice of goods and merchandize of the growth, produce, or manufacture of Great Britain and Ireland, annually exported to India and China, by the Company alone, including naval and military stores, which are also of our own manufacture, taken for the average of the last six years, have amounted to upwards of £.900,000 per ann. *exclusively of bullion*; and that the export of goods to China, in barter for teas, has in that period been greatly increased, while that of bullion has decreased in an equal or greater proportion; and it is computed that the Private Trade, registered and not registered, has amounted, for the same period, to £.750,000 per ann. at the least, taking it only at the low computation for thirty ships annually, of £.25,000 each; so that the exports of British goods to India and China may be computed at £.1,650,000 per annum.

IMPORTS.

The goods imported by the Company from *India* consist chiefly, of muslins, callicoes, and other piece-goods ‡, raw-silk, cotton, indigo, pepper, salt-petre, ophium, and various sorts of drugs; and from *China*, tea, coffee, and japan and China ware: other articles are doubtless brought both from India and China, but they are of a trifling comparative value: *Sugar* has occasionally been imported in small quantities, but it has been the policy of Government, in order to discourage (as it is thought) the introduction of sugar from the East Indies, as an article either of commerce, or for consumption, to the injury of the *West India* Planters, to lay a protecting duty on it of £.37 16 *s.* 3 *d.* at *the selling price*, while the West India sugars pay only after the rate of 15 *s.*

† The First Report is confined to the Trade with India; the Second, to that of China; and the Third, to Japan and Persia. In the two last are contained connected narratives of our commercial intercourse in those parts, the nature and extent of our trade with China, and the delicate footing on which it stands; with Remarks, shewing the dangerous tendency of making new experiments with the Chinese: And in the third Report are shewn the difficulties which obstruct the extension of British commerce with Persia and Japan.
* Accounts presented to the House of Commons in February 1793.
‡ *Wrought Silks, Bengal Stuffs mixt with Silk*, or *Herba*, and *printed Callicoes*, brought from *India, China*, or *Persia*, are prohibited from being worn in Great Britain. But they pay a duty, though they are again exported. The importation of *Thrown Silk* is also prohibited.

per one hundred weight. This difference in the duty at the prefent enhanced price of fugar, with the high freight paid by the Company on their Bengal fhips, virtually deftroys all competition, and amounts in effect to a prohibition: Otherwife, it is afferted that, Bengal alone, might, in a few years, be made to furnifh far more fugar than would fupply our own confumption; and that, fetting afide the duty, the fugars of the Eaft Indies might be imported, both for confumption and exportation, to the profit of the importers, and reduction in the prefent enormous price of that ufeful, not to fay neceffary article of life. But if any great quantity were to be brought from Bengal, until produced by new plantations, it would doubtlefs be felt by the Natives as a grievance, depriving them of a principal means of rearing their children, whofe fupport, while young, depends very greatly upon the fugar-cane.

To fhew the *immenfe gain* derived to this Country, by the import trade of the Eaft India Company, (a gain which diffeminates itfelf through every branch of manufacture, and affords, in all its confequences, a conftant employment to fome thoufands of our valuable artificers and workmen,) we will endeavour to ftate the whole in as clear a point of view as poffible, taken on the average of the years 1788, 1789, and 1790, and alfo on the average of the years 1791, 1792, and 1793, giving diftinctly the totals of the fums paid by the Company for prime coft, and the cuftoms and excife thereon, and the freight and demorrage, and charges of merchandize, with the total of thofe articles collected; and laftly, the amount of fales for the fame period. But it muft be remembered, that though the gains to the community may be computed from this datum, thofe of the Company cannot, as they depend on various circumftances, which require a diftinct inveftigation.

Average of the Company's own Trade, from 1ft March 1787, to Ditto, 1790.

Invoice, or Prime Coft abroad.	Cuftoms.	Freight and Demorrage.	Charges of Merchandize.	Total.	Amount of Sales.
£.	£.	£.	£.	£.	£.
2,547,848	521,883	736,275	270,675	4,076,681	4,511,262

Average of the Company's own Trade, from 1ft March 1790, to Ditto, 1793.

£.	£.	£.	£.	£.	£.
2,550,728	612,231	717,453	306,185	4,186,597	5,103,094

N. B. The Company do not infure their Ships or Merchandize, and therefore no premium of infurance is included in the charges of Merchandize, nor any intereft for the capital employed.

To the preceding are to be added the imports on the *Private* and *Privileged* Trade. The freight and demorrage, and charges of merchandize are included in the above account. Their prime cost can be known only to the parties concerned; but their sale amount, and the customs paid, taken on the average for the following periods, were as follows:

	Customs. £.	Sale Amount. £.
The annual average of Private and Privileged Trade, from 1787 to 1790, being three years, was	150,482	855,796
Ditto from 1790 to 1793, average of three years,	100,873	773,376

Besides the duties of customs contained in the above accounts, the following further duties were paid, amounting, on the average of each year, taken for five years from 1st March 1787 to ditto, 1792, to the sums following:

Excise on Arrack, &c.	Inland Duties on Pepper consumed in England.	Customs and Inland Duties on Tea and Coffee.	Customs on Wines.	Totals.
£.	£.	£.	£.	£.
81,765	14,930	334,960	6,894	438,549

The whole average amount of the customs, and inland duties on the import trade of India and China to Great Britain, may therefore be fairly estimated at £.1,050,000 per annum, and the sale amount thereof at £.5,850,000 per annum. It is computed, that the sale amount of the Company's own imports, for the current year, will amount to 5¼ millions.

The duties, however, here stated, do not wholly stop at the Exchequer. A great proportion of the merchandize from India, and probably about one tenth part of the tea imported from China, is exported to Ireland, and foreign parts; the drawbacks and bounties on which, considerably diminish the amount of the duties paid by the Company on their importation. It would, for many obvious reasons, be extremely difficult, if not impracticable, to discover with exact certainty, the nett amount of the duties on the merchandize of India and China, which has remained after those deductions. An account of this nature was made for the year 1788, and by an actual and very laborious collection from the books of the custom house, it was computed that out of £.750,000 paid by the Company for customs, on the imports sold at their sales, £.330,000 had been repaid for drawbacks and bounties*. We are not, however, to conclude, that either the revenue or the country are ultimately injured by the diminution. The export of India goods forms no inconsiderable part of our carrying trade to other countries, giving additional employment to our shipping, and affording commercial profits to our merchants, who, in return for the India goods exported, bring other valuable commodities, sufficient to return in customs, a sum probably equal to that, which may have been paid in drawbacks and bounty. Other advantages also result to the dealers, and others, by the profits on the re-sales, by carriage and agency; and the Port of London being thus made the chief depôt for the supply of Europe, and of many parts of Africa and America, of the merchandize of the East, is necessarily resorted to by foreign merchants for its purchases, who, at the same time, buy various commodities of our own manufacture, which would probably not otherwise have been called for, by all which the national prosperity is promoted.

SHIPPING.

Ninety-two Ships are at this time employed by the Company, abroad and at home, in the Carrying Trade to India and China, the measurement of which is 81,179 Tons. The average complement of Officers and Subordinates is 30, and of Seamen 100 for each Ship, making 2,760 Officers and Subordinates, and 9,200 Seamen. Besides these, the Shipping employed in the Asiatic Seas, in what is termed "*the Country Trade*," is very considerable. The Reader will readily conceive, that to keep so numerous a Fleet of large Merchantmen afloat, for such long voyages, must create employment for a vast number of artificers in various branches of trade, and also occasion the consumption of a great quantity of materials manufactured and unmanufactured, not to mention the expences of victualling, &c. The extent of the employment it affords, and of the materials it consumes, may be estimated by the amount already given, of what has been paid by the Company under the head of Freight and Demorrage.

* It may be taken for granted, that, upon the average of five years, the annual returns of duties in drawback and bounty, are equal to two parts in five of the whole amount of customs and inland duties paid on East India and China goods.

Since the former Edition of this Tract, we have been favored with a most comprehensive and satisfactory detail of the sales of the Company's imports, including private Trade, the quantities thereof exported, and the quantities retained for home consumption for four years, with the totals of the drawbacks. A paper so useful, and coming as it does from the most respectable authority, cannot fail of being highly acceptable to the reader; we have therefore given it a place at the end of these sheets. To this the Public are indebted, as indeed they are to the many improvements introduced in the mode of keeping the accounts of the King's duties, by which alone satisfactory information on similar subjects of intricacy can be obtained, to the zeal talents and assiduity of Mr. Irving, the Inspector General of the Customs.

In

In bringing forward the foregoing Statements of the Import and Export Trade and Shipping of the India Company, which, it is trusted, will stand the test of the strictest scrutiny. The Writer is not influenced by any selfish or partial motives, but purely by a desire of communicating to his Readers a faithful account of the nature and extent of this branch of British Commerce, that every man, by knowing its nature and magnitude, may be properly impressed with a just estimate of its immense value and importance, in whatever view it be considered, whether as furnishing a regular permanent supply of raw materials for our Manufacturers, and a uniform annual export of their productions; or as affording constant employment and livelihood to a considerable proportion of the inhabitants of this country, or as aiding our public revenues and the Carrying Trade of the country in re-exportation to Foreign Parts, and furnishing various articles of comfort and luxury to all ranks and degrees of people, of the production of the East, at reasonable prices; from which it is easy to perceive the necessity there is for the greatest degree of circumspection being used in the introducing of any Change of System, which might hazard the loss, or divert the channels of this very valuable and important branch of British Commerce.

CHAPTER XI.

Respecting the Profits derived by the Company from their Trade.

THE accounts which have been published do not furnish the means of computing, with any degree of accuracy, the Profit and Loss upon *the Export Trade*. This defect is occasioned by the merchandize being blended with military and warlike stores, and the want of a specification what part of the stores was sold or what part of them was converted to the use of the forces and garrisons. The charges of merchandize are also blended with the expences of raising and maintaining recruits, and conveying them to India; and with gratuities, pensions, law charges, and other disbursements of various kinds. In the year 1780 it appeared, that the Export Trade, and the Company's duty on Private Trade, had, upon the medium for some years before, cleared a profit equal to an annual dividend of £.2 12s. 6d. per cent. on the old capital of £.3,200,000; the profits derived by the Exports to China * since that time have not been ascertained; and with respect to the Exports to India, it may be doubted if they now yield any real profit. For although warlike stores, and metals, ammunition, and other articles, produce something considerable, that profit is, in a great degree, if not intirely absorbed in the losses on other goods, damages and charges of merchandize, and interest of the money paid on the outfit.

* The profits on these have been computed at £.65,000 per annum.

Of the † *Import Goods* from India and China for the years 1791, 1792, and 1793, the produce of the Sales appears to have exceeded the invoice thereof, with the customs, freight, and charges of merchandize paid thereout, by £. 2,749,491, the yearly average whereof is £. 916,497.

The next article of profit arises from a duty so called of £. 5 per cent. which the Company are authorised by law ‡ to take towards the expences of supporting the Factories, maintaining Ambassadors, &c. in India, on the value of India Goods imported by the *Private Traders*. The *privileged* as well as the *private Trade* of the Company's Officers pay this duty, and also 2 per cent. more *ad valorem* for warehouse room and in lieu of other charges of merchandize on these goods, and the *privileged Trade* pays the Company at the rate of £. 15 *per ton* homeward for freight and demorrage; from hence the Company derive about £. 70,000 a year, besides the £. 15 per ton for freight, and although the sum produced may in appearance form part of their mercantile Funds, as an article of profit, it has not in reality a feature of real profit in it; because if the private and privileged Trade were to be charged with a due share of the expences of supporting the Settlements and Ambassadors abroad, and warehouses, &c. at home, apportioned by its amount *ad valorem* to the Company's own Trade, the Sum falling on the private and privileged Trade would be much larger than it is *. And it is owing to the manner in which this duty making 7 per cent. is charged in the Company's Accounts, that gives it the appearance of a profit, when in reality it is only part of the sum charged against their own Trade, under the heads of Freight and Charges of merchandize, and ought more properly to be subtracted from them. We have been thus particular in explaining the nature of this duty, because the custom house officers have complained of it as holding out an additional temptation to the smugglers of private Trade, to avoid the customs and this duty likewise. And we must confess, that if the private and privileged Trade were to be charged, in lieu of freight and other charges, a duty of tonnage, which should not depend as the Company's duty now does upon the actual lodgment of the goods in the Company's warehouses, the excitement to running the goods would in some degree be lessened.

The only further article of profit at home is the unsold part of the Company's *Annuity* from Government, and the Allowance for Management, making together £. 37,913 16 s. per annum.

The *old Settlements* of the Company in India properly form a part of their Commercial Estate. But the revenues of them, since the obtaining the Dewannee of Bengal, have been so blended with those of the Dewannee, and other conquered or ceded territories, as to make it impracticable, to state what they amount to at present. It does, however, appear, by the printed Reports

---

† Printed Papers, No. 28.   ‡ By act 9 & 10 W. 3. ch. 44. s. 76.
* The Commercial Charges, at the several Settlements in India, amount to 8 per Cent. on the Cost of the Investment; and the Charges of Merchandize at Home to 6 per Cent. on the Sale. Printed Accounts No. 3. & 4. of 20th February, 1793.

of 1772 and 1782, made by different Committees of the House of Commons, that the Company's *own landed Property, Customs and Port Duties*, produced so late as 1780, a gross revenue of at least £.590,000 a year, from which there must be deducted £.70,000 a year paid to the Soubah *Nizam Ally*, for the rent or Farm of the *Circars*. Supposing these possessions were to contribute to the general expence of the Empire in India, on a proportionate footing with those of the Company and of Arcot and Tanjore, there would still remain a very large annual income from them, probably to the * amount of more than *four per cent.* per annum on the Capital Stock of *Five Millions*.

The result of the enquiry into the annual profits of the Company appears to be, that, with a temporary use only of part of the surplus of the public Revenue of Bengal towards the purchase of their goods, the Company are in possession of a yearly income derived by Commerce, and by Rents and Customs, as follows:

The profits by import goods from China and India —	£.900,000
By the contributions of Private and Privileged Traders, towards current expences — — — —	70,000
By their annuity from the Public for their unsold part of the debt of £.4,200,000	38,000
And by rents, customs, and port duties in India, at the least	250,000
Total per annum —	£.1,258,000

* Third Report Committee of Secrecy, 1772, p. 61. Company's Lands and Customs possessed before 1757, produced in ten years (as follows):

	£.	
Bengal — — — — —	235,882	Clear of Charges of Col-
Madras — — — — —	641,440	lection, Commission to
Bombay — — — — —	565,075	Servants, Jagheers and
Bencoolen — — — — —	21,457	Stipends.
	1,463,854	

The annual average — — — — —		£.146,385
Purgunnahs, fourth Report, 1772, p. 100		115,000
Four Northern Circars, six lacs pagodas, fourth Report, 1782, p. 19		240,000
Add Guntoon Circar, at nine lacs of rupees		90,000
		591,385
Deduct the rent to the Nizam		70,000
	Remains	521,385
Suppose expences of all sorts —		271,385
	Nett —	£.250,000

Which

(35)

Which income (except the temporary use of the sum necessary to be realized in Great Britain for the benefit of the Public, through the medium of the Company's Commerce) is unconnected with, and independent of, the Dewannee revenues of Bengal, Bahar, and Orissa, and the new acquisitions from Tippoo Sultaun in the Carnatic, all belonging to the Public; and the only deductions to be made from it are, the interest on the bond debt, and on bills of exchange and occasional loans, and such other articles of disbursement, as have not been already placed under the head of Charges of Merchandize, the whole of which cannot exceed, communibus annis, on a very liberal estimate, £.200,000 per annum.

We are unable to state with certainty the profit on goods exported to China; it must, however, be observed, that the amount of that profit can be realized only by the sales of the Teas in England; although it has been estimated that there is a profit on the sale of those exports of £.65,000 a year, nothing is included, on that account, in these statements, there being no official document to refer to.

CHAPTER XII.

A concise View of the Company's Affairs, in their distinct Capacities of Sovereigns *and* Merchants.

ON the Compact* of 1781 for enlarging the term in the exclusive Trade, the funds arising by the *net surplus of the Territorial Revenues and profits of Trade*, after payment of a dividend of 8 per cent. to the Proprietors of India Stock, were to be applied, *three fourths* to the Public, and *the remaining fourth* to the Company. By the continuation of the war, and the increased establishments, civil and military, in India, between 1779 and 1782, those funds fell greatly deficient to defray the expences. In 1783 the Public agreed to forego any participation of the above funds until certain debts should be discharged; and by *the Relief-Act* of 1784 the participation, as settled in 1781, was to be resumed, as soon as the debts therein specified were paid, and the bond debt reduced to £.1,500,000. The Peace with *Tippoo Sultaun* was not concluded till March 1784, and it was a considerable time after the treaty before the troops were completely reduced to the peace establishment, and properly stationed. It has since proved, that if the whole of the debt incurred by the war, beyond the revenues which had been received, could have been brought forwards at an early period, they would not have fallen much short of *Eleven* Millions. Upwards of *Four* Millions of it have been since discharged or transferred home, and from the accounts lately printed by order of the House of Commons, it may be

* Acts 21 Geo. III. Ch. 65.———23 Geo. III. Ch. 83.———24 Geo. III. Ch. 34.

collected

(36)

collected, that after allowing for the cash in the treasuries abroad, and bills of exchange due, and such other assets as may be deemed good and available, there will still remain a debt of upwards of *Six Millions*, besides £.1,384,050 due on bills granted on account of the India Debt upon the Company at home, including interest thereon, to March 1794. The *Political* or *War Debt* of the Company remaining to be paid, or provided for, may therefore be taken at about *Seven Millions and an Half Sterling*. From the Circumstance of the Paymaster of the Forces laying before the House of Commons an ‖ Account of sums advanced relative to the Forces of His Majesty serving in India, it is not improbable but the debt will be increased by the Demands of Government under that head. The total of the sums advanced on this account, for four years, is £.258,994.

The Commercial Assets *in India alone*, without taking into the account the value of *Stores*, or *Sums* owing to the Company of a doubtful nature, appear to exceed their *mercantile debts there*, by One Million Sterling or more, and the balance of Assets in their favour in China is £.770,000. Their bond debts, and other debts at home relating to their trade, amount to about £.6,250,000. Their available Assets in merchandize and good debts, including the unsold part of their annuities, to about £.8,500,000, leaving an overplus of £.2,250,000, which, with One Million of Assets in India, and the £.770,000 in China, makes a balance in favour of the Company, after providing for their *Commercial Debts*, of £.4,000,000 towards securing their Capital Stock of Five Millions.

In addition to this sum, the Proprietors of India Stock have the following further security for their property, viz.

1st. The Military Stores abroad, valued at £.980,910 *.

2dly. The Buildings † and Fortifications at the several Settlements, including St. Helena, which appear to have cost the Company £.7,320,559.

3dly. In Plate, Household Furniture, Plantations, Farms, Slaves, Sloops, Vessels, and Stores, in India, £.1,091,705 ‡.

4thly. All their Landed Estates and Customs, (viz.): Calcutta and its Purgunnahs, Madras and its Jagheer, the Five Northern Circars, the Islands of Bombay and St. Helena, Cuddalore, Pinang, and Bencoolen, producing a gross income § of £.520,000 a year, or £.400,000 a year net income, being at least £.250,000 a year after allowing its due proportion for the general defence, as before stated.

5thly. The Produce of the Cargoes of the India and China Ships already cleared from England, beyond their prime cost.

‖ Printed by Order of the House, the 12th February 1783.
* Printed Papers, House of Commons, No. 2.
† Stock by Computation, No. 17.   ‡ Ditto.   § Ditto.

6thly.

6thly. The produce of the Cargoes above their invoices, which shall hereafter arrive from India and China.

7thly. The India-House, Warehouses, and other Buildings in London, valued at £.355,780 †, and their Ships and Vessels, valued at £.37,050.

Lastly. The Sum on Balance, justly chargeable to the Use of the Company on the *Dewannee Revenues* in India, which shall be found to have been paid by them out of their Commercial Funds, beyond what has been produced from the *Dewannee Revenues*.

CHAPTER XIII.

Recapitulation of the present State of our Trade with India and China, and the Rights of the East India Company. The Nature and Grounds of the various Objections expected to be made in Parliament, to the Continuation of the Trade on its present System. Reflections on the Effects of Innovation.

AT a time when the Company are threatened with a serious opposition to the continuance of their exclusive Trade with India and China, it is of importance, that not only the Members of the Legislature, but every individual in society, should have a competent knowledge of the nature and extent of the Company's acknowledged Rights, and the manner and authority, whereby they were obtained and are upheld, and, above all, of the extent to which their Trade has become advanced, that it may be clearly seen how far the interests of the Nation are more immediately concerned in its support, or connected with it. It was to that intent that we have gone into the detail; and we shall beg the indulgence of our readers, while we endeavour to bring the whole into a concise, but more connected view, conceiving that a concern so momentous and weighty cannot be too well understood, or too firmly impressed on the mind.

The Rights of the Company are held under the immediate authority of Parliament, and embrace all those of the Old Chartered Company, which subsisted from the year 1600 to 1708, when they became vested or absorbed, with all their Fortresses, Settlements, and Factories, and other property, real and personal, in the present United Company, (their body politic, and their power of converting the Trade into a mischievous monopoly excepted). They are a perpetual Corporation; and although their exclusive Right to the Trade, and their power of administering the government and revenues of India, were to be determined (both which it is in the power of Parliament to do after March

† Printed Papers, No. 24.

1794), they would still remain an incorporated Company *in perpetuity*, with the exclusive property and possession of *Calcutta, and Fort William, Madras and Fort St. George, Bombay, Bencoolen, and St. Helena*, and various other Settlements and landed Estates in India, and also a right of trading thither, *with a Joint Stock*, together with all their repositories and other conveniencies adapted to their commerce, and the preservation of their merchandize, both abroad and at home. The only privileges they can be constitutionally deprived of, are those of trading *to the exclusion of others*, and of *governing* the countries, and collecting and appropriating the *revenues* of India. Whether, in the event of the *sole Trade* being determined, individuals would be able to carry on a successful trade to India, if the Company were to debar them the use of their *Ports* and *Factories*, may require a serious consideration.

The exports of the Company in woollens, metals, warlike stores, and other goods, of the growth, produce, or manufacture of Great Britain or Ireland, have gradually increased since 1757, from £.230,000 to 900,000 a year, and the private trade is computed at £.750,000 more, making together £.1,650,000. Great exertions have been made, and are still making, to open new channels in the Eastern Seas for a further increase of exports of our manufactures. The imports have been extended in a greater proportion than the exports. Before the year 1757, the sales of imported goods produced only about £.2,000,000 a year; and in 1767, not more than £.2,300,000 a year including the duties on teas. During the last eight years the imports have amounted to nearly *five millions* a year, exclusively of those duties, besides Private Trade, which has produced £.800,000 per ann.; and this year the Company's sales are estimated at * upwards of 5¼ Millions, exclusively of all private and privileged Trade. The annual payment to ship owners, for freight and demorrage, have been extended in an equal proportion; and on a yearly average for the last four years, it has exceeded £.800,000 a year, and other charges of merchandize paid to individuals have exceeded £.360,000 a year. The gross annual amount of customs and excise on the goods imported by the Company's ships, including the Private Trade, has exceeded £.1,000,000 a year, and though probably £.400,000, or £.430,000 a year of that sum has been repaid in drawbacks and bounties, on the exports of goods, partly unmanufactured and partly manufactured in England with the raw materials of India, it hath been amply repaid to the Community by the employment afforded to our own manufacturers, by the gains made by exporters and dealers, by profits arising from carriage and agency, by the means to which the exports from hence of Asiatic merchandize have contributed, towards securing the general Balance of Trade in our favour; and, lastly, by the returns brought back of valuable articles of merchandize, liable to customs and inland duties.

* Printed Paper, N° 10, computes the sum to be received by sales between March 1793 and March 1794 at £.5,400,000. The sale amount cannot therefore be estimated at much short of 5¼ Millions.

(39)

The British shipping employed at this time by the Company, exceeds 81,000 tons; the number of ships is ninety-two; their whole complement in officers and subordinates 2,760, and of seamen 9,200; of the latter, not less than 7,000 are in constant employment.

Each of these officers and subordinates has a limited privilege of trading, both outward and homeward, according to their rank or birth in the ship, and their number being added to the Proprietors of India Stock, (consisting of more than 2,700 persons) and to the servants of the Company abroad, who have also indulgences of trading, the whole number of persons, who participate directly and immediately in the India and China Trade by the Company's ships, may be fairly computed at 6,000; and whilst this immense Trade has been maintained and supported at the sole risk of the Company, whose Members have received no other benefit, than moderate interest for the capital employed, the Public have derived, in direct revenue, and in various different shapes, every other * species of profit and advantage produced by it.

The superior advantages resulting from the system of regularity, established for the conduct of the Company's Trade, over a loose precarious outfit, are also numerous. The demand for manufactured goods is regular and uniform, affording constant work to the hands employed in the making of them. Those, with whom the Company have dealings, are certain of liberal treatment, and punctual payment. Tradesmen, artificers, and manufacturers, emulate for their custom. The number of families in London and its environs, whose whole support is dependent on the Company's Trade, is great beyond conception. Their mercantile establishments in England and Abroad, though conducted (if we except the article of freight) upon strict rules of economy, are immense. The India House, and their numerous warehouses, are filled with persons bred up to the business from their infancy; and if they were to be deprived of it, the greater number, men of respectable characters and irreproachable conduct, must be reduced to want or distress. It would be almost endless to enumerate the tradesmen, artificers, and others, who, by the means of this regular, and as it were, fixed trade, earn and obtain honest livelihoods in building, rigging, and careening of ships, and furnishing guns, anchors,

---

* The Company's profits by a dividend of eight per cent. on a capital of five millions, is per ann. £.400,000 only.

Paid to the merchants and ship-owners on an average of five years	800,000
Paid for charges of merchandize ditto ditto	360,000
Paid for export goods sent abroad, including Private Trade	1,650,000
Paid for customs and excise on an average of four years	1,060,000
Annual benefit to the nation	3,870,000

Exclusively of the advantages derived by the raw materials of India manufactured in Great Britain, and the profits by exporting India and China merchandize.

timber,

timber, iron, sails, cordage, and various other sorts of implements and tackle used therein.

Well calculated, however, as the present system may appear, for securing a continuance of the advantages, we have endeavoured to describe, the Company, when they come to Parliament with their Proposals for an extension of their term in the exclusive Trade, will probably find themselves surrounded by many opponents, and on various grounds. Merchants and ship owners from different quarters, but more particulary from the Out-ports, may urge, that their exclution from a participation in the benefits of the Asiatic Trade, is repugnant to the spirit of the British constitution, which declares, that the seas shall be free and open to all; and that it is highly injurious to the commercial interests of the rest of the Three Kingdoms, that this Trade should be limited, in all its imports and exports, to the metropolis alone. Manufacturers of various descriptions may think it for their interest, to unite their support with the merchants, on these general and plausible grounds, for an Open Trade. They may likewise, according to their different views of aggrandizement (in the event of the failure of their most favourite plan) insist on the justice and expediency, of laying the Company under various restrictions and prohibitions. The cotton manufacturer may be anxious to destroy all competition and rivalship to his trade, both at home and abroad, more particularly in the article of muslins; to what extent he will claim or expect this indulgence, whether to the putting a stop to the making of muslins in India, or only a prohibition against their being worn in England, time will discover. The woollen manufacturer may complain of the partiality, which he experiences (a partiality inseparable from an exclusive Trade), by the option it leaves in the conductors of it, to deal with particular customers to the exclusion of others. The ship owners may, on similar grounds, revive their complaints, and urge the propriety of laying the Company under an obligation, to charter their ships according to the lowest offers. And as the Company, like other exporters of woollen cloth, are in the habit of buying it, in an unfinished state, and employing pressers and packers to perfect it, the manufacturers of it may possibly think, that the Company ought to be restricted, in that respect, in order to add to his profits, those of the packer and presser. The tin merchant, and miners in Cornwall (regardless of the services so recently afforded them, through the medium and at the risk of the India Company, whereby alone their distresses could be effectually* relieved), may think it but a small and reasonable sacrifice, for the Company to make in their favour, to be laid under an obligation, to purchase and export all the tin they may raise, at some fixed price, or in the alternative, that the ships of individuals may be licensed to take it abroad, and barter it for teas and other China commodities. Other descriptions of persons, on similar grounds of profit and aggrandizement, may, in like manner, come forward, and urge pretensions for

---

* Alluding to the immense export of Tin by the India Company to China at a time when most of the miners, for want of employment, were in great distress, and the repositories of the tin merchants filled with tin without any prospect of their finding purchasers for it.

other

other regulations or restrictions, not yet foreseen. We know, by every day's experience, that nothing is more easy than to procure hands to Petitions, and when presented to Parliament, the petitioners have, one and all, a right to be heard, and have an equal claim to its patience, its candour, and its justice; nor can any doubt be entertained, but their petitions, and the proofs they shall adduce, will have every consideration paid to them, that may be found due to their merit.

On the grand point, that of opening the Trade altogether, we have as yet seen no specific well digested plan offered to the public eye. It, however, can hardly be supposed, that even the most zealous advocates for a new system, can be desirous of seeing the present mode of conducting the Trade determined, and the future Trade left *to hazard and chance.* A measure more preposterous and absurd, nor any so fraught with ruin and mischief to the general interests of the empire, as affecting the *political,* the *mercantile,* and the *financial* concerns, both of *Great Britain* and *India,* could not be devised or imagined by an enemy to both. A new exclusive *Joint Stock Company* (without adverting to the consideration, whether any better than the present could be framed) could not, we think, be established, but in direct subversion of those principles of justice and public œconomy, which, by analogy to other cases, where the property or interests of individuals are made to give way to the accomplishment of great and important designs, essential to public convenience and utility, have ever guided and governed the conduct of the British Senate. To such as may contemplate a new *Joint Stock Company,* it may be asked, if the public purse can be made chargeable for the value and amount of the property and immoveable effects of the present Company, abroad and at home? Or, can a new subscription be expected to succeed equal to the amount both of their *Value* and *Capital* necessary and sufficient for a trading Stock? And, how or by what *Tribunal,* or after what *Detum* shall a *Value* be fixed on the antient possessions and estates of the Company in India, and on those *indefinite Rights,* which must unavoidably be made to cease, upon the creation and investiture of any new exclusive *Joint Stock Company*; and in what respect have the present Company so forfeited that *preference* to the public favour, which their long possession of the Trade, and the services they have rendered to the community, seem so justly to intitle them to, if they shall be desirous of continuing it; subject, however, to any further regulations and restrictions, which may be thought needful, and not being degrading to the character and pre-eminence, they have so long held and supported in India?

With regard to a regulated Company, unless it were known on what principles it were intended, and whether to the exclusion of the present Company, or for the purpose of rivalship and competition, it would be premature to offer any remarks upon it.

We have hitherto confined our observations to what has relation only to the Mercantile Character and Concerns of the Company; but in deciding on the expediency

expediency of the question, whether any change or innovation (beyond mere matter of regulation) can with safety be adopted, it is essentially necessary to inquire, in what degree it might have a tendency to shake Public Credit, by rendering the revenues derived from the Trade of Asia precarious and uncertain. At present, as far as the Company's *own merchandize* is concerned, the Duties and *Customs* have been and will doubtless continue, secure from all possibility of fraud. By a few wholesome provisions, the Duties on the *private* and *privileged Trade*, we think, may be equally protected. Some of the most valuable of the articles, and on which the Duties are highest, lie within so narrow a compass, as to make them easily portable; and if the fact be true (as it has been alleged and is generally believed) that a major part of these articles, and often others, though more bulky, are clandestinely imported from the Continent, by which the Public are defrauded of duties, to a large amount, it must be left to our Readers to judge, what pernicious effects might not be produced on the Revenue of Customs, if the Trade was to be so far laid open, as to admit of the landing the goods of India and China at any of the ports of Great Britain or Ireland, at the option of the owner or master. Under any other mode of Trade, whether open, or under a regulated Company, there seems to be but one way of guarding against this evil, and in that the remedy would probably be deemed worse than the disease. It is by lowering the duties, so as to render them unequal to the risque and insurance of the smuggler. This, however, might obviously defeat the very intent of imposing the present duties, whether prohibitory or protecting. And here we cannot help adverting to the complaint of some of the Cotton Manufacturers, who vainly think, that by prohibiting the importation of India Muslins, their consumption here might be prevented. To encourage that new branch of Trade, *raw Cotton* is already allowed to be imported *free from duty*; nor is British Muslin liable to any (unless dyed of more than one colour), whilst India Muslins pay a protecting Duty of *eighteen per cent. ad valorem, on importation*; and if they are exported, only *ten* of it is returned *in drawback*. This Duty has at all times been more than * sufficient to cover insurance by the smuggler to the dealer. It is therefore obvious, that if the consumption of India Muslins is at present injurious to our own Manufacture, the lowering the duty, though it may be the means of securing and increasing the Revenue on Muslins, must have the effect of increasing the consumption, and of course the evil complained of will remain unremedied. And such we think (in deference to the better judgment of those who complain) must for ever be the case, until British Muslins can obtain a preference in the Market to those of India in their texture and price; or unless the poor Natives of India shall be forbid to reap any fruits by their ingenuity and industry. For undoubtedly, while the Natives are not prohibited from making Muslins, and while their Goods are

* It is universally known, that the insurance on India Muslins, smuggled from Ostend or Dunkirk into a dealer's shop in London, rarely exceeds £.14 per cent. in which every expence is covered. It is computed that we pay four millions of pounds sterling per annum for cotton, and that the goods manufactured with it sell for sixteen millions, while the whole quantity of India Muslins sold for Consumption, has fallen considerably short of £.400,000. It is the fineness and excellence of the Indian Goods that can alone preserve the fashion.

preferred

preferred to British Muslins, they will find their way to Europe in spite of any laws we can make; and prohibitions will only have the effect of transferring the benefit now derived by the Trade in *India Muslins* from the Company and the dealers and exporters of them, into the hands of Foreigners. The prohibition might also have the effect of making Muslins unfashionable to the utter ruin of the Trade.

That under a regulated Company, it would be impracticable to frame provisions, for securing the Duties in general from frauds, we by no means assert. It seems sufficient, to point out in what respect they may be improved under the present Company, and on the other hand how they may become more exposed than at present to evasion and fraud, and more particularly if the Trade shall become diffused, and conducted at many different ports by various hands.

Above all, it will be expedient to consider how far any material innovation on the present system of our Asiatic Commerce, may have a tendency to affect the political connection between Great Britain and India. It is well known, that the affairs of Government, Revenue, and Commerce, in the Provinces abroad, are become blended and intimately connected, each in its turn aiding and supporting the others, and that they cannot be separated without putting the whole to hazard, nor in any event without incurring considerable inconvenience and certain loss. At the time of our first obtaining these territories, it required no extraordinary degree of penetration to foresee, that *ten* or *eleven* millions of people, situate at so distant a part of the globe, attached to laws and institutions founded on superstition, and widely differing from those of their Conquerors, were not likely to submit to a New Government, and New Laws, administered in the Name of a Christian Prince, as their Conqueror, resident they knew not where but by name. To reconcile their minds, by quieting their fears and apprehensions, and to prevent, as much as possible, their feeling the change of their condition, the wise and politic as well as benevolent medium, was adopted of surrendering back, in appearance, the conquered territories to their native owners, and accepting, as a kind of trust from the reigning Mogul, the office of Duan, or High Treasurer and Collector of the Revenues arising from them, upon an engagement to protect the Country from enemies, to pay the expences of the *native* Civil Government, and to contribute to the splendor and authority of the Mogul's Court, and the Defence of his Empire, leaving the Civil Government to go on and be administered in the name of the Mogul and his Subah or Nabob. Conformably to this engagement, the Government of the Provinces has been continued to the present time. The British influence is indeed paramount, but in the public Archives of the Country, all matters which relate *to civil and criminal Judicature* appear as if conducted solely by, and in the name of, the Mogul or his native officers; and all municipal concerns are decided by the Laws of the Natives, those between Mussulmen by their Magistrates, and according to the Laws of the Koran, and those between Hindoos and Gentoos by the Shaster; nor of late time have the Company's Officers interposed their authority over the Native Magistrates, but with a sparing hand, and on urgent occasions.

The revenues of these territories, namely, of Bengal, Bahar, Orissa, Benares, Madras, and Bombay, with the subsidies of the several Nabobs and Rajahs, received by the Company, have amounted yearly, taken on an average of three years from 1787 to 1790, to about £.6,900,000 Sterling. The expences, civil and military, paid out of those revenues, and the interest of outstanding debts, with the expences of the establishments at Fort Marlbro', Pinang, and St. Helena, are computed at about £.5,800,000, leaving a net annual surplus of about £.1,100,000 *. Of the gross income, part of it arises from the Company's own proper territories and revenues, as before is stated; the remainder of it from the Dewannee lands, and by subsidies. It is universally admitted, that India having been already in a great degree exhausted of its specie, it is not possible for any part of this *surplus* to be realized in Great Britain, but *through the medium of commerce*; nor could the revenue itself b made good, but through the aid given to the collection of it, by articles of Indian manufacture, annually provided for the *China and European investments*. It would answer little purpose to go much at large into an explanation, of what in itself is intricate and tedious. Suffice it to observe, that the Company employ overseers at their Aurungs in India, and in providing their manufactured goods. The collectors of the revenue advance money to those people out of the collections, for the purchase of raw materials, and for supporting the manufacturers and workmen employed. The money has a rapid circulation; it passes instantly from the Manufacturer to the Ryot, or cultivator of the lands, for rice and other food; from thence to the Native Collectors of the village for rent, who pay it over to the superior Landlord or Zemindar, through whom it again reaches the Company's Collector. What is paid for the raw material reaches immediately the occupier of the Cotton Grove or Poppy Garden, and is circulated through a like medium till it comes to the English Collector. Such being the course of circulation established in all those parts of India, where piece goods, ophium, indigo, or other articles of merchandize, are manufactured, and the condition of the Natives employed in them, being so abject as to require a regular supply, to keep them from emigrating or starving, it should seem that either in case, of diverting the revenue to any other purpose, or depriving the inhabitants of this means of supporting their families, neither Revenue, nor manufactured Goods, could be obtained; and if revenue could not be obtained, there must soon be an end to the influence of the British government in Hindostan; the political connection between the two countries would be destroyed, and all commercial intercourse would most probably perish with it.

* *N. B.* According to the Memoir of the Carnatic, just published by Major Reynell, the revenue of the countries ceded by Tippoo Sultaun, amount to £.411,500 per ann. Whatever nett income is produced from thence must be added to this surplus of £.1,100,000.

Under

Under thefe circumftances, it fhould feem that every man, whofe mind is not biafled by an undue prejudice, or by views of perfonal aggrandizement, will perceive the imminent danger to which our Poffeffions, our Trade, and our Revenues in India, may become expofed, by abolifhing the prefent fyftem, and fubftituting another, which may prove unfuccefsful. All material innovations upon eftablifhed ufages and forms, more particularly in fuch as relate to matters of Government, Public Revenue, or Commercial Connection, are ever attended with inconveniences and difficulties, and can only be juftified upon the ground of unavoidable neceffity. The flighteft difcontent amongft the natives may lead to fuch extremities, as we may be neither prepared to meet, nor have ability ultimately to repel; and we may have to lament, when it is too late, that we have fuffered our reafon to be led aftray, by the plaufible arguments and falfe reafonings of interefted fpeculators; and, what will not add much to our confolation, will be the reflection of having fuffered ourfelves to be deluded, although warned of the impending danger, by every fucceffive Governor of Bengal, and particularly by Mr. Haftings, who emphatically tells * us, that " our exiftence in India has, on many occafions, vibrated to " the edge of perdition; and that it has at all times been fufpended by a " thread fo fine, that the touch of chance might break, or the breath of " opinion diffolve it."

In this difcuffion we have carefully avoided quoting any of the arguments † ufed upon former occafions, for and againft an exclufive Trade, becaufe, by the acquifition of Kingdoms and Provinces, the Afiatic Trade has, fince thofe times, undergone an entire change, infomuch that the order and fyftem, which formerly obtained in the conduct of it, feem now to be perfectly inverted. The point contended for on thofe occafions was fimply mercantile. The fubject now fpreads itfelf into a wider field; it attaches to it *political* concerns of high importance, as well as thofe of *Commerce* and *Finance*. At thofe times, a change in the exifting fyftem was of little comparative confequence; the Exports and Imports were *fmall*, and the Revenue by *Cuftoms*, if it had fuffered, could have been eafily made good; for the *National Debt* was then moderate, the objects left for *taxation* were numerous; and the real and perfonal affets of the Company were more than fufficient, after the difcharge of their debts, to make good the value of their capital Stock; it became therefore a queftion, fairly determinable by the weight of public opinion, how the India Trade might be beft conducted, without involving in its confequences, thofe important rights and interefts, which feem now to depend on the continuance of the prefent fyftem of conducting the Government, Revenues, and Trade in all its effential parts. It may be alfo material to obferve, that although the Eaft India Company have a clear indifputable right to continue *to trade for ever to India, with a joint Stock, in common with the reft of his Majefty's Subjects*, it does not follow as a neceffary confequence, that they will continue to do fo, further

* See his Review of Bengal, 1785.
† They are inferted very much at large in Anderfon's Hiftory of Commerce.

than

than may be necessary for winding up their affairs, unless such terms are granted them as they may think it for their interest to accept. They have certainly an option, and can in no respect be compelled, or indeed be expected to continue the responsible Agents of the Public, in the Administration of the Government of India and its Revenues, if individuals be authorised to start up in every part of Hindostan, even at their own Ports and Factories, as their rivals and competitors; or if laid under unreasonable restrictions at home, by which the ship owner, the manufacturer and the tin miner may become the dictators, what ships they are to employ, rates of freight they shall pay, in what state or condition they shall purchase their commodities, what sorts they shall be restricted from importing, and what quantity of metals they shall be compelled to take, and after what rate of price; if restrictions of this nature be imposed, the Company may think it for their interest to withdraw, and after disposing of their property to others, may relinquish the important trust. The consequences of their doing so, are more proper to be weighed by others, than to be described by us.

Upon the whole, we must confess, that until a better plan than any we have hitherto seen, or are capable of suggesting, shall be devised as a substitute for that which exists, whereby the true interests of the Public may be manifestly and substantially improved, and permanently secured, in unison with those of our fellow-subjects, the Natives of India, we hope to see no changes introduced to shake the present system; and that if any well digested plan, such as we have described, shall hereafter be brought forwards, deserving public approbation, the well known justice of Parliament may be relied on for an indemnification to the East India Company, and their creditors, in conformity with those principles which have ever guided and governed the conduct of the British Senate, when it has judged it necessary to sacrifice private Rights to public Utility.

It has been said that *the Merchants of Ireland* have a plan for opening a free Trade in the Indian Ocean. Not having seen it we forbear to make any comments on that subject. She has certainly emancipated and separated herself from Great Britain and her laws; and, as far as we are capable of judging, has as much right to try her fortune in the India Trade as any other *foreign nation*. But if her Trade should be carried on with *British Capitals*, and on the risque and account of *British Subjects*, those subjects will do well to look to the *Laws and Statutes*, which inflict severe penalties on such as have any dealings or concerns with Foreigners of any denomination in the Asiatic Trade: both they, and his Majesty's Irish subjects, will also do well to consider, ere they begin, if their means of carrying on a Trade to such distant regions, are more efficient, than were in the power of those other *foreign* Companies or individuals, who, though possessed of long established Settlements and Factories, and the other advantages, we have before described, appear to have been ruined in the attempt. If *Irish* ships still partake of the privileges of *British* ships as formerly, then will they be liable to seizure and confiscation for trading to India, as British ships are, and the penalties of the law will attach upon their owners and others concerned.

If

(47)

If they are not deemed *British ships*, then will those concerned, being *British subjects*, incur the penalties of the law, for becoming adventurers in *foreign ships* employed in the India Trade.

CHAPTER XIV.

Practical Means of securing to the Private Merchant and the Public, the ultimate Benefits of Trade within the Company's present exclusive Limits, without endangering the Chain of our political Connection with India, or materially disturbing the present System.

FREIGHT.——The advancement of the India Trade, both Export and Import, seems greatly to depend on the attainment of what has been long fruitlessly attempted, *namely*, a conveyance of goods to and from the *East Indies at a reasonable and moderate rate of Freight*, such as may encourage the Manufacturers and Merchants, on their own risque and account, to adventure therein. It will be difficult for the Directors of the India Company to persuade the British Manufacturers that they do not know what is most for their own advantage, or that the Directors know it better than themselves. It is at the same time but reasonable, that the Manufacturers and Merchants should have the liberty of making the experiment they so ardently desire of opening new Channels of Trade for an increased Export of British Manufactures, and that those, who are willing to supply the shipping, should be encouraged to do so. The good effects, which must result by the carriage of goods *at a reduced and moderate freight*, are very obvious and very numerous. Amongst other advantages, it will secure to us the benefit of the Carrying Trade to and from the East Indies to a greater extent than we have hitherto enjoyed it, to the exclusion of Foreigners, who have notoriously participated in it in an unreasonable degree: The public Revenue * will become improved, by the duties left on the goods exported from hence: Both the Public and the Company will be benefitted by the saving of expence :† The quantity of India goods for foreign markets will be increased, and, by the reduced price of the carriage, our competition in the sale of the productions of Asia in the markets on the Continent of Europe may become the more successful. There is, however, some difficulty in effecting this desirable object, in a mode that may be consistent with the general Freedom of Trade, and the common Rights of Mankind. To make it obligatory upon, and not optional with, the Managers for the Company, to charter ships, of a particular description, at the lowest rates that may be offered, might be thought a constraint, degrading on the mercantile character of the Company; might expose

* On the Export of some of the India Manufactures little more than half the Customs are returned in Drawbacks, and on some others no Drawback is allowed.
† We have before stated, that by the Acts of 1781 and 1784, the Public are intitled to three fourths of the nett surplus by Trade, as well as Revenue.

them

them to frauds and perpetual controversies; might prove injurious to the Commerce itself, and might, perhaps, in the end be productive of so many unforeseen *inconveniencies* as to drive the Company to the expedient of building their own ships. To preclude them from the power of doing so, we are persuaded can never be intended. And yet something must be done, to put an end to the improvident practice, which has but too long prevailed, through the powerful influence of what is called *The Old Shipping Interest*, in the extravagant rates given for Freight, to an amount probably of £.150,000 a year, if taken on a medium or annual average, from the end of the last war. The rejected offers at lower rates have been published, and the prices at which ships can be afforded, equally adapted to the conveniency and safety of the Trade, both of India and China *, as those which the Company have taken up, are well known. No reasonable man will wish to introduce new plans to the injury of the owners of ships already built or employed. The Public, as well as the Company, being doubly interested in the effect to be produced by lowering the freight, it should seem expedient and useful, that some of the members of the executive Government should be invested with an appellant authority. Care being first taken to secure the owners of ships already engaged from losses, we would recommend that the highest price of Freight to and from *India*, and to and from *China*, distinctly, which shall in future be given by the Company, shall be fixed by the new Act, as well for time of *war* as of *peace*, leaving to the Company a latitude and option of contracting with any Ship Owners they please, so that they exceed not those prices. Let all persons be permitted to make their offers of ships, upon previous notice of the number and tonnage wanted, to be given by the Company in the London Gazette; and let the Directors be obliged to keep a Book of Orders *for their Affairs of Shipping*, distinct from all other business; in which shall be entered the *substance* of every offer, and the *causes* for rejecting such of them as shall not be admitted; let this book be open to public inspection; and if any ship owner shall think himself aggrieved by the Directors, let him have his appeal to the members of the Executive Government, who should be either *the Board for India*, or *the Board of Commerce*, whose order, in a summary way, might be made conclusive and binding.

EXPORTS AND IMPORTS.—Let all merchants and manufacturers have permission to export, in the Company's ships, any goods of *British* or *Irish* produce or manufacture, with an exception only of *ammunition, and military or warlike stores, and the heavier articles of marine stores*, (both which should, for obvious reasons, be ever reserved to the Company,) so that notice be given to the Company of the quantity of tonnage, both out and home, at or before a certain day in every season, to be fixed in the act. The tonnage *homewards* ought never to exceed the quantity engaged for *outwards*. The *rate of Freight* to be the same, which the Company shall pay, over and besides a reasonable con-

---

* It being admitted on all hands (as we conceive) that the China Trade cannot be opened, but must of necessity remain exclusively with the Company as at present, we have confined our views entirely to the Trade of the East Indies, in the Regulations we have ventured to recommend.

tribution

(49)

tribution for the expences of warehouses, wharfage, support of factories and settlements, &c. &c. which may be put on a footing similar to the present Private Trade. *One third* at the least of this sum ought to be paid down, and a security given for the payment of *the other two thirds* at the ship's return. The import trade to be confined to such *raw materials*, and other articles to be enumerated, as shall not too much interfere with the Trade of the Company. The Company to be in no respect liable to actions for *damages or losses* in respect to the Private Trade, but their officers and servants to be liable. All Private Trade to be brought into the Company's warehouses, and put up to sale *by inch of candle*, as other India and China goods are at present. An *appeal* might be given to the same Board, as is proposed in the case of freight, to settle or adjust any disputes that may arise under this head.

PRIVATE AND PRIVILEGED TRADE.—Let this remain on its present footing, with the single variation in the mode of payment of the Company's Duty of £.7 per cent. which should be converted into a Tonnage Duty, and paid by the parties, without any regard to the *quantity or value* of the goods imported, as a means of effectually destroying the temptation of *running* the goods, to avoid the payment of that duty.

FACTORS.—Let the Company be obliged to licence any reasonable number of persons to reside at their Settlements abroad, for the management of the concerns of *private merchants* trading thither, on their entering into covenants similar to those of licensed Free Merchants. This matter also may be settled by appeal, if the Directors and the Merchant should disagree.

DIVIDENDS OF THE PROPRIETORS.—As the Company's property must ever be at hazard, to a very large amount, it seems highly reasonable and just, that their *Dividends* should bear some moderate proportion to the net income of their own Landed Property in India, and to their Profits of Trade; and this the more especially after the latter shall have been opened to the extent proposed, for the benefit of the private Trader. The Company are also in a great measure responsible for the Administration of the Government abroad, and the due collection of the Dewannee Revenues; what surplus they afford, or a great share of it, is intended to be drawn home to this Country, through the medium of the Company's Commerce. It has been shewn that after every allowance whatever, and after bearing the due proportion of the expence of the general defence of British India, the Landed Estates and Customs properly belonging to the Company may produce a net income of £.250,000 a year at the least; which with the net annual profits of their Export and Import Trade, after making some allowance for the injury it may be supposed to sustain from the private Merchants, may be fairly rated at One * *Million Sterling per annum*, clear of every charge

* Landed Revenues		£.250,000
Export and Import Trade (as before explained, page 33 and 35.)		700,000
Private and privileged Trade		70,000
Annuity		38,000
		1,058,000
Allow for lessening of profits by the Trade of Private Merchants		58,000
	The Company's own Income clear	£.1,000,000
	Dewannee Revenue	£.750,000
	Total	£.1,750,000

G whatever,

(50)

whatever, unless indeed the expence of *Insurance* were to be calculated, which is not done, because the Company are their own Insurers.

It is pretty well known *now*, with respect to the Debts owing in India, that the greatest part is due *to the Natives*, which accounts for no more of it having been drawn home upon the Transfer Plan. It is evidently wise and politic to leave a considerable debt amongst the Natives, at an annual interest. If the Revenues produce a net surplus of £. 1,100,000, they will afford *one million a year* to be drawn home by investment of goods, over and besides the produce of our own Exports, and Certificates given to the officers of the Company's ships, payable in England, and leave enough to accumulate in the Treasuries in India, either as a fund for the support of wars, when they shall be inevitable, or if it be thought better, the overplus may be applied as a sinking fund for the the discharge of the debt there.

Thus will there be £. 1,750,000 *per annum* brought into this country, which, if divided according to the acts of 1781 and 1784, and the subsequent acts for the increased capital, would stand thus :

	£.
A dividend on five millions, at 8 per cent.	400,000
The surplus left would be	1,350,000
One fourth of that sum would belong to the Company, being — £. 337,500	
And *three fourths* to the Public, being — £. 1,012,500	
	1,350,000

But before the Public are to participate in this fund, these acts provide, that the Bond Debt shall be reduced to £. 1,500,000, and Bills of Exchange to £. 300,000. Provision might be easily made out of this immense income for such reduction, without postponing the whole of its benefit to the Public or the Company to a future time. Each might contribute its due proportion, to be set apart as a sinking fund, for the reduction of the debts, and ample means would be left of adding to the public revenue, and to the Proprietors dividends. The Exchequer might be content with receiving £. 450,000 a year, and the Proprietors £. 150,000 a year in additional dividends, until those debts shall be reduced to their proper standard, which the remaining fund would effect in a short space of time. Thus might the dividend be extended to *Eleven* per cent. and according to the income by revenue, and profits of Trade, beyond those sums, so should be the proportionate future payments to the Public, and to the East India Proprietors.

However flattering this conclusion of our labours may appear to our Readers, in favour of the *Public* and the *East India Stockholder*, it is no more, than we are fully warranted to give, by the authentic documents we have had occasion to quote or refer to in the course of this work, as well as by our own knowledge of the Financial Concerns of the Company.

POSTSCRIPT.

POSTSCRIPT.

As given in the former Edition in February, 1793.

SINCE the foregoing sheets went to the press, the Company have published a Statement of their Affairs, to shew what will be the probable net annual surplus of the territorial Revenues in India, and the profits on their Trade, in times of profound Peace. In forming this Statement, they have not been governed by the medium or average, either of actual receipts or actual disbursements for any former period, but have given their reasons for departing both from the one and the other. In consequence, the receipts are not increased, though the new ceded Countries of Tippoo Sultaun are brought into the account, whilst the probable disbursements are augmented. The result of the whole is, that the probable net Revenues, of the Indian possessions, including the new cessions, are estimated only at £.1,621,050, from which £.561,923 per annum is to be deducted for the Interest of the Indian Debt, leaving a net surplus of £.1,059,127. To this sum they add £.350,000 a year for the produce of Imports and Certificates in India, making £.1,409,127, from which sum they take £.1,127,000 for an Investment of Indian Goods, and £.250,000 towards an Investment of China Goods, leaving a surplus in India of £.32,127 a year. With these aids they compute on such yearly Sales, as with their Annuity, and Profits on Private Trade, will produce a net surplus in England of £.1,207,114, after payment of a Dividend of £.8 per cent. on the present Capital Stock of 5 Millions, and the Interest of their Bond Debt, the expences of Recruits, and all other current charges at home, and the Establishment for St. Helena.

The difference, however, between the Surplus, according to the Directors' Statements and our own (theirs being £.1,207,114, whilst we make it £.1,350,000) ought not, in any degree, to vary or affect the Rule established by the Legislature for its appropriation. If the Public take £.450,000 a year of it, the Proprietors, under the participation settled by the Acts of 1781 and 1784, are intitled to £.150,000 a year; and any increase to the Public ought to be accompanied by an increase of Dividend to the Proprietors of India Stock, after the same proportion.

The Directors, in forming their estimate of the net Surplus, have, from prudential motives, computed on the lowest probable receipts, and on the highest probable disbursements, the surest way of preventing disappointment; while that which we have given, is the result of actual receipts and actual disbursements on the average of three years. The Directors have in particular rated the Sales at half a million per annum less than the Estimate of their own Officers in other accounts before Parliament. They have, however, fairly admitted a prospect of increasing the Surplus, by lessening the Interest of the Debt in India. Under these circumstances, and by the Savings in the Rates of Freight, we trust we shall not be found too sanguine in our expectations, that a Surplus will hereafter be realized to justify our own Estimate of it at £. 1,350,000 per annum. And, indeed, one of the most experienced of the Gentlemen in the Direction, whose prudence and caution will secure us from being misled by any thing he would advance, has publicly declared in Debate, that the Surplus is more likely to exceed than fall short of £. 1,500,000 per annum.

CHAPTER XV.

The Question as between the Crown and the East-India Company, in respect to the Property of the Town, Port, and District of Masulipatam, and also in respect to the Northern Circars, on the Coast of Coromandel, stated and discussed.

THE period of the compact, made with the Public in 1781, whereby the East-India Company were continued for a further time in their Exclusive Trade, as well as in the Government of the Countries acquired in India, being near its expiration, His Majesty's Ministers, with a view of continuing the present system of Government and Administration in India, have recently offered certain propositions to the Company for that purpose, and for making a new partition between the Public and the Company, of the net revenues of the Territories in India, as well of those acquired by conquest, as of those which are the independent property of the Company, and also of the net surplus, arising from the profits of the Company's trade.

The reasonableness of this partition, upon the terms proposed, must depend in some degree on the rateable proportion, which the Revenue of the conquered Territories bears to the Revenue produced by the Company's own proper Estates in India. It therefore seems highly essential, if not absolutely necessary, that means should be used, to discriminate betwixt the Revenues of the Public and those properly of the Company, antecedent to the establishment of any specific appropriation; for unless that is done, the Company must be acting altogether upon conjecture.

The Territories and Revenues of India, may be properly classed under three descriptions. First, Those which the Company possessed, prior to the year 1755, with respect to which their exclusive right has never been questioned, nor can it be in any degree liable to impeachment: The extent of them is known to a certainty, and their income was fully investigated by the Secret Committee of the House of Commons of the year 1772, as will appear upon reference to Third Report of that Committee, wherein their annual produce, for a series of time, will be found amply detailed.

Secondly, The Territories and Revenues ceded to the Company by the Mogul, the Nabob of Bengal, the Soubah of the Decan, and the Nabob of Arcot, by Grants and Treaties after the year 1755. These consist chiefly of the Pergunnahs at Calcutta, the ceded Lands so called in Burdwan, Midnapour and Chittagong, the Town and District of Calcutta, the Town, Fortress, Port and District of Masulipatam, the Five Northern Circars, and the Jagheer Lands at Madras. The property of these may be debated on distinct grounds, each having been acquired by the Company in consequence of the influence resulting from their

Military

Military Establishments, and the valour and success of their arms after that period.

Lastly, The Provinces of Bengal and Bahar, and that part of Orissa which is terminated on the South by the Cattack Countries belonging to the Maratta States, the District of Benares, and the Countries in the Carnatic, and on the Malabar Coast, lately obtained by the Treaty with Tippoo Saib. These are claimed on the part of the Public, as the property of the State, on a maxim of Law, that all Territories acquired by conquest vest in the Crown.

Although it should seem essential to the Company, that their exclusive Claim to each of the debatable Districts should be investigated and finally decided upon, we shall, for the present, confine our inquiry to the merits of what relates only to the Town, Port, and Districts of Masulipatam, and to the Five Northern Circars. We have given these a preference, from a persuasion that in point of Revenue, Extent and Situation, they will be found to be intrinsically of greater importance than any of the others with which they are classed; and because, by a full and minute investigation and discussion of the merits, whereon the legal right to these Districts seems to depend, it is not improbable, but some rule or principle may be established with regard to all, or some of the others.

The magnitude and importance of the question of Right between the Public and the Company, whether as applicable abstractedly to the Revenues of the Circars, or as establishing a precedent in Law for determining the Claims of the Company upon other Territories already, or which may in future be obtained and held upon titles of a like sort, have induced us to think it more prudent to hazard the imputation of prolixity, in the Statement we are about to give, rather than by curtailing it of circumstances, which might otherwise have been deemed inapplicable, or not pertinent to the merits of the question, incur a charge of partiality or negligence.

For the case of our Readers who may be desirous of applying the Law to the facts, in the order of their detail, according to the Rights of the respective Claimants, we propose to arrange our Tract after the following method: First, To state what we conceive to be the legal and acknowledged Rights of the Crown, by virtue of its known perogative, in so far as they relate to the present subject. Secondly, The power of the Crown to transfer its Rights to others. Thirdly, How far the Crown has transferred its Rights to the East-India Company, or otherwise enabled them by Law to acquire, hold, defend and dispose of Lands and Territories within the limits of their Trade. Fourthly, A succinct narrative of the facts and circumstances which preceded or accompanied the acquisition of Masulipatam. Fifthly, A similar narrative in respect to the acquisition of the Circars. And lastly, We shall conclude with some remarks on the merits of the Question in point of Law.

Prerogative

Prerogative Rights.

AMONGST the numerous Rights appertaining to the King's Prerogative, arising to him "from the reason of the Common Law," (as we find it aptly expressed in a great * authority) are those of making War and Peace; an interest in his Subjects, and a Right to their service; the command of all fortresses and places of strength; so that none but by the King's Licence can legally build, erect, or fortify a castle or other place of defence; the sole Coinage of Money; the Property in all Mines of Gold or Silver wheresoever found; the erecting of Courts of Judicature; a general Right of Sovereignty over the Lands of all his Subjects, and a Right to the absolute Property, as well as Sovereignty over foreign Territories acquired by conquest, whether it be by his own regular Forces, or by any of his Subjects not trained or so employed, but acting on their own will; or acquired by Grant or Treaty obtained by Influence of Arms, or even by any Treaty or Grant of Dominion made to any of his Subjects by a foreign Potentate. It is also a Right coeval and inherent in the Prerogative of the Crown, to delegate to, and invest its Subjects with such Powers and Rights as may be deemed necessary to be exercised for giving vigour and effect to the protection and security of the Empire, the Extension of its Dominions, and the enlargement of its Commerce. Neither the Power of Delegation, nor the Right of Granting, has ever, that we can discover, been denied, or questioned, or limited, where the known Laws of the Land have not been impugned or exceeded. It was under Delegations of this description, that many of our foreign Dominions were obtained; and it is under Grants, flowing from the Prerogative, that our Nobility and Gentry, at this day, derive their titles to their landed Property in the Three Kingdoms. The proprietary Districts of America, and the Lands in the West India Islands were thus conveyed; nor is the Crown debarred (that we know of) from alienating any of its foreign Territories, either in possession, or reversion, or dependent on any expectancy or contingency. The Restraining Act of Queen Anne, and the Civil List Act of His Majesty, are limited to the demesnes and hereditary Revenues of the Crown at home.

Company's Rights.

WITH respect to the Rights and Privileges of the United Company, it will be found that the Old Company, erected and incorporated by Queen Elizabeth, were legally seized of the Islands of St. Helena and Bombay, and of sundry Forts, Factories and Settlements, and were also possessed, and in the exercise of extensive Authorities and Privileges in India; all which, on the Union of the two Companies in 1702, were transferred to the United Company. Their Union was ratified by Queen Anne, under the great Seal of England, and the

* Staundf. Prerog. Reg. Plowden 314.

Rights and Powers thus conveyed, together with those which had been granted to the New Company, have been repeatedly sanctioned by subsequent Acts of Parliament made on the several compacts between the Public and the Company, for the continuation of their Exclusive Trade; on which occasions, the Company paid to the Public such pecuniary considerations, as at the time were deemed adequate in value to the Rights and Immunities purchased, or agreed to be held and enjoyed by them. Amongst which are these that follow:

To be a Corporation or Body-politic, and to have perpetual succession, with ability to hold and retain Lands and Tenements of any kind, nature, or quality whatever, and again to sell, alien, or dispose thereof; to make Settlements in India, without any limitation in their value and extent; to build Castles, Forts, Fortifications, or other Places of Strength; to appoint Governors and Commanders; raise, train, and muster Forces; repel Wrongs and Injuries on their Property; make Reprisals on their Invaders, or Disturbers of their Peace; coin Money, and erect Courts of Judicature. So * ample were the powers for enabling the Company to preserve Discipline amongst their Military, that they were authorized in all their Settlements, in cases of Rebellion, Mutiny or Sedition, or refusing to serve in War, flying to an Enemy, forsaking Colours or Ensigns, or other offences against Law, Custom and Discipline Military, to use and exercise all the Powers of Captain General. And by one of the Charters it was expresly declared, that these Powers and Immunities should extend to all Territories which the Company should at any time purchase or acquire within the limits of their Trade; and by another † Charter it was granted, that the Company should have the sole Rule and Government of all Forts, Factories and Plantations, already, or which should thereafter be settled by or under them, and exercise Martial Law therein; and by ‡ another, they are impowered to fit out Men of War in times of hostility. In these Charters and Grants the Sovereignty of the Crown alone is reserved.

Under the Rights and Powers thus conveyed, the Company acquired by purchase from the Moguls, or other of the Native Princes and States, sundry spots of ground on the Peninsula of India, on which they erected Factories and Houses of Trade; and for the better defence of their property against the incursion of banditti and casual depredation, they had long anterior to the conquest of Bengal, fortified the Island of Bombay, and their Factories at Madras, Vizagapatam, St. Davids, and on the river Ganges, and garrisoned them with their forces; and in general exercised the several other authorities and privileges derived from their Charters. The mildness of their Government within their Factories, the equal administration of Justice at their Courts, the punctuality and uprightness observed by their Servants in their dealings, the simplicity of their manners, and their quiet and inoffensive deportment, endeared them to the Natives, and induced many of the Hindoos to settle within, or near their districts. The Soubahs of the country bestowed on them exemplary marks of their favour, until

---
* Charter of 27th September, 1669.   † 9th April, 1683.   ‡ 12th April, 1686.

at length the Company had obtained Territories which produced in Land Rents and Port Duties, a confiderable income, fufficient at leaft to defray their eftablifhments, as long as they were permitted to obferve a ftrict peace or neutrality amongft the Native States; nor from the firft erection of the Company by Queen Elizabeth, till the accidental Conqueft of Bengal, had the Right of the Company been called in queftion, to acquire, by any means they could devife, Settlement, Territory, or other Property in India for their own benefit. It was the magnitude of that conqueft, which firft excited Public attention, and a general maxim of law, of which, perhaps, no inftance or occafion for its being exerted or acted upon had happened for centuries, if ever, in this Kingdom, was now enforced by Parliament, with a faving however of Rights, fo as to leave the queftion open to litigation at fome future period.

Situation of Mafulipatam and Circars.

Before we proceed in our narrative, it may not be amifs to give the Reader fome idea of the extent, fituation, and income of Mafulipatam and its diftricts, and we cannot do this more fatisfactorily, than by reference to Mr. Orme's Hiftory of Hindoftan. The following is a literal quotation * from his work.

" Thefe † acquifitions added to Mafulipatam, and the Province of Con-
" davir ‡, made the French mafters of the Sea Coaft of Coromandel and
" Orixa, in an uninterrupted line of 600 miles from Medapilly, § to the
" Pagoda of Jagernaut ‖. Thefe countries are bounded by a vaft chain of
" mountains, which run nearly in the fame direction as the Sea Coaft, and are
" in moft places about 80 or 90 miles diftant from it, although in fome few not
" more than 30. They are covered with impenetrable forefts of bamboes, and in
" the whole extent there are not more than four paffes which, according to
" Mr. Buffey's account, may be defended by 100 men againft an army.

" The Province of Condavir extends between the River Kriftna and Gon-
" degama, which gains the fea at Medapilly. The limits of the other Four
" Provinces are not exactly afcertained; neverthelefs it appears, that Mufta-
" phanagur joins to the North of Condavir; that Elore lays to the north weft
" of Muftaphanagur; that Rajahmundrum is bounded to the fouth by thefe two
" provinces, and that Chicacole, much the largeft of the four, extends 250 miles
" from the River Godaveri to the Pagoda of Jagernaut. The revenues of the
" Four Provinces were computed at 31,00,000 rupees; of Condavir at 6,80,000;
" and the dependencies of Mafulipatam were fo much improved that they pro-

---

* Firft Vol. p. 334.
† The Circars of Muftaphanagur, Elore, Rajahmundrum and Chicacole.
‡ Another name for the Guntoor Circar.
§ The northern extremity of the Carnatic on the Coaft of Coromandel.
‖ The fouthern extremity of the Mahratta dominions in Cartack, lately under Modajee Boofla one of their chiefs in Orixa. His dominions extend northwards upon the Coaft, to the extent of about 240 miles, where they adjoin to that part of the Britifh poffeffions in Orixa which are under the Prefidency of Bengal.

" duced

" duced this year (1753) 5,07,000, in all 42,87,000 rupees equal to more
" than £.535,000 sterling per annum. All these rents, excepting those of
" Masulipatam and its dependencies, which seemed already to be carried
" to the height, might be greatly improved; so that these territories ren-
" dered the French masters of the greatest dominions, both in extent and
" value, that had ever been possessed in Hindostan by Europeans, not ex-
" cepting the Portuguese when at the height of their prosperity; nor were
" commercial advantages wanting to enhance the value of these acquisitions;
" for the manufactures of cloth, proper for the European markets, were made
" in this part of the Decan of much better fabrick and at much cheaper rates
" than in the Carnatic. In Rajahmundrum are large forests of teak trees, a
" wood in every respect equal to oak, and produced in no other part of the
" Coast of Coromandel and Orixa. Chicacole abounds in rice and other grain,
" of which great quantities are exported every year to the Carnatic."

And speaking of the Soubah's proposals to the Madras Government in 1756, for their assistance against the French in the Decan, he says, * " Nothing could
" be more acceptable to the Presidency than this invitation; for since the dis-
" appointment of the expedition which the Company had projected to be
" carried on from Bombay, they despaired of having another opportunity of
" striking at the French influence in the northern parts of the Decan, on which
" nevertheless the very existence of the English, on the Coast of Coromandel,
" seemed to depend.

Monsieur Dupleix, speaking of the nature of the Soubah's last grant, to Mr.
Busley, in his famous Memoir says, " I persisted in demanding the four beau-
" tiful provinces of Ellore, Mustaphanagur, Chicacole, and Rajahmundry,
" which suited us in every respect, and I obtained them. They were given in
" full sovereignty to the Company, at the charge of keeping with the Nabob, a
" body of French troops, after the manner of the Mogul Lords or Mahrattas,
" to whom the Emperor or the Nabob grants Jagheers."

Narrative of the Acquisition of Masulipatam and its Dependencies.

The war which broke out between France and England in 1745, soon spread itself to India, where the Companies of the two nations had raised native corps of troops, and sacked or besieged the Settlements of each other. Advices of the peace, concluded in 1748, reached India just at the time of our raising the siege of Pondicherry. The British squadron, under Admiral Boscawen, soon returned to England; but neither of the Companies discharged their troops. Chunda Saheb, competitor with Anawarden Caun, and afterwards of his son Mahomed Ally, for the Nabobship of Arcot, had agreed to take those of the French into his pay, and they waited his arrival in the Carnatic to be united with his army. It was not long after this period that the two Companies became auxiliaries on opposite sides to these rival Chiefs.

* First Vol. p. 434.

The Carnatic forms part of the Mogul Empire, conſtituting one of the Provinces, or a Nabobſhip of the Decan, which had been long governed by the Soubah Nizam ul Mulk, as the Viceroy of the Mogul. To him belonged the nomination of the Nabob. On the death of that Soubah in 1748, different competitors, his ſons or deſcendants, had laid claim to the Government of the Decan; the Mogul was not in ſtrength to interpoſe his authority with effect; otherwiſe there can be but little doubt but the Nizam's eldeſt ſon, Ghazi ul Dien, who was at that time the principal Miniſter to the Mogul at Delhi, and had been named as ſucceſſor to his father in the Government of the Decan, would have been eſtabliſhed in it. Nazir Jung, another ſon of the late Soubah, (but ſtiled by the French a baſtard) and who at that period commanded his father's army, had taken poſſeſſion of his immenſe treaſures, and pretending that Ghazi ul Dien had ceded to him the Soubahſhip, (preferring a reſidence at the Court of Delhi) he aſſumed the reins of Government, keeping his three younger brothers little better than his priſoners; whilſt Muzafa Jung, a favorite grandſon of the deceaſed Soubah, claiming the right, under a pretended will of his grandfather, appointing him his ſucceſſor, raiſed an army in the Country weſt of Golconda, and claimed the Soubahſhip.

Such was the ſtate of parties and of the country when a ceſſation of hoſtilities between the two Companies took place in 1749. It was about this time that Chunda Saheb and Muzafa Jung had united their Forces under a ſolemn ſtipulation, never to ſheath their ſwords 'till the one was put into compleat poſſeſſion of the Carnatic, and the other eſtabliſhed in the Government of the Decan. They ſoon after fought the famous battle of Amboor, where the ſuperior diſcipline of the French army overcame all obſtacles, and obtained a deciſive victory for their employers over Anawarden Caun, Nabob of the Carnatic, who was himſelf ſlain, and his eldeſt ſon Muzafa Caun taken priſoner; Mahommed Ally his younger ſon, the preſent Nabob, narrowly eſcaping the ſame fate.

Muzafa Jung was immediately proclaimed Soubah at the head of his victorious army, and Chunda Saheb declared Nabob of the Carnatic. The Engliſh forces had not hitherto interfered in theſe diſputes, but the news of the victory, and the preparations making by the French and their allies for extending the influence of their arms through the Decan, brought down the Soubah Nazir Jung into the Carnatic; nor did he ſtop 'till he encamped with his army at Velſtour, within a ſmall diſtance of Pondicherry, where he was met and oppoſed by that of his nephew and his auxiliaries. The Madras Government, now perceiving for the firſt time with certainty, that Nazir Jung was the actual reigning Soubah, they ſent Meſſrs. Lawrence and Dalton, with a ſmall corps of Engliſh troops to pay him their homage; they were received with politeneſs, and permitted to encamp near him. A parley took place between the uncle and the nephew, which naturally occaſioned alarm to the French, leſt by a reconciliation the Native Chiefs ſhould unite their forces and turn their arms againſt them. They therefore ſuddenly withdrew themſelves from the camp, and retired towards their own Settlement. It was in vain that Chunda Saheb endeavoured to diſſuade Muzafa Jung from liſtening to the propoſals of his uncle. That Chief therefore

withdrew

withdrew himself to Pondicherry, and the infatuated nephew, allured by the solemn protestations of the Soubah, both of affording protection to his person, and of placing him in the Government of certain Provinces of the Deccan, proceeded to the Soubah's tent; where, in violation of the ties of honor, justice, and his pledged faith, the Soubah instantly loaded him with irons, and falling suddenly on his unsuspecting adherents, both they, and such of the French as could be overtaken were miserably butchered.

At this period neither the English nor French possessed any thing more at Mafulipatam than their Factories or Houses of Trade. The French, sensible of the importance of that Port for the purposes of commerce, had obtained a promise from Muzafa Jung of a grant of it with its dependencies, a circumstance which probably had reached the ears of Nazir Jung; for shortly after the affair at Vellour, he caused his Officers to seize the French Factory and effects at Mafulipatam, though it does not appear he meddled with any other, (for they had other Factories in his dominions); and Dupleix, highly exasperated at this act of tyranny over the private property of innocent and helpless individuals, vowed severe vengeance.

The Soubah with his army took up his residence at Arcot for the Monsoon. In the mean time Chunda Saheb and Dupleix were indefatigable in their preparations for war. Before the Soubah began to stir, they made themselves masters of Gingee, and also of Mafulipatam, and appeared in such force in the Carnatic, that the Soubah, as the condition of being permitted quietly to withdraw himself from its confines, found it prudent to grant to the French the absolute property of Mafulipatam and its dependencies; and to make them other concessions. He however still kept Muzafa Jung a prisoner, which Dupleix highly resenting, found means to corrupt certain of the Patan Chiefs, who formed the body guard, and agreeably to a plan concerted, the French attacked his camp by surprize, when the unfortunate Soubah, quitting his tent, fell a victim to French treachery, and the villainy of his own people. His head having been exposed, Muzafa Jung was taken from prison, and proclaimed Soubah by the unanimous voice of both armies; and one of the first acts of the new Soubah, in gratitude for his release and advancement, was to confirm the grant of Mafulipatam, with its dependencies, to the French. According to Mr Orme, they were to be held in vassalage; though, if we may credit the relations of Mr. Buffey and Mr. Dupleix, they were granted in compleat sovereignty for ever.

In the Appendix to Mr. Dupleix's celebrated Address to the French Nation, will be found an accurate account of the revenue produced from Mafulipatam, distinct from the places dependent on it, as well as from their subsequent acquisitions in the Northern Circars. If they had been otherwise before, it is evident that, from this time at least, Mafulipatam and its dependencies formed a distinct district from the Five Circars, producing a revenue of about £.38,000 a year.

A few months had only elapsed before Muzafa Jung also fell a sacrifice to the treachery and avarice of the same Patan Chiefs, who had assassinated his uncle. Three other of his uncles, Salabut Jung, Nizam Ally, and Bazalet Jung, had been continued prisoners in his camp. Mr. Dupleix set them at liberty, and raised Salabut Jung, the eldest of the three, to the Musnud of the Decan; and for a considerable time after, the influence of Mr. Dupleix wholly prevailed over the Councils of the Soubah. His person was constantly guarded by the French soldiers, who fought and conquered by his side in several conflicts with the Mahrattas; the French commanders dictated the terms of the successive conventions, for suspension of hostilities; and in 1753, they planned the triumphant entry of the Soubah into his capital of Aurungabad, where he rewarded the French Company with grants first, of the Guntoor, and soon afterwards of the other Four Circars; and although by an invitation of Jaffeer Ally, one of the discarded Zemindars in the Circars, some of the neighbouring Mahrattas broke in and devastated the most fruitful parts of the country, they soon retired, and in 1754 the French were left to enjoy, without interruption, the fruits of these valuable acquisitons.

The Company's troubles in the Carnatic and in Bengal, at the time of the rupture in 1756 with France, had obliged them to weaken their little garrison at Vizagapatam. The Fort and Factory at that place, and also Madepollam, Bandermalanka, and Ingeram, fell an easy prey to Mr. Bussey, and the forces he kept in the Circars. In the mean time, by the intrigues of Nizam Ally, and Bazalet Jung, assisted by Shanavese Khan, their brother's Duan, the influence of the French became weakened at the Soubah's Court. The French detachment however still accompanied him, and most probably saved his life, at the time the two brothers possessed themselves of his Seals of State, and assumed to themselves the reins of the Government, which, however, they administered in his name. This revolution must have have happened about the time of Bussey's capture of the English Company's Factories. He had no sooner accomplished that object, than he hastened, with what force he could collect, to the assistance of Salabut Jung at Aurungabad. It consisted of 700 Europeans, 500 Sepoys, and 10 field pieces; and though at his arrival he found the Soubah surrounded by three armies under the command of his two brothers, to whom he could be considered as little better than a prisoner, he so managed as to procure the Seal to be restored. Nizam Ally, unable to brook what he feared openly to resist, but resolving in some degree to avenge himself for what had happened, procured the assassination of Hyder Beg, (the new Minister) imposed on his brother by Bussey, and then fled to Brampour. The friends of Hyder Beg immediately revenged his death by the murder of Shanavese Khan, and his son Mahommed, the Emperor's Duan, and all their adherents; so that Bussey was again left to direct the Councils of the Soubah. He was, however, shortly after called to Pondicherry with his forces for the relief of that place then besieged by the English Company. He quitted the Soubah, leaving a force for the defence of Matulipatam and the Circars.

After the death of Vizeram Rauze (the Zemindar who had superceded Jaffeer Ally in the Rajahmundrum Circar, and who had also been manager for that of Chicacole) Busfey had imposed such new arrangements and conditions on his nephew and successor the Rajah Anunderawze, as to excite his resentment. He therefore took the opportunity of Busfey's departure to avenge the supposed injury, and to recompence himself by seizing on the garrison of Vizagapatam. Fearing his own ability to retain it, he sent advice of what he had done to Madras, offering a surrender of it to the Company. He afterwards made a like offer to the Presidency of Bengal, proposing to join his forces with any detachment they should send for driving the French from the ceded provinces. Lord Clive accepted of the offer, and immediately re-established the English Factory at Vizagapatam. He likewise sent 500 Europeans, and 2500 Native troops, under the command of Col. Ford, to unite with the Rajah against the French. It was agreed between the Colonel and the Rajah, that all plunder should be equally divided, that all the inland countries which should be conquered should be delivered to the Rajah, who was to collect the revenues; but the sea ports and towns at the mouth of the rivers, with the revenues annexed to them, were to belong to the English Company; no treaty for restitution was to be made but by mutual consent; and the Rajah was to supply half a lack of rupees monthly for the expences of the troops; and 6000 rupees, to commence from their arrival at Vizagapatam, for the particular expences of the officers.

In December 1758, the united forces gained a complete victory over the French commanded by M. Conflans, who retreated first to the city of Rajahmundrum, and afterwards to Masulipatam, followed by Colonel Ford; and the campaign ended with the siege and capture of that place by storm, in April 1759.

The tardiness of the Rajah in bringing forward his troops from Rajahmundrum to Masulipatam, and his backwardness to advance the money for the detachment, had induced Col. Ford to agree to the following variation in the agreement which had been made with him in the preceding November, (namely) that whatever sums the Rajah might furnish, should be considered as a loan; and that the revenues of all the countries which might be reduced on the other side of the Godavery, excepting such as belonged to the French, either by establishment or grant in propriety, should be equally divided between the Rajah and the English.

Whilst Colonel Ford was before Masulipatam, the Soubah, at the entreaty of Conflans, brought an army into the Circars, of such a force, as united with the French, might have easily raised the siege, and compelled the English detachment to have laid down their arms. The Soubah, however, neither joined the French nor interrupted Col. Ford, but encamped about 40 miles from the fort, waiting the event of the siege. All he did was to call upon the Rajah and the Zemindars, that were with Ford, to repair as his vassals to his standard; and it was not without difficulty they were prevailed on to disregard the summons. Some part of the French forces, after their defeat, had separated from
those

those who took refuge in Mafulipatam, and being formed into a small army of observation, were encamped at no great distance from the Soubah. Colonel Ford perceiving his danger, and in defpair of efcaping, planned the bold effort of ftorming the fort, though with little expectation of fuccefs: To amufe the Soubah in the interval, he fent Mr. Johnftone to pay him his homage, which the Soubah took in kind part, and received him in his camp. On the place falling into the Colonel's hands, the Soubah advanced within 15 miles of the fort, and the Rajah and Zemindars not doubting but the Soubah intended to reduce it, feparated from the Englifh and retired into the country; but Salabut, after fome conference with the commander of the French army of obfervation, agreed to receive Colonel Ford in his tent, and to grant him certain requefts, and to fwear to the performance of them.

This engagement has been treated as a grant, and erroneoufly confidered as the foundation of the Company's title to the Five Northern Circars. It may, however, admit of a doubt, whether aided as it was by the Soubah's oath for its obfervance, it had the efficacy of a grant or treaty. The power of the Soubah to make any grant of, or to alienate a part of the Soubahfhip, is in the firft place very queftionable. Secondly, He had already granted the fame diftricts to the French. Thirdly, The Sunnuds promifed by it, and which by the Conftitutions of the Empire (admitting the power) would be a mere nullity, unlefs paffed under the Seal of State accompanied by a variety of ceremonies and regifterations, do not appear to have been ever obtained. Fourthly, In military or feudal tenures, (and this at beft could be confidered in no other light) a new invefliture becomes neceffary on every change of the fupreme power who makes it, fo, that in no event could the Sunnuds have been valid beyond the life or removal of Salabut Jung. And laftly, the requeft extended only to a diftinct part of the Circars. The form in which the Soubah's engagement is printed by the Company, differs materially from, and is far more extenfive in refpect to the territories defcribed in it, than what is given as the agreement by Mr. Orme; his again far exceeds what the Madras Government, at the time, defcribed to be the extent of it, in their advices to Bengal of July 1759. The Company's printed copy contains a promife of Sunnuds, for giving to the Company the Circar of Mafulipatam with eight diftricts, and the Circar of Nizampatam, and the diftricts of Condavir and Wacalmanner, in the fame manner as was done to the French. Mr. Orme defcribes the grant to be of the whole territory dependent on Mafulipatam, with eight diftricts and jurifdiction over the territory of Nizampatam, and the diftricts of Condavir and Wacalmanner, all which were to be held without the referve either of fine or military fervice. The Governor and Council of Madras, immediately after the communication to them by Colonel Ford of his interview with the Soubah, defcribe the grant to be no more than " of the port of Mafulipatam, with the " dependencies thereto belonging;" recommending it to Lord Clive to obtain a confirmation of it from the Mogul, or at leaft a renewal of the Company's old Firmaund for Divi Ifland, and their factory in the town of Mafulipatam. Whatever

(64)

ever might be the extent, it is evident that the port, town, and citadel of Mafulipatam were all that the Company retained. The Circars at large, were left in the Soubah's poffeffion as their immediate fuperior, under a promife that Anunderauze fhould be continued in the management of the Chicacole Circar, upon the terms which his anceftors had held it from the former Soubahs. Colonel Ford with the Englifh forces were foon after withdrawn from the Circars, a very fmall number only being left in the garrifon; and fo far were the Company from retaining the poffeffion of any thing beyond the port and town, and dependencies, that it appears that fo early as June 1760, Nizam Ally, who, in confequence of his brother being deferted by the French, had affumed the Soubahfhip, vifited the Circars, and was attended at Rajamundrum by Mr. Alexander, the Chief of Mafulipatam; where he urgently requefted a body of the Company's troops to act againft the Mahrattas; offering to pay one lack of rupees monthly, and if they beat the Mahrattas, and difpoffeffed them of the country belonging to him, he would then agree to give the Englifh the Circars of Rajahmundrum, Ellore, and Muftaphanagur; and that, on the propofal not being accepted, he had left thofe Circars under the management of Huffein Ally, and had granted the Guntoor or Condavir Circar, in Jagheer, to his brother Bazalet Jung; continuing Vizeram Rauze (fon of Anunde Rauze) in that of Cicacole; and in a letter from Madras of April 1766, it is exprefsly faid, that after Colonel Ford had taken Mafulipatam, and put an end to the authority of the French in the Decan, all the Five Circars were reftored to the dominion of the Soubah.

It is obfervable, that Salabut Jung's firft grant to the French was of Mafulipatam only. Mr. Orme has given us the income of it, diftinctly from that of the Circars. It was the only part of the country which the Company retained from 1759, till they obtained the grant of the Circars in 1765. From thefe circumftances it is pretty evident, that Mafulipatam was confidered as a diftrict of itfelf from any of the Circars, or perhaps as forming a Sixth Circar. The other Five take their names from the capital of each. Condavir or Guntoor from the towns bearing thofe names. Ellore from that town, and fo of the reft. And hence it was that Huffein Ally's authority over Ellore, as the manager or renter thereof to the Soubah, might be perfectly compatible with the Company's enjoyment of Mafulipatam.

From thefe facts we think ourfelves warranted in the following conclufion (namely) that the diftinct diftrict of Mafulipatam, with the fortrefs and port belonging to it, were obtained BY CONQUEST; and from the moment of the capture of the fort by Colonel Ford, they became vefted in full and intire property as well as fovereignty in the King; and at this day continue the eftate of the Crown, to be kept or granted as His Majefty may think fit.

Should it be objected that becaufe Mafulipatam had been held by the French as a fief of the Indian Empire, and that the change of hands could not alter

the

the rights of the Mogul or his Soubah, as the paramount lords, we are ready to admit that the King, by his prerogative, muſt of neceſſity be the *ſummus dominus ſupra omnes* over all territories held by him; that lands in his poſſeſſion are free from every tenure; that he can neither be a joint tenant with another, nor hold of another. But with this amiſſion, and though in fact the Soubah had taken no part in the-hoſtilities between the Engliſh and the French, yet we conceive that the levying war in the Decan againſt the French, they being feudatories of the Soubah, muſt, to every legal intent, be held as levying war againſt that power alſo; and that by the conqueſt, the ſovereignty as well as the ſoil became inſtantly annexed to the Crown of England. If the French had themſelves the ſovereignty, the legal effect would have been the ſame. The ſubſequent agreement by Col. Ford with Salabut Jung, could not change or vary the nature of the King's title to Maſulipatam once acquired, nor under the Charter of 1757 could the Company reſtore it, becauſe they were reſtrained from ceding back any acquiſitions belonging to the European ſtates. The treaty of Peace, in 1763, completely eſtabliſhed the right of the King; the French having thereby renounced all their acquiſitions on the Coaſt except their Factories, which alone were reſtored to them.

The Acquiſition of the Circars.

THE new Soubah Nizam Ally, derived his right to the Government of the Decan under a grant from the Mogul; he was preſſed on all ſides by the armies of the Mahratta States and of Hyder Ally, and was in the utmoſt diſtreſs both for money and ſuccours. He appears from the firſt commencement of his acceſſion, to have anxiouſly courted our alliance, as the ſureſt means of furniſhing himſelf with protection againſt the French, whom he both feared and had offended, and againſt the ambitious views of his troubleſome neighbours. We have already ſeen that he made his firſt overtures to Mr. Alexander at Rajahmundrum in 1760, immediately after he had depoſed his brother. In 1761 he repeated them, with an earneſt deſire to be aſſiſted with troops, and an offer of the Circars by way of ſubſidy. At this period it would on many accounts have been deſirable for the Company to have complied; but the period was critical, and European forces could not be ſafely ſpared. In the mean time many of the Zemindars and Renters in the Circars, taking advantage of the weakneſs of the Soubah's Government, and the unſettled ſtate of the Decan, had become refractory, had with-held their tribute, and had bid defiance to the authority of Huſſein Ally the Soubah's manager; and to render the anarchy the more general, the more powerful of the Zemindars had waged war againſt each other. Unable to ſend aſſiſtance from Hydrabad, the Nizam, in the autumn of 1762 deputed his Miniſter Huſſein Ally, to the Preſidency of Fort St. George, with *grants or funnuds* for the Four Circars in the nature of a ſubſidy, again repeating his requeſt for a European force. The war with Spain had been juſt commenced, and the expedition againſt Manilla undertaken, ſo that the Madras Government were unable to comply. They, however, did not chooſe to hazard the giving the Soubah offence,

offence, by an abrupt rejection of the Sunnuds, nor a positive refusal, fearing he would admit the French again to their possession of those districts; pressed by Hussein Ally to lend him a small body of Native troops to support his authority in the Circars, and persuaded that it was the general disposition of the Zemindars and Renters, to submit to any reasonable proposals if sanctioned by the Company's authority, and that their name alone would go far in drawing them back to their allegiance, the Madras Government, with Hussein's consent, proceeded to publish the Sunnuds in the Circars, and though no force was used, the Zemindars and Renters came immediately in and settled for their rents with Hussein Ally and the Company's civil officers. It appears however, that a small body of Sepoys was sent from Madras to Masulipatam, to have enforced obedience to the Sunnuds if it had been found necessary. But the submission of the Zemindars was spontaneous and immediate, and it does not appear that these Native troops had occasion to stir from their place of landing.

In the mean time the Soubah despairing of our assistance, found means to appease, in some degree, the Mahratta army. Full of resentment at the conduct of the Company, for their breach of the confidence he had reposed in them by the publication of the Sunnuds, without a compliance with the condition annexed to them, he meditated revenge both on the Company and on his own Minister. The Madras Government therefore submitted to restore both the Sunnuds and the country; and as soon as the expences of the troops had been discharged, they were withdrawn. The Nabob of Arcot interposed his mediation with the Soubah for his forgiveness of Hussein Ally, who by dint of a large present lent for the purpose to Hussein by the Nabob, or advanced by the Company's servants, was reinstated in his master's favor; and, recovering his former influence, he returned into the Circars, cloathed with efficient powers for the Government of those districts.

No sooner had the Company withdrawn their succours, than the Zemindars and Renters again fell from their allegiance to the Nizam, who finding that nothing but the Company's influence could keep his subjects there in any degree of subordination, now came forward with a direct requisition for their assistance, and an agreement being settled for the subsidy to be paid for their hire, wherein the charge of the garrisons of Masulipatam and Vizagapatam was included, a body of forces with artillery was again sent from Madras upon that service, and they no sooner made their appearance, than all the Zemindars and Renters quietly submitted; order was restored, and Hussein Ally's authority was fully re-established.

The French had lately returned to their factories on the Coast, and a general rumour prevailed that they were preparing to re-assume their possessions of the Circars under the article in the treaty of Versailles for mutual restoration [*]; the French ministry having refused, as it was said, to admit the propositions of the Duke of Bedford, relating to India into the final treaty.

[*] The affairs of India had escaped notice 'till some time after the preliminaries were signed.

Although

Although this report had no foundation in fact, it neverthelefs, for the time, was believed, and gave great alarm to the Company's fervants; who, well knowing that if the French were to be re-eftablifhed in their authority and influence in the Decan, former contentions would inftantly be renewed, came to the refolution in any event, of refifting any attempt that might be made for that purpofe. At the end of 1764, they opened a new negociation with the Soubah for a grant of the Circars, upon payment of a ftipulated fum annually. They knew that he had hitherto realized but a trifling income from that part of his dominions, and they flattered themfelves that as the Zemindars had ever refifted his authority, while they had fhewn an anxious difpofition to remain under the Company's protection, the Soubah might be induced to yield to their application, at a rent inferior to what the Zemindars could afford, and were willing to pay to him. In their firft overtures they offered him five lacks of rupees for the firft year; ten for the fecond; and fifteen every year after. But fo great was their anxiety to feclude the French, that without waiting the event of their firft offer, they fent a fecond meffenger with a new one, of a prompt payment of five lacks, and to give fifteen lacks per annum from the commencement. The Soubah ftood for twenty lacks, which exceeding the authority given to treat upon, was rejected; whereupon the Nizam immediately granted a Sunnud of them to Huffein Ally, at that or fome other large rent, as we have before obferved. The zeal of the Madras Government to obtain poffeffion of the Circars, kept pace only with the inftructions from the Directors and the advice of Lord Clive. The difficulty was how to affect it without a rupture. The Company had in 1762, 1763, 1764, and 1765, repeated their earneft wifhes to obtain them, but at the fame time deprecated new wars and troubles, and in particular cautioned their fervants how they infracted the treaty of peace, even in the event of the French procuring a new grant of the Circars; and in fome of their letters they expreffed their concurrence to any agreement with the Nizam, though attended with an engagement to furnifh him with the forces he wanted, if weighty reafons or the neceffity of the cafe fhould require it. Lord Clive was in the mean time anxioufly contemplating on the means of effecting the favorite plan he had formed, of uniting our poffeffions on the Coaft with thofe in Bengal. The reluctance of the Soubah to accept the Company as his tributaries on reafonable terms, with the abfolute neceffity there appeared for feeluding the French, drove that able commander to folicit a grant from the Mogul, conveying to the Company the intire property of the Five Circars; and in 1765 he obtained it. At the time of the grant reaching Madras, the troops we had lent to the Nizam were ftill in his pay and fervice in the Circars, and the Madras Government, with the concurrence of Lord Clive, came to the decifive refolution of availing themfelves in any event of the grant. Their forces were already on the fpot to maintain or enforce the claim. War however, was if poffible to be avoided; treachery, chicane and bribery were fubftituted as the fafer inftruments. Huffein Ally, the manager for the Soubah, was in the firft inftance dealt with, and fuccefsfully, to betray the interefts of his mafter, and for the promife of a Jagheer (which was actually fettled on him afterwards by the Company) and a promife of fupport

and

and protection, and also of being continued in his renterſhip, he agreed to act with the Company. A very ſmall additional force to what was already there, was then ſent into the Circars. The 800 Native troops under Ibraham Beg the Soubah's military commander were, by the management of Huſſein Ally, inliſted into the Company's pay. Vizeram Rauze was alſo brought over by aſſurances of leſſening his rents, and having traiterouſly delivered up the Forts of Rajahmundrum and Coſſim Cotah, which had been in his charge, he retired to his own Circar of Chicacole. In the mean time a deputation was ſent to Hydrabad, again to offer terms of becoming tributaries for the Circats to the Soubah, who was as yet a ſtranger to the grant of the Mogul. The Fort of Condipilla was deemed a neceſſary poſſeſſion to cover the principal paſs from Ellore to Hydrabad; and, while the deputies were negociating with the Nizam, General Calliaud ſeized upon it. This place is ſituate between the mountains bordering on the Ellore diſtrict, and was taken by ſtorm; four Sepoys being wounded upon the occaſion. This was moſt probably a deviſe concerted to create a panic in the Nizam; for by the agreement then ſubſiſting, our troops were to have poſſeſſion of any of the Soubah's Forts as the means of ſubjecting the inhabitants, and Huſſein Ally was ſole governor. So little was the reſiſtance at this Fort, that if there was any, it was deemed too trifling to be worthy of notice by the commanding officer in his letters of the time mentioning the capture of it. The Mogul's Sunnuds were now publiſhed, and every Zemindar immediately acknowledged the Company as their ſovereign. After a ſlow and tedious negociation at Hydrabad, and by dint of money advanced to the Soubah and preſents to his * miniſters and officers, his own grant of the Circars was obtained for the Company at a rent or annual tribute or gift of nine lacks of rupees, and under an engagement to furniſh a body of forces when called upon; and thus was the Company firmly eſtabliſhed in the poſſeſſion of the Circars, except of the Guntoor, for which they were to wait either the death of Bazalet Jung or his breach of faith, in either of which events the Company were to have the poſſeſſion of that Circar alſo; and in the interval two lacks of the rent was to be abated. The Nizam reſerved to himſelf the diamond mines and the villages near them, and alſo the Kildarry and Jagheer of Condapilly.

It had been agreed that our troops ſhould join thoſe of the Nizam and the Mahrattas, and proceed to the conqueſt of Hyder Ally's dominions. The troops were accordingly ſent, and they remained with him ſome months; but Hyder by a large bribe brought the Soubah over to his own purpoſes, and our troops were in conſequence withdrawn. Before they quitted the Nizam, a promiſe was obtained that the tribute (for ſo it is called) of two lacks per annum for the Chicacole Circar ſhould be relinquiſhed; and in July 1767, the Soubah gave a Sunnud for the remiſſion of it. In Auguſt following the Nizam threw off the maſk, and openly joined Hyder's army at Bangalore; from whence their

* One lack was given to the chief miniſter, half a lack to the ſecond, and preſents to the inferiors.

horſe

horse made excursions and ravaged the Carnatic as far as Arcot. In September, Colonel Smith drove them from the Carnatic, and in December following, the Nizam separated from Hyder Ally, and soon afterwards confirmed, by a new treaty the Mogul's grant of the Circars, and also his own Sunnud for the remission of the tribute for Chicacole, reserving the other tribute of five lacks, and two more for the Guntoor Circar, payable only when possession should be had; agreeing also to allow out of those tributes 25 lacks of rupees for the expence of the war.

After the death of Bazalet Jung, Lord Cornwallis liquidated all accounts with the Nizam, and obtained possession of the Guntoor. The Company paid him a large balance for arrears, and entered into engagements for the regular payment of the whole annual tribute of seven lacks.

In deciding the question of right to the soil and revenues of these Circars, under the peculiar circumstances by which they were obtained, it is necessary to have recourse to first principles; for the right of sovereignty in the present case seems equally disputable with the right of soil. The reason or principle whereon a right attaches to a sovereign over conquered territories, bears a strong analogy to the cases of escheats. By the operation of law, the legal estate (as it is called) in the lands of a bastard or other person dying intestate without heir, devolves upon the Sovereign, because in the very nature of the case, the legal estate can go no where else, and it must be vested somewhere. So of a conquest, the former owners are driven out, and the legal ownership must, by the necessity of the thing, vest in him who has the right to the services of his subjects the conquerors; and as is before shewn, the Sovereign has a right to their service. In such a case, the legal property could otherwise exist in no one; a fluctuating body being by Law incapable of taking an interest in lands. On the other hand, if there be any thing intermediate that prevents the property passing in a direct channel to the Crown, that circumstance compleatly interrupts the operation of the principle we have described. Thus, if a bastard dies intestate, seized of a copyhold of inheritance, it shall not go to the King, but to the Lord of the Manor; and so on an attaint of blood, if the convict has previously transferred the legal interest in his inheritance over to another the King is barred, and shall not take it by his prerogative.

The question then becomes reduced to the simple fact, whether at the time of, and anterior to the Company's taking possession of the Circars, the legal estate in the soil was in them. If it was, it remains so still, and the term of conquest in so far as it has any relation to, or connection with the question of right, is inapplicable to the subject. Every force used however necessary and just, to help any lawful owner to his own, might equally be termed a conquest. In viewing and comparing the case of the Circars with those of Masulipatam and the final conquest of Bengal, for the purpose of discovering the operation of law with respect to the property in the soil, the difference (and a very great one indeed it is) consists in this, that in the former instance the grant was *antecedent* to the possession; it was made by the lawful owner to a party (the East-India Company)

K

pany) capable and authorized by law to accept and hold the lands so granted, whereby the legal estate and title became transferred to the Company in the first instance, and they have done no act whatever to divest themselves of it, but have obtained possession as they lawfully might, and have ever since retained it. Whereas in the other cases, the grant being made *subsequent* to the conquest, the law instantly cast the legal estate by the conquest upon the King; and any grants made subsequent to the King's title once acquired, though made by the conquered party and former owner to the real conqueror, are unavailable, and cannot operate to divest the King of what he had previously been invested with.

To raise a question at this day upon the efficacy of the Mogul's grant to the Company, would be absurd and preposterous, as striking at the very root of their titles to various parts of our possessions in India, and particularly to the settlements of the Company; and because if the grant be bad, it will not make a title in the King.

With respect to the means used for obtaining the grant in question, it will be also nugatory to enter upon the enquiry, since no part of the claim of the Public is founded upon an imputed forfeiture; and because by the jurisprudence of England, the King must shew a legal title in himself to support his right; no equitable circumstances can avail him in such a case against his subjects. Besides which, if a fraud, however gross and atrocious it may have been, were to be proved or admitted in respect to the means used to obtain the grant, it could give no right of resumption here, nor assist the claim of the Crown or the Public. If by the enormity of the fraud, the grant could be vitiated and set aside, the lands must revert to the grantee upon whom the fraud was committed.

That the Company were capable, and must so continue 'till the law is altered, of acquiring landed property by grants from the country powers to an indefinite extent, is evident both in the letter and the spirit of their Charter, and no man will be hardy enough to deny it, after the high legal authority we have before quoted at large in the Third Chapter upon that very point.

Lest what we have already said should not be thought sufficient for supporting the exclusive claim of the Company to the Circars; and lest the claim of the Public should be again brought forward as for a country obtained by conquest, it may be right further to discuss the fact.

That fraud and every species of corruption, chicane and artifice, were practised to create fears and apprehensions in the mind of the Soubah, as the means of influencing and bringing him into our views for effecting our purposes; and that we corrupted his ministers and commanders to gain them over to our interests, will not be denied. Practices of a nature which would never have been admitted in the Councils of the Company's servants, under other circumstances than the very peculiar ones which at that critical juncture existed. But

we

we see in this nothing like *conquest*. The forces we had in the Circars, except a very few that had been added for shew more than actual service, to attend the publication of the Mogul's grant, were at that time in the pay and service of the Soubah himself, and we were in perfect amity with him. The bare act of taking possession of the defenceless Fort of Condapilly and the pass, cannot surely be deemed a conquest of the Circars. It is much to be doubted, if that Fort is deemed a part of the Circars, nor does it clearly appear that it was garrisoned by the Soubah's forces. It may rather be presumed to have been held by a Zemindar, as those Forts were which we obtained by corrupting Vizeram Rauze. But admitting it was the Soubah's, it will be found situate at the extremity of the Circar of Ellore, between the hills, which form the north-west boundary of it. As well might it be argued that by the capture of Breda, the French had accomplished the conquest of the United Provinces, as that a country six hundred miles in length on the sea coast, was conquered by taking this hill fort, situate at the Western extremity of it. The Government of Fort St. George, the moment they knew of the Mogul's grant, had undoubtedly resolved to seize and keep the Circars upon many considerations both political and commercial, and had concerted and taken their measures to meet the event of the Nizam ultimately rejecting their proposals, or of his resisting their attempts to keep them by force. But both justice and policy dictated the propriety of holding them as fiefs of the Empire under the Native Sovereigns, by a rent and military tenure, rather than to involve the country in a new war; and their plan succeeded. They purchased, of the Soubah, a confirmation of their possession by a fine, a yearly rent or tribute, and an engagement to furnish a body of forces when required. They acted upon this agreement by an actual supply of troops immediately after, and they have paid the stipulated rent. It may be said, and perhaps truly said, that the Soubah's mind was influenced in making the grant more by panic and the fear of resentment if he should refuse, than by any advantages he could expect to derive by his compliance. But the motives for his conduct can in no way be admitted to affect the decision on the question of right, nor will they admit of proof; still less ought we to presume that because the Company's servants pursued improper means to gain their point, those means failing, the conquest of the Circars must of necessity have followed ; as well might it be argued that though the grant was obtained, the Company instead of being permitted to take the fruits of it, shall be considered as having done that, which they did not in fact do, and which their ability to have done, must have depended altogether on the precarious events of war.

With respect to the treaty of 1768, whereby the Soubah in effect ratified the two former agreements ; nothing material appears to us to arise from it to alter the question of right, and therefore we forbear to enter into any discussion of it. The Company's tenure and their possessions remained as before.

It has been noticed that by *conquest*, the sovereignty, as well as the soil, passes to the Crown. If the Law Officers in India had conceived that the Circars were
held.

held in right of conquest, they could have had no difficulty in advising their constituents to have obtained from the Crown a Charter of Justice for those parts of their possessions. The want of Courts of Judicature there, has long been a subject of very serious complaint. That none have been instituted, can alone be ascribed to the circumstance of our not holding the Circars by right of conquest, but as Jagheerdars and tributaries to the Native Princes. The Law officers of the Company have given it as their opinion, that the sovereignty remains in the country powers, and that no Courts can be instituted but by the authority of the Mogul or his Soubah. If the sovereignty is not in the King, it must follow that the property in the lands or revenues cannot be vested in him; and although the Crown cannot hold by the tenure of another, it is very consistent for the Company to do so, and in fact they always have so held from the time of their obtaining their first Firmauns from the country powers.

Upon the whole, we retain the opinion formerly given in the Third Chapter,* that in point of law the Crown or the Public have no claim against the Company in the northern Circars, and that they are held by the Company as Jagheerdars to the Mogul, (a species of military tenure, by which they are to furnish a number of cavalry, determinable by the Emperor's books) paying at the same time by voluntary compact, a fixt tribute to the Soubah of the Decan, who is the nominal viceroy and representative of the Mogul in those parts.

How far so large a territory may be necessary for the purposes of commerce, and in that respect proper to be kept by the Company, or for any political purposes to be taken from them and placed in the Crown, it is not our province to determine. The Legislature are the proper judges in that respect. All that we mean to contend is this, that the Circars never were conquered by the East-India Company; that their title to them is by grant, and that there is no law existing by which they can be taken out of their hands, or by which they are liable to account for the revenues of them to the Public, otherwise than according to the terms and conditions of their existing compact for the continuance of their exclusive trade, by which a temporary participation has been established of the Revenues of the British Territories in India at large, of which Masulipatam and the Circars form a part, with a mutual saving of Rights from being prejudiced by that partition.

* Vide the opinions of the Company's Advocate General and Solicitor General at Fort St. George, given in July, 1783.

An ACCOUNT of the Value of the Goods, diſtinguiſhing the principal : the Value of the Exports of Eaſt India Goods, eſtimated at the ſame Rate as the Imports ; n of Four Years.

	Years.	Walking Canes.	China Ware.	Coffee.	Pepper.	Stuffs, indigo.	Red Sanders.	Shellack.	Saltpetre.
		£.	£.	£.	£.	£.	£.	£.	£.
Value of Goods ſold at the Company's Sales	1789	16,755	39,124	29,720	95,438	5,589	4,847	4,152	100,067
	1790	13,668	38,959	14,928	163,097	,107	3,441	609	87,041
	1791	4,425	54,550	54,015	175,223	,564	2,279	—	85,692
	1792	918	45,201	47,919	149,189	,351	—	1,296	160,913
Total Value ſold in the Four Years		35,766	177,834	146,582	582,947	,611	10,567	6,059	433,713
Medium Annual Value ſold		8,941	44,458	36,645	145,736	,152	2,641	1,514	108,428
Ditto exported		5,657	12,684	14,503	100,472	,011	812	3,365	5,434
Medium Annual Value remaining for Home Conſumption		3,28.	31,774	22,142	45,264	,141	1,829	—	102,974
Medium Annual Value retained for Home Conſumption, excluding the Duties		2,587	16,682	12,278	25,194	,141	1,829	—	86,514

	Years.	Mother of Pearl Shells.	Silk, Bengal Raw.	Silk, China Raw.
		£.	£.	£.
Value of Goods ſold at the Company's Sales continued	1789	3,323	289,271	235,5
	1790	—	302,991	217,7
	1791	—	321,882	236,1
	1792	2,322	318,440	148,5
Total Value ſold in the Four Years		5,645	1,232,584	837,6
Medium Annual Value ſold		1,411	308,146	209,2
Ditto exported		720	46,620	14,0
Medium Annual Value remaining for Home Conſumption		691	261,526	195,6
Medium Annual Value retained for Home Conſumption, excluſive of the Duties		573	233,883	145,5

RECAPITULATION of the preceding Account.

Medium Annual Amount of East India Sales, including Duties paid by the Company and the Purchasers, viz. in Goods £. 5,015,180; in Duties £. 1,060,692; in all £. 6,075,872. The above Sum of £. 6,075,872 consists of the following Articles, including the Duties.

1st. Walking Canes, China Ware, Coffee, Pepper, Sago, Tea, Turmeric, manufactured and unmanufactured Goods, and sundry small Articles	£. 2,756,262
2dly. Drugs and Cowries	14,391
3dly. Indigo, Red Sanders, Saltpetre, Mother of Pearl Shells, Bengal and China Raw Silk, Cotton Wool, and sundry small Articles	704,256
4thly. Callicoes, Muslins, and Nankeens	500,683
Total Amount retained for Home Consumption, including the Duties	3,975,592
Goods exported, including the Duties	2,114,378
Total	6,089,970
Deduct the Amount of those Articles, the value of which on exportation exceeded the value sold, arising from a greater quantity of these Articles having been on hand at the time the Account commenced, than at the period in which it terminated	14,098
	6,075,872

RECAPITULATION, exclusive of the Duties.

Medium Annual Amount of East India Sales, exclusive of the Duties	£. 5,013,239

The above Sum of £. 5,013,239 consists of the following Articles, exclusive of the Duties.

1st. Walking Canes, China Ware, Coffee, Pepper, Sago, Tea, &c. as above	£. 2,370,027
2dly. Drugs and Cowries	11,288
3dly. Indigo, Red Sanders, Saltpetre, Mother of Pearl Shells, &c. as above	606,201
4thly. Callicoes amounting to £. 77,877; Muslins £. 294,831; and Nankeens £. 21,820; making in all	394,528
Total	3,382,044
Deduct the Amount of those Articles where the Export exceeds the Sale	14,098
Medium Annual Value of Goods retained for Home Consumption	3,367,946
Amount of Goods exported £. 2,114,378	
Deduct Drawbacks repaid to the Exporters 433,601	
	1,680,777
Total	5,048,723

The difference between the Value sold, exclusive of the Duties, and the Value, thus accounted for, amounting to £. 35,484, arises from a variety of circumstances, a detail of which, in figures, would greatly tend to complicate the Account.

RECAPITULATION of the preceding Account.

Medium Annual Amount of East India Sales, including Duties paid by the Compan{y by}
the Purchasers, viz. in Goods £. 5,015,180 ; in Duties £. 1,060,692 ; in all £. 6,075{,872}
The above Sum of £. 6,075,872 consists of the following Articles, including the D{uties}
1st. Walking Canes, China Ware, Coffee, Pepper, Sago, Tea, Turmeric, manufac{tured}
and unmanufactured Goods, and sundry small Articles   £. 2,756,262
2dly. Drugs and Cowries - - - - - 14,391
3dly. Indigo, Red Sanders, Saltpetre, Mother of Pearl Shells, Bengal and China Raw Silk, Cotton Wool, and sundry small Articles - 704,256
4thly. Callicoes, Muslins, and Nankeens - - - - 500,683

  Total Amount retained for Home Consumption, including the
    Duties - - - - - 3,975,592
  Goods exported, including the Duties - - - 2,114,378

  Total - - - - - 6,089,970
Deduct the Amount of those Articles, the value of which on exportation exceeded the value sold, arising from a greater quantity
  of these Articles having been on hand at the time the Account
  commenced, than at the period in which it terminated - 14,098
                                                                           —————— 6,075,{872}

RECAPITULATION, exclusive of the Duties.

Medium Annual Amount of East India Sales, exclusive of the Duties - £. 5,013,{239}
The above Sum of £. 5,013,239 consists of the following Articles, exclusive
  of the Duties.
1st. Walking Canes, China Ware, Coffee, Pepper, Sago, Tea, &c.
  as above - - - - - - £. 2,370,027
2dly. Drugs and Cowries - - - - 11,288
3dly. Indigo, Red Sanders, Saltpetre, Mother of Pearl Shells, &c.
  as above - - - - - 606,201
4thly. Callicoes amounting to £. 77,877 ; Muslins £. 294,831 ;
  and Nankeens £. 21,820 ; making in all - - 394,528

  Total - - - - 3,382,044
Deduct the Amount of those Articles where the Export exceeds
  the Sale - - - - - 14,098

Medium Annual Value of Goods retained for Home Consumption   3,367,946
Amount of Goods exported - - £. 2,114,378
Deduct Drawbacks repaid to the Exporters - 433,601
                                                       ————— 1,680,777
Total - - - - - - —————— 5,048,{723}

The difference between the Value sold, exclusive of the Duties, and the Value
accounted for, amounting to £. 35,484, arises from a variety of circumstances, a deta{il of}
which, in figures, would greatly tend to complicate the Account.

An ABRIDGMENT of the Act for settling the Government and Trade of INDIA, and for the Appropriation of the Territorial Revenues and Profits of Trade.

THE CONTROUL AT HOME.

THE Act provides for the continuation of the Board of Controul for the Affairs of India in all its parts, except, that instead of the Secretary of State being the President, the person first named in the King's Commission is to be the President; and, instead of the Commission being limited to six Privy Counsellors, the number is indefinite, resting on the King's pleasure; of which, however, the two principal Secretaries of State and the Chancellor of the Exchequer are to be three: and His Majesty may, if he pleases, add to the list two Commissioners, who are not of his Privy Council.

By the former Act, no salaries were given to the Commissioners for India; and those of their Secretary and other Officers were to be paid out of the Civil List. By the new Act, the King may give £. 5,000 a year amongst such of the Commissioners as he pleases; which, together with the salaries of the Secretary and Officers, and other expences of the Board, are to be paid by the India Company, and not by the Civil List. The whole is not to exceed £. 16,000 a year, the Commissioners Salaries included.

Oaths are prescribed for the Commissioners and their Officers. The office of a Commissioner or Chief Secretary, is not to be deemed a new office, to difable their fitting in Parliament. The appointment of a Commiffioner not having a falary, or of a Chief Secretary (if a Member of the Houfe of Commons) is not to vacate his feat; but the appointment of a Commiffioner, with a falary, will vacate his feat. Three Commiffioners muft be prefent to form a Board.

The powers of the Board are, in fubftance, the fame as under former Acts of Parliament. They are to fuperintend, direct and controul all acts, operations and concerns which relate to the Civil or Military Government and Revenues of India, fubject to the reftrictions hereafter-mentioned. They and their Officers are to have accefs to the papers and records of the Company, and to be furnifhed with copies or extracts of fuch of them as fhall be required. They are alfo to be furnifhed with Copies of all proceedings of General Courts and Courts of Directors, within eight days; and with Copies of all difpatches from abroad, which relate to Matters of Government or Revenue, immediately after their arrival. No orders on thofe fubjects are to be fent by the Company to India until approved by the Board, and when the Commiffioners vary or expunge any difpatches propofed by the Directors, they are to give their reafons; and all difpatches are to be returned to the Court of Directors in fourteen days. The Directors may ftate their objections to any alterations, and the Commiffioners are to reconfider them, and if they interfere with what the Directors may deem matters of Commerce, the Directors may apply to the King in Council to determine betwixt them. But the Board are reftricted from the appointment of any of the Company's Servants. If the Directors, on being called upon to propofe difpatches, on any fubject relating to Government or Revenue, fhall fail to do fo within fourteen days, the Board may originate their own difpatches on that fubject.

The

The Board are not to authorize any encreafe of falaries, or any allowance or gratuity to be granted to perfons employed in the Company's fervice, except the fame fhall be firft propofed by the Company, and their intention and reafons for fuch grant are to be certified to both Houfes of Parliament thirty days before the falary can commence.

The Directors are to appoint three of their members to be a Committee of Secrecy, through whom difpatches relating to Government, war, peace or treaties, may be fent to, and received from India. The Secret Committee, and the perfons they employ to tranfcribe fecret difpatches, are to be fworn to fecrecy.

Orders of Directors concerning the Government or Revenues of India, once approved by the Board, are not fubject to revocation by the General Court of Proprietors.

THE GOVERNMENTS ABROAD.

The prefent Forms of Goverment over the Prefidencies of Bengal, Fort St. George and Madras, are continued in all their effential parts. For Bengal, by a Governor General and three Members of Council. For each of the others, a Governor and three Members. Thefe latter, in refpect to treaties with the native Powers of India, levying war, making peace, collecting and applying Revenues, levying and employing forces, or other matters of civil or military Government, are to be under the controul of the *Government General* of Bengal; and are, in all cafes whatever, to obey their orders, unlefs the Directors fhall have fent to thofe fettlements any orders repugnant thereto, not known to the Government General; of which, in that cafe, they are to give the Government General immediate advice.

The Court of Directors are to appoint to thefe feveral Governments; namely, the Governor General, the two other Governors, and

and the the Members of all the Councils; and likewise the Commander in Chief of all the forces, and the three provincial Commanders in Chief. None of the Commanders in Chief are, *ex officio*, to be of the Council; but they are not difqualified from being fo, if the Directors fhall think fit to appoint them, and, when they are Members of the Council, they are to have precedence of the other Counfellors. The civil Members of Council are to be appointed from the Lift of Civil Servants, who have refided twelve years in the fervice in India.

The Directors may appoint to any of thofe offices provifionally, but without falary, till the perfons appointed fhall actually fucceed in poffeffion. Any vacancy of Governor General, or Governor, when no provifional fucceffor is on the fpot, is to be filled by the Senior of the civil Counfellors, till a fucceffor fhall arrive, and the vacant feat in Council, thereby occafioned, fhall be temporily fupplied from amongft the Senior Merchants at the nomination of the acting Governor General, or Governor, if only one Counfellor fhall then remain. The Governor General and Governors may fupply vacancies in Council from the Lift of Senior Merchants, until fucceffors, duly appointed, fhall arrive to take their feats. In all thefe cafes, the falaries and allowances are to follow the acting Members while in office. If the Directors fail to appoint to vacancies in two calendar months after notification thereof, the King may fupply them, and the Directors fhall not remove any perfon fo appointed. In all other cafes the Directors have the power of recalling or difmiffing any fervants; and the like general power is vefted in the Crown. Appointments made before the Act are not to be thereby difturbed.

The Commander in Chief of all the forces, when at either of the fubordinate fettlements, is to have a feat at the Council Board, but is to have no falary in refpect thereof; and if the Provincial Commander is a Member of that Council, he may continue to deliberate

rate, but his voice shall be suspended, as long as the other shall remain.

Provision is made for supplying the place of any Member of Council, disabled from attending by any casual illness or infirmity.

The departure of any Governor or Member of Government, or Commander in Chief from India, with intent to come to Europe, or any written resignation delivered in by them shall be deemed an avoidance of office, and the coming into any part of Europe shall be a sufficient indication of that intent. No salary shall be paid or payable to any Officer, or his Agent, during absence, unless employed on actual service; and if any officer, unless absent on service, never returns, the salary is to be deemed to have ceased from the day of his quitting the settlement.

The Act prescribes the order and method of conducting business at the several Council Boards. Matters propounded by the President, shall be first proceeded upon. He may adjourn the discussion of questions put by the Members of Council, but not more than twice, nor beyond forty-eight hours each time. All orders are to be expressed to be made by the Governor General *in* Council, or Governor *in* Council. Powers are given to the Governor General or Governors, to act contrary to the opinions of the other Members of Council, taking upon themselves the sole responsibility. On such extraordinary occasions, the Governor General, or Governor, and Counsellors are to communicate to each other their opinions and reasons by minutes, in writing, and to meet a second time; and if both retain their first opinion, the minutes are to be entered on the consultations, and the orders of the Governor General, or Governor, are to be valid, and put in execution.

If the Governor General shall visit any subordinate presidency, he shall appoint a Vice President to act in Bengal during his absence fence, who, with the Council, may act for that Presidency alone. The Governor General's authority, and that of his Council over such subordinate settlement, shall be transferred to the Council Board of the Presidency where he shall be present; except in judicial cases. And whilst he is in a subordinate Presidency, the Governor thereof shall have only a voice in Council. His other authorities, except in regard to judicial matters, shall be suspended. If the Governor General shall be in the field without a Council, all the Governments and Officers shall obey his orders, and he alone shall be responsible.

These extraordinary powers shall not extend to the imposing any tax, nor to any act which might not be done by the whole Council, nor to any judicial case, nor to the suspension of any standing order of Government, nor shall those powers be exercised by persons casually succeeding to the temporary Government; and the Directors, with the approbation of the India Board, may suspend these extraordinary powers, and again revive them; and all the Governments are laid under restrictions to prevent war or extension of dominion in India, unless hostilities against the Company, or their allies, shall render war unavoidable; and the Members of the subordinate Governments, acting contrary to this Act, or to the directions of the Government General, may be suspended or dismissed by that Government, and further punished. The subordinate Presidencies are also required to communicate all matters of importance to the Superior Government, with all dispatch.

The Governor General, and the other Governors, are vested with powers of apprehending persons suspected of illicit correspondence. Witnesses are to be examined and cross examined, and their evidence recorded; and the parties may be tried either in India or sent home: in the latter case, the depositions of the witnesses are

also

also to be sent home, and are to be received in evidence, subject to impeachment in respect to the competency of the witnesses.

To the acting President of the several Council Boards, is given a casting vote in all cases of equality of voices.

PATRONAGE AND RULE OF PROMOTION.

The Directors are to appoint so many Cadets and Writers only, as to supply vacancies according to returns from abroad. Their ages shall not be under fifteen, not exceed twenty-two, unless any Cadet shall have been one year in the King's service, and then his age is not to exceed twenty-five years. All shall have promotion by seniority of service only. Three years service qualifies a civil servant for a place of £.500 a year; six years for one of £.1500; nine years £.3000; twelve years £.4000 a year or upwards. None to take two offices, where the joint emoluments shall exceed this rule. All Collectors of the Revenue are to take the oath prescribed in the Act against the acceptance of presents, and for faithfully rendering to the Company all they shall receive.

The acceptance of any present, by any servant of the Crown, or of the Company in India, is made punishable as for extortion (with a saving of fees to professional men) and the Court, before whom such offence is tried, on any conviction, may return the present to the party who gave it, or dispose of any fine in favour of the prosecutor.

Disobedience of orders of the Directors by servants abroad, is made punishable as for a misdemeanor, and so is any breach of trust or duty, or making or being party to any corrupt bargain concerning any office or employment, whether by a King's or a Company's servant; and all the King's subjects in India are made amenable

amenable to all Courts of competent jurisdiction abroad, and at home for all crimes committed by them in India. The Company may compound civil actions, now depending, or hereafter to be brought at any time before judgment, but in criminal cases they are absolutely restricted from compounding or remitting any judgment or sentence whatever.

Servants of the Company, after five years absence, cannot return with their rank, nor serve again, unless detained by sickness; or unless it be by leave of the Company on a ballot of three parts in four of the General Court. In case of sickness, the Directors are the judges in the Civil Service, and in the Military the Directors and the Board of Controul jointly are the judges.

THE TRADE.

The Company's term is extended for 20 years, from the 1st of March 1794; subject to be determined at, or after that period, on three year's previous notice by Parliament, signified by the Speaker of the House of the Commons; subject, however, as to the trade to and from *India*, to the following limitations in favour of such private Merchants, as may choose to trade thither. In other respects, and to and from *China*, and other places beyond the Cape of Good Hope, the former restrictions against private Traders are continued in force; and if the exclusive trade thus limited, shall be hereafter discontinued, the Company are still to retain their corporate capacity, with power to trade with a joint stock in common with other people. If, however, any new settlement shall be obtained from the Chinese Government, separate from the Continent of Asia, an export trade thither is reserved to private Merchants, under certain conditions and regulations; and there is also a clause to preserve the Southern Whalers in the benefit of

their

their carrying trade into the Pacific Ocean, by the way of Cape Horn, to the northward of the Equator, limited to 180 degrees weft longitude from London; and ſhips from Nootka Sound are to be licenſed to trade from thence with Japan and China, but are not to bring any goods of the produce or manufacture of thoſe Countries to Great Britain.

LIMITATIONS ON THE EXCLUSIVE TRADE TO AND FROM INDIA.

All perſons may export and import goods to and from India in the Company's ſhips, except that they ſhall not export military ſtores, ammunition, maſts, ſpars, cordage, anchors, pitch, tar, or copper; nor import India callicoes, dimities, muſlins, or other piece goods, made or manufactured with ſilk or cotton, or with ſilk or cotton mixed, or with other mixed materials, unleſs it be done by leave of the Company. If the market ſhall not be ſufficiently ſupplied with the excepted articles of import or export, with an exception of military ſtores and copper, the Board of Controul may open that trade alſo to individuals. If the Company ſhould not export 1500 tons of copper annually, private Traders may export copper, in the Company's ſhips, to the amount of the deficiency.

The Company are to furniſh private Traders, till 1796, with 3000 tons of ſhipping yearly, computed on the ſame principle as the Company's own tonnage is computed. The quantity may be increaſed by order of the Board of Controul, to meet the demands of the private Traders; and if the Board order more than the Company approve, they may appeal from the order to the King in Council. And the Company are reſtricted from charging any higher freight than £.5 per ton outwards, and £.15

per ton inwards, except in time of war, or in circumstances incidental to war, or preparations for war, when they may charge an increased rate of freight, in a due proportion to the rates at which they shall take up their own shipping, but the proposed increase can only be made by the consent of the India Board, to whom the Directors are also required, in 1794, and in every third year afterwards, to lay a statement of the affairs of shipping, and to abide by their order, touching any continuance, encrease, or abatement of the rate of freight on private trade.

Private traders are required to notify to the Company's Secretary, at home, and to the proper officers in India, at a time limited, the quantity of tonnage wanted by them for the ensuing season, with the place of destination, and the time when the goods will be ready for shipping. At home, this notice is to be given before the 31st August for the ships of the ensuing season, and before the 15th September they are to deposit the sum for the tonnage, or give security to the Directors for payment of it. Before the 30th of October, they are to deliver a list of the sorts and quantities of the goods intended to be sent. In failure of having them ready, by the day specified in the notice, they are to forfeit their deposit or the security, and also their tonnage for that turn. Similar rules are prescribed for shipping, &c. goods in India; but it is left to the Governments there to fix the times, and to name the officers, to whom notices are to be given. The Company is to have the benefit of all forfeited and vacant tonnage, and if more is demanded for private trade than the quantity limited, every person is to have his due proportion; and notice is to be given him thereof, seven days before the day for making the deposits. All Private Trade is to be registered in the Company's books, and, in default of being registered, it is to be considered as illicit trade, and punishable accordingly.

The

The restrictions of the law against the Company's Servants, or others, from acting as factors for foreigners, or lending money to foreign Companies, or on bottomry of their ships, or assisting them with remittances by bills, are repealed. And all legal impediments to the recovery of debts, under any pretence that they were incurred illicitly, and against the letter of these abrogated laws, are removed; and all persons in India, not specially prohibited by the Company, or restricted by their covenants, are authorized to act as mercantile agents for any who may choose to employ them; and if there shall be a want of Factors (properly qualified and authorized) the Company are to licence free merchants, with the approbation of the India Board, so that there may be always a proper supply of agents for conducting the Private Trade abroad. But the becoming factors is not to exempt any persons from being amenable to the general authorities of the Governments in India; and all Agents are restricted from going beyond ten miles from some principal settlement without special leave.

As a further relief to Private Traders, the duty of 5 per cent., granted by an Act of King William, on Goods imported in Private Trade, is, in respect to the India Trade, repealed; and the Company's usual charge of 2 per cent. discontinued, and in lieu of these, and in satisfaction of the expences of unshipping, hoyage, cartage, warehouse room, sorting, lotting, and selling private goods, the Company is to have £.3 per cent. on the gross amount of the sales of Private Trade, the customs thereon included. The repeal, or the allowance thus substituted, is however not to extend to special engagements made between the Company and any of their Officers, touching their privileges.

For the case of manufacturers, who may import any articles of raw materials, Rules or By-Laws are to be framed and established for bringing them to as early a sale as possible, and for preventing any undue preference in the sales of the same commodity amongst any of the importers, whether the goods belong to the Company or to Individuals, the sales are to be open and public, by inch of candle; and the whole consignment bought in by the private importer, is to be delivered out to him, on payment only of the duties and other dues thereon. All other goods imported in Private Trade are to be sold, and treated as heretofore, according to the By-Laws of the Company; and all goods in Private Trade are to pay to Government the same customs as goods imported by the Company on their own account.

And inasmuch as the allowance of 3 per cent., and the rates of freight, will be insufficient to indemnify the Company their actual charges upon Private Trade, the Legislature hath thought it just to exempt the Company from actions for losses or embezzlements, which a common carrier might, in ordinary cases, be liable by law to make good to the owner. But the Act provides that the Company's Officers, and all persons through whose means or negligence any loss shall happen, shall be liable to make it good to the owner, and it gives a further remedy to the owner, in certain cases, to recover satisfaction, by enabling him to prosecute under the written engagements or securities taken by the Company for the safe keeping of their own merchandize. All the laws prohibiting the import of goods from any other place than that of their growth, and for continuing all prohibitory laws in respect to the consumption or wearing of foreign manufactures are continued.

APPROPRIATIONS.

First; in India. The territorial revenues are to be applied, in the first place, in defraying all charges of a military nature. Secondly;

In payment of the interest of the debts there already, or hereafter to be incurred. Thirdly; In payment of the civil and commercial establishments. Fourthly; In payments of not less than one million per annum for the Company's investments of goods to Europe, and remittances and investments to China; and the surplus, if any shall remain, is to be applied in the discharge of debts, or such other purposes as shall be directed from home. The sum allowed for investments, may from time to time be increased to the extent of the diminution made in the annual amount of the interest of debts which shall be paid in India or transferred home; for which transfer, provision is made to an extent of £.500,000 a year, by bills of exchange to be drawn upon the Company: and if the creditors shall not subscribe to that amount, other persons may subscribe, and the money advanced by them for bills is to be applied in discharge of such debts; and this rule is to be continued till the India debt shall be reduced to two millions. The Company may increase these transfers home, but the Governments abroad are restricted from exceeding the above amount, without their orders.

Secondly at Home. The net produce of the Company's funds at home, after payment of current charges, are thus appropriated: First; In payment of a ten per cent. annual dividend, on the present or any increased amount of the capital stock of the Company. Secondly; Of £.500,000 per annum to be set apart on the first March and the first September, half yearly; and applied in the discharge of the before-mentioned bills of exchange, for the aforesaid reduction of the India debt. Thirdly; Of a like annual sum of £.500,000 to the Exchequer, to be applied by Parliament for the use of the Public, and to be paid on the 1st of January and first of July, half yearly, by equal instalments. And, lastly; The surplus may be applied in the more speedy reduction of the India debt, till reduced

to

to two millions; or in discharging debts at home, so as not to diminish the bond debt below £.1,500,000. Subject to these appropriations, and after the debt in India is reduced to two millions, and the bond debt at home to £.1,500,000; *one sixth* part of the ultimate surplus, is to be applied to an increase of dividend on the capital stock, and the remaining *five sixths*, is to be made a Guarantee Fund, or collateral security for the Company's capital stock, and their dividend of ten per cent. until such Fund, by the monies paid by the Company, and the interest thereof, shall have amounted to twelve millions; and after that time, the said *five sixth* of the surplus is to belong to the Public in full right. These *five sixths* are to be paid into the Bank, and laid out in the purchase of redeemable annuities, in the names of the Commissioners for the reduction of the National debt, who are also to receive the dividends, and lay them out in like manner, until twelve millions have been invested. That being accomplished, the annual dividends of the stock purchased therewith, are, in the first place, to make good any defalcation in the Company's revenues, to pay the ten per cent. dividend, and subject thereto, those dividends are to belong to the Public. If on the Company's exclusive trade being determined, their own assets shall prove insufficient to make good their debts, and also their capital stock rated at 200 per cent., the excess of such Guarantee Fund is to make good the deficiency, as far as it will extend, and in the event of the Company discontinuing their trade altogether, the excess is to belong to the Public. But if the Company shall continue to trade with a joint stock, then the overplus, and the annual dividends thereof, are to remain as a like guarantee, for a dividend of ten per cent. and the capital rated at £.200 per cent. as long as the Company shall trade with a joint stock; but subject to the making good any such deficiencies the said Fund is to be deemed the property of the Public.

If the bond debt at home, or the debts abroad, after being reduced to the sums before limited, shall be again increased, the former appropriation is to be revived, until those debts shall be again diminished to their respective standards before limited.

Any deficiency in the Funds to make good the £.500,000 to the Exchequer in any year, is to be made good in the excesses of subsequent years, unless it happens in time of war, or by circumstances incidental to war, in which case the deficiencies are not to be carried forward as a debt on the *annual* funds of the Company, nor be brought forward as a debt to be paid by the Company, unless only in the event of their assets, on the conclusion of the exclusive trade affording more than sufficient to make good the capital stock, rated at £.200 per cent. but any excess of such assets beyond that amount, is liable to make good the deficiency of any such payments to the Public; no interest is to be computed in the mean time on such deficiency.

The securities given by the Cashiers of the Bank, are to extend to the monies they may receive under this Act, and the Treasury is to direct the allowances for management; and if the India Company make default in any payments directed by the Act, they may be sued, and shall pay £.15 per cent. damages with costs of suit.

The Act directs the manner in which receipts shall be given, and a power is lodged in the Treasury, to give the Company further time for payment in cases of exigency. And it is declared, that neither the claims of the Public, nor of the Company, to the territories in India, shall be prejudiced by the Act, beyond the prolongation of the term in the Exclusive Trade. The act also contains a clause of mutual acquittal of all outstanding demands between the Crown and the Company, to the 24th Day of December, 1792.

The Act recognizes the rights of the Company to a sum of £467,896 7s. 4d. in money and £9,750 East India stock; (which sums constitute the separate Fund of the Company, established under the Act of 1781;) and it is observed, that it will be more for the general interest of the Company to continue that money employed in trade, computing an interest upon it, and to make it a fund for a permanent increase to their dividend, of 10s. per cent., than to draw it from their trading capital for any sudden distribution. And it then authorizes and limits the Company to make a dividend from this separate fund, and the interest thereof, after the rate of 10s. per cent. per ann. during their further term in the exclusive trade; and at the end of the term, it gives them a power of disposing of the remainder of this fund as they shall think fit.

The Company are not to grant any pensions, or new salaries, beyond £.200 per ann. to any one person, without the consent of the Board of Controul; and they are to lay before Parliament, annually, a list of all their establishments abroad, and at home, in which all pensions and new salaries are to be particularly noticed; and also complete accounts of all their affairs, receipts and outgoings of the preceding year, with estimates for the following year.

All the old Laws for preventing clandestine trade with India, and from lending to or assisting, or being concerned with Foreign Companies, or Foreign Traders, are wholly abrogated, and the following provisions are substituted in their place, observing that the penalties are made to extend only to such of His Majesty's subjects as belong to Great Britain, Guernsey, Jersey, Alderney, Sark, Man, Faro Isles, or to the Colonies, Islands, or Plantations in America or the West-Indies; and that all vessels and goods forfeited, may be seized by any of the Company's Officers in India or China.

Persons going unlawfully to India, and trafficking there, forfeit ships, vessels, goods, and merchandize, and double the value thereof; one fourth to the Informers, and three fourths to the Company, they paying thereout the costs of prosecution.

Persons unlawfully going to India, shall be deemed unlawful Traders, and subject to the foregoing penalties and forfeitures, and may also be prosecuted as for a crime and misdemeanor, and be liable to fine and imprisonment. One moiety of the fine goes to the King, the other to the Company, if they prosecute, or else to any other informer.

Persons unlawfully resorting to India, may be seized and sent home for trial; and, on arrival, they are to give bail, or be committed to prison.

Persons dismissed the service, or whose licences shall have expired, if they continue in India, are to be continued as illicit Traders, and are made subject to penalties and forfeitures of goods, &c. as such.

Goods shipped clandestinely, or such as are restricted by the Act, and goods unshipped at sea, shall be seized and forfeited, with double the value, and the Master, or other Officer, knowingly permitting or suffering the same, shall forfeit all his wages to the Company, to be deducted out of the monies payable to the owners, and be disabled from again acting in the service.

Any who shall solicit for, or accept a foreign commission, to sail to and trade in India, shall forfeit £. 500, half to the Company, and half to the Prosecutor, or the whole to the Company, if they shall prosecute.

All Governors and Counsellors are prohibited from trading, except for the Company; and all Collectors, Supervisors, and others

others employed in the Revenues of Bengal, Bahar, and Orissa, or their Agents, or any in trust for them, are prohibited from inland trade, except for the Company. The Judges of the Supreme Court of Judicature in Bengal, are absolutely prohibited from traffick; and none, without the permission of the Company, shall trade in Salt, Beetle Nut, Tobacco, or Rice, on pain of forfeiture of the goods, and treble the value, one moiety to the Company, and the other to the Prosecutor.

None shall send goods from India to the Continent of Europe, by any other channel than as allowed by the Act, on pain of forfeiture of double the value; but this restriction is not to extend to matters of agency, only on the account *bonâ fide* of any foreign Company or foreign Merchant.

The Act then prescribes the method of suing for forfeitures and penalties, and determining the legality of seizures. It gives a right of suing by Action, Bill, or Information, in any of the Courts of Westminster (in which case the venue is to be laid in London or Middlesex), or in the Supreme Court of Judicature in Bengal, or the Mayor's Court at Madras or Bombay; and in such suits the legality of seizures of persons, ships, or goods, is made cognizable. In cases of misdemeanors, the offenders are punishable by fine and imprisonment, and if abroad, they may be sent home, as part of the punishment; and a capias, for arresting the accused party, is given in the first instance, which may be compounded for by bail.

For securing to the Crown the duties for goods unlawfully trafficked with, in the cases of forfeiture of goods, the Attorney General may prosecute the offenders, or their partners, by bills in a Court of Equity, waving penalties, and the defendants shall make full discovery of their illicit traffick upon oath, and shall be decreed to pay all the duties thereupon to Government, and £.30 per cent.

on the value of the goods to the Company, and shall be relieved against all other forfeitures. The Company may, in like manner, proceed against offenders by Bill in Equity, and if they fail they shall pay costs. Defendants are to pay costs to the Crown and to the Company, when the decree shall be against them.

If a common informer, before any suit is commenced, shall make known any offence to the Company, or the Attorney General, and either of them shall prefer a Suit in Equity, in that case the informer shall be entitled to one third part of the simple value of the concern which shall be recovered. But if the Directors prefer a prosecution at law, the informer may proceed, but shall not discontinue the suit without their consent.

When the Company are the first informers, the whole of the informers shares of penalties and forfeitures shall belong to the Company, although the suit be commenced after the time elapsed for common informers to sue or prosecute the offence.

On any suit against the Company or their Servants for seizing, &c. the defendants may plead the general issue, and give the Act in evidence, and the burthen of proofs shall be on the plaintiffs, that the seizure, &c. was unlawful; and on nonsuit, verdict, or judgment, the plaintiffs shall pay treble costs.

The Acts or parts of Acts repealed, are as follow: 9 and 10 W. 3. ch. 24. f. 81. The whole of the temporary Act of 5 Geo. 1. chap. 21. and so much of the several Acts as continued it in force. The 7 Geo. 1. ch. 21. f. 1. to f. 9. The whole of 9 Geo. 1. ch. 26. The 3 Geo. 2. ch. 14. f. 9. The 17 Geo. 2. ch. 17. f. 11. The 10 Geo. 3. ch. 47. f. 1 and 2. The 13 Geo. 3. ch. 63. f. 23 to 29. and f. 32 to 35. The 21 Geo. 3. ch. 65. f. 29. The 24 Geo. 3. ch. 25. f. 3, 13, 29 and 31. The whole of the 26 Geo. 3. ch. 16. and the 32 and 33 f. of 26 G. 3. ch. 57. The repeal is not to extend to offences committed before the commencement of the Act, nor is it to affect the powers of the present Board of Controul, until a new one shall be appointed; nor to affect the powers given to the India Board by certain Acts of the 28th and 31st years of the King, concerning the forces in India.

The jurifdiction of the Supreme Court of Judicature at Fort William, in caufes of Admiralty, is made to extend to the High Seas at large, whereby a defect in the Act of 1773 for conftituting that Court is cured.

For increafing the number of Magiftrates in Bengal, Madras, and Bombay, the Supreme Court of Judicature in Bengal is to iffue commiffions of the peace, in purfuance of orders iffued in Council for that purpofe; and any of the Juftices, fo appointed, may by order in Council, fit alfo in the Courts of Oyer and Terminer, taking the oaths of Juftices in England, excepting the oath prefcribed by the Act of the 18 Geo. 2. (relating to qualification by eftate.) The proceedings and judgments of juftices may be removed to the Court of Oyer and Terminer by Certiorari, as may be done into the Court of King's Bench in England, and on fimilar conditions, but cannot be fet afide for want of form, but on the merits only. The Juftices may alfo affociate with the Judges in caufes appealed, when called upon fo to do.

The Governments abroad may appoint Coroners to take inquefts upon the bodies of perfons coming to an untimely end, and appoint fees to be paid for that duty.

The Juftices of the Peace may appoint Scavengers, and raife money by affeffinents for cleanfing, watching, and repairing the streets

streets of Calcutta, Madras, and Bombay: they may also licenfe houfes for retailing fpirituous liquors, and fix the limits of thofe towns; and none are to retail fpirits but fuch as they fhall fo licenfe, under the penalties of the laws of Great Britain.

A fpecial oath is prefcribed to be taken in future by the Directors of the Company, prohibitory of their acting as Directors, when concerned in buying from, or felling to the Company any goods; and prohibitory of their being concerned in any fhipping employed by the Company, or accepting any prefent for any appointment of office, or of being concerned in any Private Trade contrary to the Act.

The Days and Hours fixed by former Acts of Parliament *for Purchafers of Teas* to make their *Depofits*, having been found inconvenient to the Trade, the Act has, with their Approbation, fixed *Tuefdays* and *Saturdays* at the Hour of THREE for making their Depofits in future.

Profecutions for any thing done under the Act are limited to three years, or if the party aggrieved be abroad, then in three years after his return.

The Act is to commence in Great Britain as foon as it fhall receive the Royal affent, and in India on the 1ft of February, 1794, except when any fpecial commencement is prefcribed in it.

By Permission of the Right Hon. HENRY DUNDAS.
This Day is published,
In One Volume Quarto, Price One Guinea in Boards.

I.

HISTORICAL VIEW
OF PLANS FOR THE
GOVERNMENT of BRITISH INDIA, and REGULATION of TRADE to the EAST INDIES;

And Outlines of a Plan of foreign Government, of Commercial Economy, and of Domestic Administration for the Asiatic Interests of Great Britain.

Printed for J. SEWELL, No. 32, Cornhill; and J. DEBRETT, Piccadilly.

This Work is explanatory of the System for Indian Affairs which has been submitted to the Legislature. The Authorities have been obtained either from the Records of the Company and from the Archives of the State, or from the Communications of those, whose official and local Knowledge qualified them to aid their Country upon this important Occasion.

OF WHOM ALSO MAY BE HAD,

II. A HISTORY of the GOVERNMENT of the ISLAND of NEWFOUNDLAND. With an Appendix, containing all the Acts of Parliament made respecting the Trade and Fishery. By JOHN REEVES, Esq. Chief Justice of the Island. Octavo, Price 6s. in Boards.

N. B. The Profits of this Publication are given by the Author for the Relief of the Suffering Clergy of France, Refugees in the British Dominions.

III. NAVAL ARCHITECTURE. A COLLECTION of PAPERS on these NOBLE STRUCTURES, from the EUROPEAN MAGAZINE, where the Subject will be continued, with a Catalogue of Authors Ancient and Modern, English and Foreign. PART I. Price 2s. 6d.

Also, just published, the SECOND PART of a COLLECTION of PAPERS on NAVAL ARCHITECTURE. This Part contains an enlarged descriptive Catalogue by a foreign Gentleman, with several interesting Papers, new and old. PART III. Price 3s.

IV.

IV. A VIEW of the NAVAL FORCE of GREAT BRITAIN; In which its prefent State, Growth, and Converfion of Timber; Conftruction of Ships, Docks, and Harbours; Regulations of Officers, and Men in each Department, are confidered and compared with other European Powers. To which are added, Obfervations and Hints for the Improvement of the Naval Service. By an OFFICER of RANK. Price 5s.

"When profeffional men of rank and fortune, poffeffed of an independent fpirit, will ftep forth and communicate the fruits of their knowledge and experience to the Public, we feel ourfelves under a particular obligation to them. The Author of this Treatife, on a fubject moft interefting to Englifhmen, as a great maritime and commercial nation, feems to have no object in view but the public good.

"It is clear, by the ftyle and manner of this work, that the Author is not a writer by profeffion. We have therefore forborn all minute criticifm. But his intentions are certainly laudable, and his work abounds with ufeful hints and obfervations, which will, we hope, be attended to.

ANALYTICAL REVIEW, July 1791.

V. A TREATISE on PRACTICAL SEAMANSHIP; with new and important Hints and Remarks relating thereto. Defigned to contribute fomething towards fixing Rules, upon philofophical and rational Principles, for the Form and proportional Dimenfions in Length, Breadth, and Depth of Merchant Ships in general, and the Management of them; and alfo to render Navigation in general more perfect, and confequently lefs dangerous and deftructive to Health, Lives, and Property. By WILLIAM HUTCHINSON, Mariner and Dock-Mafter, at Liverpool. Quarto, 18s. Third Edition, confiderably enlarged.

This valuable book contains a treafure of naval knowledge of every kind (prefented to the world by a moft experienced, able feaman, who is at prefent finifhing his honourable career as Dockmafter at Liverpool, as a legacy of what he gathered of ufeful knowledge from a very extenfive experience), and includes, among many other moft ufeful remarks, very ingenious counfels on the conftruction of merchant-fhips and their management.

Capt. MULLER.

VI. THE SHIP-BUILDER's REPOSITORY; or, A Treatife on Marine Architecture. Wherein are contained the Principles of that Art, with the Theory and practical Parts fully explained;
and

and every Inftruction required in the building and completing a Ship of every Clafs, from the forming of the Draught to the launching into the Water, calculated to the Capacity of young Beginners. Compiled and digefted in a Manner entirely new, and laid down different from what has hitherto appeared on the fubject. The whole being intended as a complete Companion for thofe Naval Architects defirous of attaining a competent Knowledge of that important Art. London, printed for the Author (without the year), 4to. and a large copper-plate, 1*l*. 5*s*.

The theoretical part gives a concife view of the moft effential parts of the more ancient theories on the calculations of the refiftance of fhips, and of the fituations of the centre of gravity of the immerfed part, confidered as an homogene compofition, with fome general remarks on the form of fhips. The practical part, by far the largeft and moft valuable, is diftinguifhed and remarkable principally for a very extenfive table of the fcantlings of every fingle piece entering into the conftruction of a fhip; and is preferable to many others, as it contains the dimenfions of the bolts and ironwork: but the ufe of this table has this inconvenience, that it is not arranged in an alphabetical or any other manner which renders the finding the fingle articles contained in it eafy; fo that it requires a kind of familiarity with it to get directly at the inftruction wanted in a particular cafe. Very valuable are the dimenfions of a great variety of fhips (from the largeft to the fmalleft fize) given in it, for laying down the body-plans of them on the mould-loft. The inftruction for forming the draughts of fhips, exemplified on the plan of an eighty gun fhip, is very plain and fatisfactory; and the explanation of the draught of the inner parts of a fhip, moftly neglected in other works of the fame kind, deferves to be mentioned as a particular merit in this work. The laudable defign of the Author to render it more ufeful by a low price, did not allow him to give more copper-plates.

CONSIDERATIONS

UPON THE

TRADE WITH INDIA,

&c. &c.

C. Mercier and Co. Printers,
King's Head Court, St. Paul's Church-yard.

CONSIDERATIONS

UPON THE

TRADE WITH INDIA;

AND THE

POLICY OF CONTINUING

THE

COMPANY'S MONOPOLY.

"Most of the Statutes or Acts, Edicts, Arrets, and Placarts of Parliaments, Princes, and States, for regulating, directing, or restraining of Trade, have, we think, been either political blunders, or jobs obtained by artful men, for private advantage, under pretence of public good."

Dr. Franklin's Works, vol. ii. p. 415.

London:

PRINTED FOR T. CADELL AND W. DAVIES, IN THE STRAND;
AND ARCHIBALD CONSTABLE AND CO. EDINBURGH.

1807.

CONSIDERATIONS

ON THE

TRADE WITH INDIA, &c.

The trade of India has, from the earliest period of commerce, been cultivated as a source of wealth, and the possession of it has, in modern times, been eagerly disputed by the different nations of Europe.

Although some prejudices appear to have existed against this branch of commerce, it will hardly be denied that a trade which supplies commodities, for which there is an extensive and efficient demand, may be a source of profit and riches to those who engage in it. Whether such commodities serve for luxury, or as the raw materials of those manufactures, which are most necessary to the comfort of life, the trade may merit protection and encouragement, if it return, with a profit, the capital and labour it employs. That is the great test of its utility or inutility; and by that test the adventurers in it may safely be allowed to regulate their conduct.

Moralists and statesmen have sometimes given themselves the trouble to decide, what commerce should be proscribed as generating a baneful luxury, and what encouraged as beneficial. This interference, however, has generally failed in its object; and merits, at the most, the praise of that honest, good intention, which, unfortunately, is too often connected with narrow views and slender capacity.

In the complicated order of human society, it is difficult to ascertain and distinguish what division of industry deserves peculiar encouragement. Whenever we admit something beyond what is barely *necessary* (a thing indeed of itself very vague, because it is wholly comparative,) and advance to what is convenient for human life, we open an unbounded field. A state of extensive industry must be a state of extensive consumption; and that consumption necessarily supposes infinite varieties of taste, of fashion, of elegance, and refinement in the objects. In this variety it is curious and interesting to trace, as far as it can be traced, how the taste for enjoyment furnishes the stimulus to industry, by creating the demand for its produce. Throughout the whole society, labour is set at work in a thousand different ways. All ranks wish to share the comforts which circulate; and industry, among the lowest, is excited by the desire of possessing conveniences, unknown or despised, or unattainable in ruder times.

As it is very difficult, it probably is not very necessary, for statesmen to decide what species of commodities ought to be forbidden, or what kinds of commerce ought to be discouraged. It is clear that a desire to possess luxuries, the produce of foreign countries, may excite and encourage our domestic industry, and may conduce to domestic improvement. In the extensive circle of society, and its refined enjoyments, there is room, nay there is a demand, for variety; and it may be considered certain, that the introduction of new commodities from abroad, will produce new equivalents at home. The mass of exchanges is increased. Perhaps there never was much danger at any time, there is none surely in the present state of our society, that we should consume more of foreign commodities than we have means to pay for, or that our domestic manufactures should be injured by their competition. Whenever we begin to think that we ought to sell and never to buy, we get into the absurdities of the mercantile system; we strike at the root of commerce, by impairing that taste for enjoyment, and that turn for consumption, which are its source.

It is not therefore requisite to justify the commerce of India to an enlightened people, whether that commerce procure objects for our home consumption, or for that of other nations. It may be highly useful in either way; though doubtless the opportunity of laying our neighbours under contribution, and drawing from them a balance in cash, is that which affords most delight to a certain class of statesmen.

Political writers have justly considered a trade, of which the profits are small and the returns quick, as most beneficial, because it sets in motion the greatest quantity of productive labour, and affords the greatest quantity of revenue to the industrious inhabitants of a country. But in the progress of society there is a stage in which capital is prepared to go into the trade of distant returns and large profits; and that division of employment is necessary to the perfection of the social and commercial system. It is needless to inquire, therefore, whether or not the trade with India is a roundabout trade of consumption, and therefore not so advantageous as a direct trade of consumption. There is no danger that an undue proportion of our capital will go into that employment. It is the tendency of a monopoly to force more capital into a particular branch of trade, than would otherwise go; and Dr. Smith thinks that such has been the effect with regard to the colonial trade in this country. It is possible, indeed, that capital, by means of monopolies, was prematurely directed to the trade of India. In the present circumstances, however, and particularly if the trade is left free and open, there is no danger whatever of too much capital seeking that direction, or starving any more important branch. We are in that state in which the accumulation of the capital we possess ought to have every facility to go into any new channel in which it can profitably be employed.

If then the commerce of India is to be cultivated at all, every one will agree that it ought to be prosecuted in the manner calculated to afford the greatest advantage to the nation.

The Charter of the East India Company will, upon the usual three years' notice, expire in March 1814, and it is probable that some years, at least, before that epoch arrive, the propriety of renewing the monopoly will be considered and decided by the legislature. The wisdom and policy of that renewal, under any modification of the present system; or, if that system is to be retained, what limitations and conditions ought to be annexed to it; are questions that deeply involve the national interests, and demand the most careful investigation.

From the commencement of our intercourse with India, it has unfortunately happened, that almost every question concerning it has been the object of party contest. It was the ground on which Whigs and Tories fought their battles more than a century ago; and a question which, as Anderson, in his *History of Commerce*, justly observes, " should have been of no party," divided the two great contending factions in the state.

These political feuds however, if they have sometimes increased the temporary importance of India affairs, have, upon the whole, diverted men's minds from the sober discussion of them. Subjects which have been rendered interesting by the association of party zeal, appear vapid and tasteless when destitute of that seasoning. For this reason perhaps, as much as any other, the affairs of India are very little understood in England, and it is a just and common complaint, that they do not command the attention even of those who, by every obligation of public duty, are bound to study them.

We have long been amused with the most flattering hopes of wealth and power from our Indian possessions: they have been represented as sufficient to compensate all our political losses, and to remove all our financial difficulties. But these benefits seem as yet to have been in speculation, not in enjoyment. India, to use the words of Dr. Smith on another occasion, has been " not a gold mine, but the project of a gold mine." If the mine exists, it is time to prove its value.

If the advantages, which so vast a domain as India is calculated to yield, have not hitherto been realized, it probably is owing either to the impolitic monopoly under which the commerce is carried on; or the disgraceful and ruinous system by which an immense empire is farmed out on lease to a Company of Merchants.

In the following inquiry the author proposes to consider,

I. The general policy of granting any branch of trade to an exclusive joint stock company.

II. The principles and views which led to the establishment of the English East India Company, and how far they apply to our present situation.

III. What is the state of the trade with India, and its capacity of extension.

IV. What is the commercial situation of the Company, and the means by which it carries on its commerce.

V. The state of the private trade.

VI. The share which foreigners possess, or are likely to acquire; and the consequences of their competition, if the trade continue to be confined to an exclusive joint stock company.

Lastly, To examine the commercial objections raised against laying open the trade; viz. Danger of losing the trade, if it is left to individual exertion, &c.: The political objections; viz. Danger of a free intercourse with India; colonization; objections on constitutional principles, &c.

1. At the time when our intercourse with India began, it was not only the vice of government, but it was the error of the times, to render almost every species of commerce and manufacture the object of a monopoly. In the most insignificant undertakings monopolies were granted to individuals; and not unfrequently on corrupt considerations. The Crown exercised an unbounded discretion in these grants. The abuse of them was one of the most odious grievances in the days of James I. and his son, and not one of the smallest sources of the unpopularity with which the family of Stuart was overwhelmed. In those days, however, the establishment of mercantile companies was naturally encouraged at court, because it gratified the royal prerogative, and fed a needy and rapacious treasury*.

But this was not the only source of the mischief. The principles of commerce being very imperfectly understood, it was thought the wisest and the most effectual mode of prosecuting trade, to place it under the management of a company of some kind or other. It was never suspected that individuals were capable of conducting affairs which appeared of vast complexity and boundless risk. It seemed to be as necessary that men should unite their talents to secure wise administration of the concern, as to club their joint stock to supply the fund for carrying it on, or to guard the adventurers against the danger of untried experiments.

---

* Down to the Revolution it was customary for the East India Company to pay annual presents, of very large sums, to the King and to the leading ministers: the King had 10,000l. at least a year—a very large sum then. See Bruce, vol. ii.

The revival of civilization, and the improvement of human society, in modern Europe, had been considerably advanced by the privileges granted to boroughs, and by the establishment of corporate bodies*. But unfortunately these associations, so useful in the progress of society from lawless violence to civil order, and from warlike pursuits to those of peaceable industry, have in the end become, in many instances, grievous restraints upon the natural liberty of mankind, and the free exercise of that labour which is their right, because it is the source of their subsistence. The erection of almost every branch of trade or labour into a privileged company fixed a deep root of oppressive monopoly in the political body. The acquaintance men had with these associations, of the mischievous tendency of which they were not yet aware, naturally influenced their conduct in every thing connected with trade. The spirit which arranged the petty detail of handicraft occupations, infected the more enlarged enterprises of liberal commerce. Companies for foreign trade were considered as necessary as for the most trivial subdivisions of mechanical employment.

——" In longum tamen ævum
Manserunt, hodieque manent vestigia ruris."

It is not surprising, therefore, to find that every branch of trade was engrossed by a company, sometimes regulated like a corporative association, sometimes joint stock. The history of our commerce, from the reign of Henry VII. to the present day, furnishes examples of several hundreds of these companies, happily now remembered no more. At one period, the *Exeter Company of Merchant Adventurers* had an exclusive charter to carry on the trade with France. There was a Southampton Company of the same description. The privileges of the Exeter Company were confirmed by an Act of Parliament so late as the 4th of James I. It was a monopoly against the rest of the inhabitants who were not free of the Company, and the reason given for it in

* See Robertson, Hume, &c.

the statute is, " the inconveniences *that had arisen from the excessive* number of ignorant artificers, &c." who in that city took upon them to " *use the science, art, and mystery of merchandise.*"

This has been the language of all companies down to the present day. They pronounce it impossible that private individuals can understand *the science, art, and mystery of merchandise,* or practise it with effect. Happily for this country, one of the great advantages derived from the political struggles, which continued from the reign of James the First to the Restoration, was the exposure of the pernicious principles and dangerous tendency of monopolies. Those who contended for the freedom of the constitution were the advocates for the freedom of commerce. The discussions of those days, though not fully successful, or even perfectly enlightened, were of infinite utility[*]. The service is worth acknowledging, though, while we enjoy the benefit, we are apt to forget the source from whence it flows.

The most esteemed writers upon political economy have so clearly demonstrated the establishment of joint stock companies to be injurious to the interest of commerce, that it may seem superfluous to insist upon the point; yet there is such a disposition to solicit an exception, even where the principle is admitted, that the justice and wisdom of the law cannot be too much enforced.

Dr. Smith hardly admits a case in which joint stock companies can be profitably employed in any undertaking that is not of routine. If they are useful for a banking establishment or an assurance company, or necessary in the undertaking of a canal, or any work in which private capital could not embark, there seems scarcely any other case in which they deserve to be tolerated[†].

[*] In 1640, the House of Commons expelled several of its members, for being concerned in *monopolies* and *projects,* by which the industry of their fellow citizens would have been depressed.

[†] Sir James Stuart says, that companies are good in the *foreign market,* for preventing the

Indeed, the very principle of the human mind, which prompts men to the pursuit of commerce, seems to make it impossible that it can flourish under the management of a company. The feelings of the merchant have not changed since the days of Horace :—

> " Impiger extremos curris mercator ad Indos
> Per mare pauperiem fugiens, per saxa, per ignes."

Yet if the principle of trade be selfish, it is strong because it is selfish. No one, however, doubts that the pursuit of gain may be liberalized into an honourable employment. Its importance, at least, cannot be questioned. He who, for his own advantage, promotes the exchange of commodities between different countries, or different parts of the same country, is a benefactor of the human race, for he promotes that which is the parent of industry, and the source of enjoyment. But that active love of gain which inspires exertion, and which regulates its direction, is properly an *individual* sentiment. It cannot animate bodies, because in bodies there is no real moral personality. Though, in the fiction of law, a corporation may be a person, it but faintly resembles the individual character, and never does approach to it but mischievously. If such bodies were animated with the feelings of real persons, they would be too powerful: they would be Brobdignagians among the Liliputians. It would be impossible to live near them. They are only tolerable when they are torpid and impotent.

Of all undertakings, in which men can engage in common, trade, too, is that for which perhaps an association of great numbers is least

competition among citizens of the same state; and bad, because they prevent competition in selling the commodity at home. These positions might justify a doubt of the weight of Sir J. Stuart's authority: yet his argument is against companies. See his opinions at large, vol. ii. p. 182, of his works.

fitted. The interest is too dispersed, and the managers, if they have no interest distinct from that of the other members, neglect their duty. An undertaking, the object of which is not gain, may succeed under a common management. Political associations, in which a social feeling, an *esprit de corps*, may exist, can prosecute their ends successfully; but the love of gain is not a *social* sentiment. If gain then be the object, success is impossible, because the body never can be animated by that which is an individual feeling, and if the undertaking be of imperial magnitude, who can expect success? How can it be imagined that they who discharge functions of a dignity and extent equal to those of the Roman senate in the height of its glory, shall descend to the paltry details of economy, in laying in investments, or in the assortment of cargoes? How can it be expected that the agents of such a company, who rival the wealth and splendour of prime ministers and ambassadors, should submit to the detailed economy which governs the operations of a private merchant, and ensures their success?

A very ingenious Italian writer (Denina*) observes, that when the family of Medicis addicted themselves to political pursuits, their commerce was ill-managed, and became dependent on their political power. One passage is curious:—speaking of Pietro, father of Lorenzo de Medicis, he says, " The affairs of Peter were indeed at this time in such a situation, that he must have lost his mercantile credit had he lost the resource for supporting it in availing himself of the public money." Trade cannot consist with negligence, or dispense with the direct impulse of immediate interest. It is extremely well known that West India property rarely thrives under the management of agents: yet the trade of the East India Company, less under control and inspection,

* Denina, Origine e Principio di Potenza della casa de' Medici.

is to thrive under the management of a thousand irresponsible agents! It seems, therefore, contrary to the nature of man that commerce should be well conducted by a joint stock company.

It is notorious, that no joint stock company ever carried on trade, for any long period, with success. The possession of a monopoly may, indeed, support the affairs of such a company; because it often enables them to impose whatever price they please on the commodities in which they deal. But their very prosperity is, in such cases, at the expence of the country that permits their existence. They exact from their countrymen a monopoly price for their goods; they therefore impose a real tax on the community. They draw from the pockets of the consumer the exorbitant profits which enable them to trade advantageously, in spite of waste, prodigality, and negligence.

The wise and salutary maxim in commercial policy, *Laisser faire*, seems to be the last which statesmen will acknowledge. The rage for governing is so powerful, and the conceit which ministers of state have in their superior wisdom so great, that they are excessively prone to regulate and guide that which succeeds best without guidance and direction. In other countries, as well as our own, colonial commerce and the commerce of India have been committed to exclusive joint stock companies. The French government at one period consigned the West India trade in all its branches to an exclusive company; but after the *systeme reglementaire* of COLBERT had produced infinite loss and disappointment, the trade to the Antilles was made free, and the unparalleled prosperity of St. Domingo was the consequence *.

* The French Council of Commerce, constituted about the year 1700, appears to have had the most just and liberal views. In a very detailed report they condemn the conduct *of all the Companies* which then depressed the French colonies. They add, " *it is a most certain maxim that nothing but competition and liberty in trade can render commerce beneficial, and that all monopolies, or traffic appropriated to companies exclusive of others, are inconceivably burdensome and pernicious to it.*" I wish that a certain *Council of Commerce*, I could name, entertained such enlightened views of trade.

In France, too, the trade of India was, with occasional intervals of unsteady wisdom, committed to an exclusive company, and the history of the French East India Company, under which the trade was almost wholly extinguished, is a series of disasters and of disgrace.

Even the Dutch, with all the sobriety and caution of their national character, have, like their neighbours, contributed to demonstrate the folly of joint stock companies, although the constitution of the Dutch East India Company was in many respects superior to that of similar establishments in other countries, particularly in the distribution of the trade among their six principal ports. Although, too, its conduct was as free from the inevitable vices of such institutions as any can ever expect to be, it had, even before the late conquest by the French, expired, after a long period of hopeless decay, and the vain endeavours of the government, by loans, to support its credit and retrieve its prosperity.

No institution of this sort indeed can have a durable success in the management of commerce, and if successful, by means of the monopoly, that success, as has been shown, is purchased at the general expence of the whole state. Such companies either mismanage the trade, to the danger of losing it altogether, by the competition of foreigners, or, if successful as merchants, it is by the enormous prices the monoply enables them to impose. It is difficult to say, then, whether such a monopoly is most mischievous in its prosperity or adversity.

The monopoly which every European nation has established, in favour of its own subjects, with its foreign dominions, has, as Dr. Smith states, " sacrificed the interest of the colony to the supposed interest of the mother country. The monopoly of the colony trade therefore, like all the other mean and malignant expedients of the mercantile system, depresses the industry of all other countries, but chiefly that of the colonies, without in the least increasing, but, on the contrary, diminishing that of the country in whose favour it is established."

How much more mischievous must that monopoly be which is given to a company to the exclusion of all the other adventurers of the state! It depresses the industry and prosperity of the country with which the trade is carried on, and the industry of all the people of that country, who are dependent upon the monopoly for the supply of the articles in which it deals. Indeed Dr. Smith states this point so strongly that I must quote his words. " A temporary monopoly of this kind may be vindicated upon the same principles upon which a like monopoly of a new machine is granted to its inventor, and that of a new book to its author. But, upon the expiration of the term, the monopoly ought certainly to determine; the forts and garrisons, if it was found necessary to establish any, to be taken into the hands of government, their value to be paid to the company, and the trade to be laid open to all the subjects of the state. By a perpetual monopoly, all the other subjects of the state are taxed very absurdly in two different ways; first, by the high price of goods, which, in the case of a free trade, they could buy much cheaper; and secondly, by their total exclusion from a branch or business, which it might be both convenient and profitable for many of them to carry on. It is for the most worthless of all purposes, too, that they are taxed in this manner. It is merely to enable the company to support the negligence, profusion, and malversation of their own servants, whose disorderly conduct seldom allows the dividend of the company to exceed the ordinary rate of profit in trades which are altogether free, and very frequently makes it fall even a good deal short of that rate. Without a monopoly, however, a joint stock company, it would appear from experience, cannot long carry on any branch of foreign trade. To buy in one market, in order to sell, with profit, in another, when there are many competitors in both; to watch over, not only the occasional variations in the demand, but the much greater and more frequent variations in the competitors, or in the supply which that demand is likely to get from other people, and to suit with dexterity and judgment both the quantity and quality of each assortment of goods to all these circumstances, is a species of warfare of which the operations are continually changing, and which can scarce ever be conducted successfully without such an unremitting exertion of vigilance and attention, as cannot long be expected from the directors of a joint stock company. The East India Company, upon the redemption of their funds, and the expiration of their exclusive privilege, have a right, by act of parliament, to continue a corporation with a joint stock, and to trade in their corporate capacity to the East Indies in common with the rest of their fellow subjects. But in this situation, the superior vigilance and attention of private adventurers would, in all probability, soon make them weary of the trade*."

It is impossible to add any thing to arguments so invincible. Were I disposed to enter upon a discussion of the policy of the European states towards their colonies, it would throw much light on the mischievous effects of monopolies. The example of the errors into which they have fallen is highly instructive, and affords the most practical illustrations of the true principles of commerce. The narrow monopolising spirit which has, with so few exceptions, governed the colonial interests of Spain and Portugal, is sufficient to account for the little comparative advantage those countries have derived from the large and fertile provinces of South America. The less severe though jealous spirit of the Dutch, the more liberal though imperfect system of the French and English, afford striking examples of the effects of liberal policy, and the pernicious tendency of monopoly. They demonstrate, by indisputable facts, how inseparably the prosperity of the colonies and the

* Wealth of Nations, Vol. iii. p. 141.

mother country is connected with the freedom of trade, and how inevitably the baleful influence of monopoly operates to retard the advancement of both in wealth, population, and power*. I forbear, however, to go at large into the subject in a brief treatise of this kind, though the detail would afford the most decisive evidence of the ill effects of colonial monopoly, and particularly of the impolicy of exclusive companies.

11. The English India Company was formed upon the principles which prevailed in the age in which it was established. It has, through a long career, however, maintained itself after the principles to which it owed its origin have become obsolete, and the alleged necessity for it has ceased.

It cannot be uninteresting, therefore, to take a view of those principles. The discussion does not involve merely a dry historical detail, but it will serve to make us intimately acquainted with the maxims and opinions of the friends of the Company at the present day. A slight review of the rise and progress of the Company will be a sufficient answer to those who think that the patronage it has received from government is a clear proof of the policy of its establishment. This cursory review, with the reflections which the facts naturally suggest, will throw a great light upon the causes by which the Company have so long maintained their chartered monopoly against all opposition.

It is not my intention to state chronologically the different renewals of the Company's Charter. I mean only to indicate the principal circumstances attending such renewal, and the grounds on which it was supported and opposed. The connexion of matter is, perhaps, more important than the order of time.

It is certain that the East India Company was very unpopular for

* See the subject admirably treated in Brougham's Colonial Policy.

a very long period after its first establishment; and during the civil disturbances, between 1630 and 1650, is not much heard of. We know, however, that it durst not venture to assert its privileges, founded on royal charters, during some part of the above period.

In the year 1681 the public appears to have been a good deal divided respecting the policy of the Company's establishment, and various tracts were published by the adherents of the Company, and the advocates of a free trade. But the Company were put upon their defence before the privy council, in consequence of a complaint by the Levant Company. The latter, it is hardly necessary to observe, was one of those regulated companies which then existed, and exists now; the greatest praise of which, according to Dr. Smith, is, that they have been perfectly useless and harmless.

In their answer to the complaint of the Levant Company, and to the objections against their monopoly, in the year 1681, the Company defended themselves by an argument exceedingly curious and worth quoting.

" It cannot be denied, by any reasonable man, (say they) that a joint stock is capable of a far greater extension, as to the number of traders and largeness of stock, than any regulated company can be; because noblemen, gentlemen, shopkeepers, widows, orphans, and all other subjects, may be traders, and employ their capital in a joint stock; whereas, in a regulated company, such as the Turkey Company is, none can be traders but such as they call legitimate or bred merchants."

2. " The consequence whereof is, that if the trade for India were laid open, the adventurers would be fewer, by three quarters, than they are now, because those who *have skill would run away with the whole trade, as, in fact, they did between the years* 1653 *and* 1657."

This is a curious morsel of reasoning to be sure. It will be observed, however, that it contains an important admission: "*Those who had skill had run away with the trade.*"

It were a waste of time to demonstrate the absurdity of calling the holders of shares in a joint stock company *Traders*. The true character of joint stock shares, particularly those of the India Company, we shall explain hereafter. It certainly is very probable, that if the trade had been laid open, there would have been *fewer traders* in the sense of the memorial just quoted; for *noblemen, shopkeepers, widows,* and *orphans*, would not have been traders, if they can be called such as holders of a company's stock. But it is worth while to dwell a little upon the instance alluded to, of 1653 to 1657. At that time the trade was laid open; and at every period, when the renewal of their Charter has been solicited, to the present day, the directors have assumed, as decisive of their case, that the adventurers between 1653 and 1657 were all ruined. The authors of the THIRD Report on the private trade in 1802, in allusion to this æra, say, " this bold experiment terminated as might have been expected; it confirmed the PROTECTOR in the wisdom of that policy which he doubted. The monopoly was re-established, and the Company's temporary abolition became, in its consequences, their triumph." This Third Report, in every page, betrays the same gross ignorance or misrepresentation of facts. It is material, therefore, to contradict assertions so frequently brought forward, and which must have deceived those who were not at the trouble to inquire.

The truth is, that the private adventurers, between 1654 and 1657, carried on their trade with great success, notwithstanding the opposition they experienced from those interested in the monopoly at home, and from the Dutch and other foreign rivals. It was natural they should experience such hostility, for they were eminently successful. They "run away with the trade," during the time the trade was open, as the Company in 1681 admitted.

Nothing indeed was more alarming than the idea of a free trade, not only to our own monopoly Company, but to the Dutch Company. Those who were rivals in every thing, agreed in this alone, that a free trade would ruin them both. THURLOE, Cromwell's secretary, informs us, in his Letters*, that " the merchants of Amsterdam, having heard that the Lord Protector would dissolve the East India Company at London, and declare the navigation and commerce to the Indies to be free and open, were greatly alarmed, *considering such a measure as ruinous to their own East India Company*."

This passage presents matter for very important reflection. There is no doubt that the alarm was well founded, and the event corresponded with the fears of the sharp-sighted merchants of Amsterdam. Notwithstanding the success of the private traders, they were, however, deprived of their privileges by Cromwell, and the monopoly re-established. There is little reason to doubt that the usurper, who was a lover of his country, was deceived by the persons to whose representations he listened, and who were corrupted by the agents of the Dutch and English Companies.

That it was not because the experiment of laying open the trade had failed, that the Company was restored, is evident, because the period, between 1653 and 1657, could afford no fair test of the measure, even if the adventurers had at first been unsuccessful. But they had not failed.

A tract, written in the year 1680, informs us, that, " during the years 1653-4-5-6, *when the trade was laid open, the English traders*

* Vol. iii, p. 80.

afforded the India commodities so cheap, that they supplied more parts of Europe, and even Amsterdam itself, therewith, than ever was done after; whereby they very much sunk the Dutch East India Company's Actions*. This fact sufficiently accounts for the alarm of the Dutch, at the freedom of the trade in England, and its truth is confirmed by the admission of the Company above quoted, that the skilful *traders run away with all the trade*. It is material to keep these facts in view, because they prove that the privileged companies were unable to cope with the private traders, though the latter were exposed to every species of hostility and opposition.

It must appear extraordinary, then, that when the success of the private traders was so distinguished, there should have been any hesitation, in an enlightened government, to abolish the monopoly for ever.

The solution of this difficulty depends upon two principal circumstances; the ignorance which then prevailed of the principles of commerce, and the influence and corruption which, as a united faction, the Company were able to employ to gain their end. Such was the ignorance of men in general, and of governments in particular, in regard to commerce, in those times, that the very circumstance of supplying the market cheaply appears to have been considered as a proof that commerce was ill conducted. It was the object of regulation to prevent all competition in trade, as competition was thought mischievous. A very amusing instance of this mercantile spirit is to be found in a Defence of the Company, written in the year 1681 by some of the literary Swiss whom they are known to have employed.

" For who is there that hath, in any competent degree, studied and considered trade, in reference to the kingdom's interest, but knows

---
* Anderson's History of Commerce.

that all buying and selling at home, from one to another, is but a mere changing of hands, neither adding to, nor diminishing, the nation's stock or wealth. It is dear selling, or rather the selling of great quantities of our native commodities and manufactures in foreign parts, and our cheap purchasing of commodities in foreign countries, whereby our kingdom is enriched. For if we do but consider the consequence of this Barrister's* position, it will clearly appear, that particular Englishmen, traders to India, vying upon one another in the buying of cloth, &c. in England, may, for a year or two, raise the prices in England; and, on the other hand, they may lower the prices, and undersell one another, to get off their goods in India, and make returns; some, perhaps, selling cheaper than the prime cost, whilst others may not be able to put off their goods, and so, perhaps, let their ships return dead freighted, &c. What probability is there then of their continuing to send any thereafter, or that the exportation of our English manufactures should increase? whereas the present joint stock company have so well managed their trade, that from one hundred to four hundred cloths, at most, formerly exported, they now annually export four thousand whole broad cloths and upwards. And with respect to goods imported from India; the multitude of buyers in India raising the prices there, and of sellers in England lessening the prices here, cannot but be very contrary to the kingdom's interest. Because not above one fourth part of the India goods imported are consumed in England, the other three fourths being exported to foreign parts. Now, if the prices of what is consumed in England be lowered, the like must inevitably follow for the other three fourths exported: so that the nation really loses by the cheap selling of India commodities in England, and our real interest is to buy cheap in India, and sell dear in Europe."

It is not necessary in this age, we hope, to point out the falsehood of these general principles of commerce. Nothing is in theory better

---

* An advocate for the free trade.

established than that competition excites demand, and therefore secures supply; and that by the joint operation of these causes, efficient demand and efficient supply, the common interest of consumers and growers is promoted. But it is the principle of all monopoly to limit the supply and augment the price. We wish the sentiments of this author of the seventeenth century, and his patron Directors, just quoted, were really as unfashionable as they are old and absurd; but we shall see by and by, that they are the principles of Leadenhall-street at this hour.

It is no wonder then that the private traders were held in disrepute for that which we hope would now be considered merit; because they would have afforded the commodities in which they dealt at a cheaper rate. When it was the principle of commerce to enhance the price, it was only consistent to confide the business to the monopoly of a joint stock company. Relatively to that view the contrivance was admirable.

Those called interlopers, however, were so obstinate in " seeking their own ruin," that they could not be prevailed upon to abandon a trade in which, by their competition, " *they lessened the prices here contrary to the kingdom's interest.*" The Company, and their hired advocates, could not convince these unfortunate persons to give up ruining themselves. The Company, indeed, in their great liberality, spared no expence to convince them, either by argument or authority, of their error. The vindictive and oppressive proceedings against the interlopers, and the enlightened arguments of Pollexfen, in the case of Sands, against the policy and legality of the monopoly, are well known. The Company, however, availed themselves of the prerogative claimed by arbitrary power, and of the authority of Judge Jefferies, to oppress their fellow-citizens.

But there was another reason in those days (not surely remaining in ours) for keeping up the monopoly, and it was that the Directors of the Company found a private interest in the speculation. They did not indeed, like modern Directors, exercise functions of power greater than those of a Roman senate, but they had objects of ambition suited to the mediocrity of the age in which they lived. They were merchants themselves, and they were nothing else. To be at the head of a joint stock company, was to have the means of carrying on trade, not merely for the joint stock, but for their own private advantage.

In fact, such was the division of stock, that out of six hundred shares, same individuals had sixty or eighty, and votes accordingly. These active members always being in the direction, they carried on a double traffick, trading on their own private account, and receiving dividends also on the amount of their stock; advantages which the *noblemen*, *widows*, and *orphans* in the Company undoubtedly did not possess.

The opposition to the renewal of the Charter of the Company, soon after the Revolution, very nearly proved successful, but by large bribes the Court of Directors contrived to buy off some of the principal private traders, who were merchants of eminence in London. This bribery was not confined to the rivals of the Company. The most shocking corruption of members of Parliament, and of the highest officers of state, was carried on. No less than 170,000*l.* was employed in bribing members and ministers.

The following account of these villainous proceedings is so curious, that I cannot help extracting it:—

" By the new subscription of 744,000*l.* which added 781 members to the English East India Company, it might have been imagined, that they had now effectually secured themselves against the future attacks of opponents. But, as this Company had *expended vast sums of money* to courtiers, members of parliament, and others, as well for obtaining the last three Charters, as in endeavouring to divide and buy off the interlopers; and more especially in endeavouring to obtain an act of parliament for their absolute legal establishment, their enemies found means to influence the House of Commons so far against them, as to enter upon a strict examination of their practices. In the course of the inquiry they discovered, that in the year 1693 alone, whilst Sir Thomas Cooke was governor, and Francis Tyssen, Esq. deputy governor, upwards of 80,000*l.* were expended for secret services by the former, and by Sir Basil Firebrass (lately brought from the interloping interest), which two last-named gentlemen, refusing to discover to whom the said secret service money was given, were, together with Mr. Charles Bates and Mr. James Craggs, committed to the Tower of London by the House of Commons in the year 1695. And although, in obedience to an act of parliament of this year, Sir Thomas Cooke made a discovery of many things to both houses of parliament, yet it did not give entire satisfaction, as may be more fully seen in a printed collection and supplement of the debates and proceedings of parliament of the years 1694 and 1695, upon the inquiries into the late briberies and corrupt practices, (quarto, 1695,) concerning which we shall just observe, that sundry sinister arts, at that time used, were afterward practised on a similar occasion in the famous year 1720; such, for instance, as Sir Basil Firebrass's contracting with the East India Company to put (i. e. to oblige that company to receive of him) 160,000*l.* India stock at 150 per cent. when the Charter should be granted, although their stock was then only at 100 per cent.: whereupon the Company paid him the difference, being 30,000*l.*; the disposal of which last sum Sir Basil Firebrass could never be brought to discover. Great sums were also paid out for the refusal of stock at certain prices on the same supposition. Refusal of stock was a contract for having the option of demanding stock, at a fixed price; as the put of stock was a contract by which, for a premium paid down, the contractor obliged himself to take a fixed quantity of a stock, at a future time, for a fixed and higher price therein specified. These new-fangled or cant terms were first brought into use by this Company; and in this way of stock-jobbing daily bargains were made for many succeeding years, so as to be since reduced to a kind of science; but most eminently in the famous year 1720, and some years after, till all such time-contracts and bargains for stocks were made penal by act of parliament. Great sums were also laid out by the managers to answer the Company's contracts for sale of stock, &c. The House of Commons had also impeached the Duke of Leeds, then Lord President of the Council, on the said account; but the prorogation of the Parliament put an end to it. Some years after all this bustle was over, Sir Thomas Cooke had 12,000*l.* *bestowed on him by the General Court of this Company, by way of compensation for his former sufferings on their account*[*]."

Such were the profligate and corrupt arts by which a great national benefit was prevented, when the liberty settled by the Revolution ought to have confirmed to the country the full enjoyment both of its commercial and civil rights. That it was solely for the private purposes of the Directors, and their jobbing connection, that so great a struggle was made to secure the privileges of the Company, no one can entertain a doubt. At the very moment when the Directors had corruptly expended 170,000*l.* for the renewal of their Charter, and to purchase the protection of government, they were not able to make a dividend at all. When the contests between the projectors of a new, and the managers of the old Company, were renewed in 1698, the latter had not, according to Anderson, been able to make a dividend for " sundry preceding years [†]." The Directors, however, carrying on a beneficial monopoly for themselves, under the cover of that of the Company, were naturally unwilling to abandon a job, and, though the great mass of their stockholders must

[*] Anderson's History of Commerce. [†] Ibid.

have been sufferers, the managers contrived to preserve their own interest, by admitting their opponents of the new Company into the scheme of plunder. This scheme was ratified and sanctioned in 1702, and was carried into effect in 1708, under an award of Lord Godolphin.

But, notwithstanding the intrigues, the corruption and fraud by which the national interests were sacrificed to a corporation of jobbers, it was impossible to prevent the enterprise and the capital of the country from attempting to acquire a share in the trade of India. In the year 1714, the Emperor established the Ostend East India Company. The ships, the commanders, the capital, with which this undertaking was carried on, were procured from England and Holland. The English and Dutch Companies remonstrated against the Ostend Company, by the competition of which, conducted by the skill of individuals in the spirit of a free trade, they would infallibly have been ruined. These remonstrances, as is well known, succeeded after a struggle of near twenty years. Before they finally prevailed, however, the two Companies obtained the most sanguinary laws against their fellow subjects, who should embark, under foreign auspices, in a trade from which they were excluded by the injustice and folly of their own country. In Holland the penalty of death was enacted against such as should be concerned, in any manner, in the trade carried on from Ostend. The British Parliament was not so bloody; but, by the 7 Geo. 1. c. 20, very heavy penalties were inflicted upon those who should be guilty of trading to the East Indies under foreign commissions. So little able, too, was the Company to sustain the competition of the free trade at Ostend, that it was found necessary to protect their monopoly, by prohibiting the importation of tea from other parts of Europe, thereby enabling them to extort from their fellow subjects whatever prices they could get for the commodity.

But the penalties enacted against embarking in the trade to India, in foreign bottoms, were ineffectual. It was necessary to increase the code of severity, for the benefit of the Company's monopoly. By the 9 Geo. 1. c. 26, not only were British subjects prohibited from being concerned in the Ostend Company, but " British subjects found in India, unless lawfully authorized, or within our East India Company's limits, are declared guilty of a high crime and misdemeanor, and liable to such corporal punishment or imprisonment, or for such times, as the court, where they shall be tried, shall think fit." Yet all these disgraceful severities, for the protection of injustice and absurdity, were inadequate to the end. The competition of the Ostend Company compelled the East India Company to reduce their dividend from eight to six per cent. and if the English and Dutch governments had not prevailed on the court of Vienna to abandon the Ostend Company, the Dutch and English monopolies must have died a natural death.

It is not uninteresting to remark how nugatory, and yet how vexatious, penalties and prohibitions, in matters of commerce, are, when strongly opposed by the private interests of men. Capital, both English and Dutch, nay, the individuals of those nations, could not be deterred from engaging in the India trade, under the protection of the Ostend Company. Let it be remembered, too, that if our own subjects are still to be excluded from the East India trade, the Ostend Company may be revived; at any rate Ostend, or some other port, will be established to carry on Eastern commerce. It is not to be expected now, however, that the Company will be rescued from the competition of a rival, as it was in 1729, when the abolition of the Ostend Company was procured. Those times are gone. We cannot expect to shield ourselves from the consequences of our own folly, by extorting such concessions from our rivals or our enemies.

The Company, however, had now obtained a complete victory over all direct opposition at home, and, though many still doubted the policy of the monopoly, the administration was induced to patronize the institution; and the money which the Company advanced for the renewal of their Charter was considered an important financial resource.

In the year 1730, when their Charter was under consideration, the Company employed the following curious arguments:—

" The Company at present employ a vast stock in trade, their sales amounting to about three millions yearly. And the customs accruing to the public are prodigiously great, and answer the appropriations made of them by Parliament, better than most other duties; they bringing in net money, clear of all drawbacks and debentures, three hundred thousand pounds yearly. Would it then be prudent in the legislature to let these customs fall, without a certainty of at least as much in the room of them? The forts and factories at present cost the Company 300,000*l.* yearly; and doubtless the government could not maintain them for so little. Those forts and other buildings are unquestionably the property of the Company, who actually purchased them of the old Company, and are of very great value. Who, then, shall set an equitable price on them? What certainty have the government, when they are in their hands, that the proposed open trade will be always sufficient to maintain so vast an expence of customs and forts as 600,000*l.* yearly? For, as every man is, by the proposed scheme, left at liberty (and will doubtless make use of it) to trade, or not to trade, thither, as it may suit his interest, it my happen that one year there may go fifty ships for India, and another year, perhaps, not five: and these being all separate traders, the government can have no certainty nor security from them, nor indeed from any other but an incorporated body, who have a great deal to lose, and who are able to bear the ill fortune of some particular years trading, without presently laying it aside. By the competition of the separate traders in India, for the sake of dispatch, the prices of goods there would be raised so high as at length not to be worth buying. And for the like reason, at home they would so undersell each other, till the goods would not be worth selling; which was the case for the small time that the two Companies (the old and the new ones), and the separate traders, contended against each other; whereby they all did very much hurt to the trade."

On the other hand the following objections were urged:—

" That the government should take the support of the forts, factories, embassies, &c. in India, into their own hands, out of the large customs on the India trade, which should thenceforth remain free and open to all British subjects. For (say they) the more free and open that trade is, the more profitable it will be to the nation. And though it may be true that laying the East India trade open would lessen the profit of individuals in that trade, by their striving to outdo and undersell one another, yet the gain to the nation would be vastly greater, as the emulous private adventurers, by thrusting themselves into new ports and countries, in Arabia, Persia, India, China, &c. would undoubtedly occasion the exportation of much more of our manufactures and product than the Company can do. And, on the other hand, a joint stock company can never trade so frugally and advantageously, either for themselves or for the nation, being in fact but one buyer and one seller; who, moreover, manage their trade with a pride and expence more becoming the state of kings than of merchants; and their governors and agents in India live like princes. They also expect to be followed by the markets, and therefore do not stir from their warehouses. Whereas, on the contrary, private traders would follow the markets, would push into every creek and corner, and would narrowly look into the conduct of their agents in India. That the abolition of the present Company would moreover destroy the pernicious practice of stock-jobbing, so fatal to persons and families. That when almost all the maritime nations of Europe are now running into this trade, which will doubtless diminish our own commerce thither, it seems the most effectual means for driving them out of this trade to lay it open to all our people."

On this occasion also it was stated by the Company, that those who had petitioned (the merchants of London, Liverpool, and Bristol,) for an open trade "were not in the secret of the trade, and that if the Company could not be prevailed upon to communicate their lights, the trade must be wholly lost to the nation."

Upon the arguments employed by the Company on this occasion, Dr. Smith remarks,—

" In 1730, when a proposal was made to Parliament for putting the trade under the management of a regulated company, and thereby laying it in some measure open, the East India Company, in opposition to this proposal, represented, in very strong terms, what had been at this time the miserable effects, as they thought them, of this competition. In India, they said, it raised the price of goods so high that they were not worth the buying ; and in England, by over-stocking the market, it sunk their price so low, that no profit could be made by them. That by a more plentiful supply, to the great advantage and conveniency of the public, it must have reduced very much the price of India goods in the English market, cannot be well doubted ; but that it should have raised very much their price in the Indian market seems not very probable, as all the extraordinary demand which that competition could occasion must have been but as a drop of water in the immense ocean of Indian commerce. The increase of demand, besides, though in the beginning it may sometimes raise the price of goods, never fails to lower it in the long run. It encourages production, and thereby increases the competition of the producers, who, in order to undersell one another, have recourse to new divisions of labour and new improvements of art, which might never otherwise have been thought of. The miserable effects of which the Company complained were, the cheapness of consumption and the encouragement given to production, precisely the two effects which it is the great business of political œconomy to promote. The competition, however, of which they gave this doleful account, had not been allowed to be of long continuance."

The Company, however, procured the rejection of the proposal of an open trade, though recommended by the abilities and authority of Sir John Barnard, and many of the most eminent merchants of London. Indeed, the objections against the Company's monopoly were urged with a force of reasoning which we should think nothing could have resisted, except arguments similar to those employed in 1694 and 1702*.

From this period, to the acquisition of the continental dominions, nothing deserving of remark relative to commerce occurred. From the cursory view we have taken, it seems evident that the trade might have been perfectly well carried on by individuals: we have seen that the Company never could sustain the competition of the interlopers, and that had the Ostend Company, or a free trade at that port, continued, both the Dutch and the East India Companies must have been ruined. It is manifest, therefore, that a joint stock monopoly company, instead of being well qualified to carry on the trade of India, could not carry it on at all, without sanguinary and oppressive penalties against the competition of their fellow subjects, and without the means of sup-

---

* Of these practices take the following additional illustration. " Reports were brought to the House of Commons of elections that had been scandalously purchased by some who were concerned in the new East India Company. Instead of drinking and entertainments, by which elections were formerly managed, now a most scandalous practice was brought in of buying votes with so little decency, that the electors engaged themselves by subscriptions to choose a blank person, before they were trusted with the name of their candidate. The old East India Company had driven a course of corruption within doors, with so little shame that the new Company intended to follow their example, but with this difference, that, whereas the former had bought the *persons who were elected*, they *resolved to buy elections*. Sir Edward Seymour, who had dealt in this corruption his whole life-time, and whom the old Company was said to have bought before at a very high price, brought before the House of Commons the discovery of some of the practices of the new Company. The examining of these took up many days. In conclusion, *the matter was so well proved, that several elections were declared void; and some of the persons so chosen were for some time kept in prison, after they had been expelled the house.*"

TINDAL, vol. xv. p. 79.

pressing the free competition of foreigners. But in addition to all these circumstances, the state of this country, the state of Europe, and the state of India, has altered so much since the first establishment of the Company, that the arguments on which their monopoly was formerly justified, even had they been well-founded then, would now appear supremely ridiculous.

When the Company first was established, the Portuguese were, though indeed in considerable decline, in possession of the trade to India. To attempt opening a trade with a country then little known to us, under the disadvantages of a competition with the Portuguese, who had extensive and flourishing settlements on different parts of the coast of the peninsula, was an enterprise of great risk. The adventurers had to encounter, not merely the commercial rivalship, but the military force of the Portuguese in India. They had to encounter the opposition of the Dutch afterwards upon the same principles, for it was the custom of those days to fight for trade as for a prize. Commerce was wholly militant, and the Indian seas were stained with the blood of the parties contending for that which is the offspring, and ought to be the bond, of peace.

If any thing could justify a joint stock company, it seemed to be a state of things which rendered all private adventure impossible; but yet in a few years we have seen private traders labouring to establish themselves, not only against the competition, and the hostility of other nations, but against those of their bitterest enemy, the English chartered Company. The smallest military protection from the government would have supplied all that was necessary to enable the private traders to manage the commerce of India with complete success. Those unfavourable circumstances are now at an end. The government of this country is both able and willing to protect its commerce in every quarter of the globe. Commerce may now lay aside the sword and become peaceful. The government will give it security, and if, on extraordinary occasions, it must defend itself, it can do so without the aid of a monopoly.

After the acquisition of the territorial dominions, a new æra in the history of the Company commenced, and this country became distracted with disputes about Indian affairs, as it had been at the end of the preceding century. The disorders committed in India, and the distresses of the Company, brought their conduct before parliament, and scarcely any public question ever excited so much faction and division in the state. I purposely forbear from any discussion of the transactions between 1767 and 1785. Commerce seemed to be little in view. During that period, the Company was, at different times, brought to the bar of the nation as a criminal and a delinquent. Though they escaped the forfeitures they had incurred, they were always dismissed under strong, though inadequate, securities for their good behaviour.

Their affairs, since 1785, have fallen into a form of more quiet and regular mismanagement. Their misconduct and their embarrassments, now excite less *eclat*. They seem, indeed, to have required a sort of prescriptive right to dilapidate the national resources and their own. Their affairs, too, are involved in a degree of obscurity, notwithstanding the parliamentary review to which they are annually subject, that few understand them, and almost all revolt from the attempt to learn. People indeed seem to wait quietly for that inevitable crash which will rouse attention, or, for some measure which, proposing to apply the national resources to the Company's aid, will display the juggle and the fraud of that institution to every man in the empire.—That period is very fast approaching.

Leaving these things to their natural course, I now proceed to consider the present state of the trade with India.

III. Previous to the Company's acquisition of the territorial* domi-

* Before the war in 1757, the Company had, on the coast of Coromandel, Fort St. George,

nions during the seven years' war, their relations with India were purely commercial. The trade was carried on with funds raised by the credit of the Company, and fed by the profits which were made. It appears that, upon the whole, notwithstanding the extravagance, the negligence, and the ill management incident to a joint stock company, the trade being at last reduced nearly to a strict monopoly as to British subjects, and the foreign companies being still more mismanaged than our own, yielded a profit, and enabled the Company to pay a moderate dividend to the proprietors of stock.

The trade with India was at that time carried on chiefly by exportation of bullion, the exports of English commodities being then more inconsiderable than at present. The Directors, in their Second Report on the Private Trade, say, " From the remotest times of which we have an account, down to our own days, the manufactures of India, fit for the European market, were set on foot by money imported into that country." This certainly appears to have been the case ; but it proves the wretched system of government in a country possessing great industry and resources. It proves that, with great means of producing capital, so baneful was the system of the government, that the accumulation of stock was prevented ; and the most abundant springs of wealth which nature, and industry, and art could furnish, were choaked up and destroyed. At this hour no steady, regular capital is employed in those articles of manufacture which come to Europe. Advances are still made by the agents of the Company, or by private merchants, to the native manufacturers, to enable them to furnish the articles in demand.

It is perhaps impossible to fix upon any criterion which could more

Madras, and Vizagapatam ; the settlements of Fort William and Calcutta on the Ganges. On the Malabar coast, Bombay. They had also the four northern Circars, the Jaghire lands, and Pergunnahs, together with some other factories of less importance. Since 1757 the territorial acquisitions are of a magnitude hardly credible ; but they unquestionably belong to the crown.

strongly evince the miserable state of the people of India, who, industrious in a high degree, and distinguished for ingenuity in the finest manufactures of the loom, are yet so beggarly and poor, that they are supported by the precarious advances made by their employers. Capital has never, among them, been steadily vested in the manufactures which Europe consumes. There are artificers, but no persons of capital to employ and direct their industry. Nothing can show more strongly the want of confidence which prevails, and the active oppression which prevents the natural union of capital and labour. This state of things reminds us of that barbarous situation of agriculture in some countries, where the mendicant farmer sows the ground with seed advanced by the landlord, and whose stock, and even instruments of labour, are his master's. When such things exist, we may be assured that there are radical vices in the constitution of the society and the character of the government.

The new interest, which, as lords of the soil, the Company obtained in the prosperity of Hindustan, ought to have inspired them with more liberal views of traffick, and have led them to consider commerce, not merely as a source of wealth to themselves, but as the means of improving their territories. Their views, however, do not appear to have extended with their situation. The characters of sovereign and merchant have been strangely blended; and, without being a beneficent sovereign, the Company has become a worse merchant than ever. The wars of India, the impolitic administration of the territories, the Company's affairs often on the verge of bankruptcy, form the eventful history of the period in which the monstrous junction of commerce and sovereignty has subsisted.

In the character of sovereign of the soil, the East India Company ought to lament the miserable and depressed situation of their subjects. But as merchants, we find them jealous of the trade, which would improve the resources and encourage the industry of Hindustan. They are blind to the advantages to be derived from enlarging and improving the productive powers of their dominions, lest rival traders might interfere with the paltry profits of their own shop.

The Company have at different times complained, that if competition of British subjects existed, the trade would be ruinous to those who embarked in it. That is, they complain of that which it is the policy of every wise government to encourage. The wretched argument against competition, which, as has been stated, Dr. Smith treats with such merited scorn, occurs again in the Reports of the Directors, respecting the private trade. In the Second Report they make the following remarks:

" Thirdly, with regard to the competition which a great enlargement of private trade may occasion in the India commerce—That the law of every market should be a free permission to those who enter into it, to buy and sell, need not to be disputed; but it is a question, not of commercial principle, but of the policy of states, whether their subjects shall be *encouraged to enter into competition with each other at any particular foreign market.* There can be no doubt that a great increase of demand and of purchases in India would enhance the cost of commodities there, and that a like increase of the quantities sold here, though this mart should be the largest, would, on the whole, *lower the prices.* The consequence from both branches of competition would therefore be evident and direct disadvantage to this country, and disadvantage, not to be compensated, in this case, by the extent of the trade."

The spirit displayed in this quotation, ought not to escape without censure. I do not insist upon the ignorance of the true principles of commerce which it betrays. We have seen what Dr. Smith thinks of such reasoning. But let it be remembered, that the people of India are our subjects. We exact the fruits of their toils, and surely we are bound to encourage the industry which supplies the ability to pay. But the Directors seem to be afraid lest their own subjects should derive any advantage from an increased demand for their produce. They would sacrifice the people of India entirely to the supposed interest of this country. They would sacrifice the grower wholly to the selfishness of the sovereign consumer. Can any thing, in the spirit of monopoly, be more flagrant and more odious than this?

Let it be considered, too, that the state of the people of India seems particularly deserving of encouragement and aid from every mercantile source.

It is admitted by the Directors, that the Company's commerce was intended to be carried on chiefly by the tribute, though in fact there has been no clear surplus tribute. They tell us in their Reports that, besides the surplus tribute, and the fortunes of British individuals, there is at this day " no capital in those territories applicable to an extension of their exports to Europe." They take it for granted, that there are no means of extending the commerce of India upon any great scale, " *consonant to the ideas held out of improving our possessions, but by capital transferred thither in bullion from this country.*" They then decide peremptorily that it would not be good policy to employ British capital in such enterprises.

The worthy Directors do not seem to have been aware how pointed a condemnation they pass upon the India trade, such as it was carried on before the territorial acquisitions, nay, such as they are obliged now to carry it on themselves. They have just told us that it was supported by importations of bullion from Europe. Do they mean to say, however, that the trade was a bad one, because it was carried on by means of bullion exported? The trade that is carried on with bullion may be gainful, and to suppose the contrary, were to recognise as truths, the most exploded errors of the mercantile system.

At the worst it is only a round-about trade of consumption. If the goods brought from India are sold in Europe at a price which fully replaces, with a profit, the stock, and pays the wages of the labour employed in bringing them to market, there is no danger that the merchant shall want that supply of bullion, which is the instrument by which the trade is carried on. If the people of this country have a taste for the commodities of India, they must procure the means of indulging that taste by an increase in their own industry and produce. They are thus stimulated to exert themselves to procure equivalents for those things they wish to enjoy. We do not necessarily lose, therefore, upon the whole, by such a trade. On the other hand, if a great surplus of the goods imported from India be re-exported to foreign countries, the bullion is supplied to us by foreigners, to the infinite comfort of those miserable valetudinarians of commerce, who, like the man in the Spectator, are perpetually weighing the exports and imports of the country in their mechanical chair, and watching the changes of the balance of trade with such sickly anxiety.

What may be the amount of the trade in the commodities of British India, or of what extension it is susceptible, it may not be easy to ascertain. The demand for those commodities we know has been, and is, very great in Europe. We know that it is considerable in America and the West Indies, and there is every reason to believe that it is capable of being greatly extended, if not in the articles now considered the staples, at least in others. That it can be extended under the management of the Company is not to be expected.

The policy of employing British capital in the trade of India must depend solely upon the returns which the trade affords. If the trade is a lucrative one, there can be no reason for not employing capital in it as well as in any other. The Directors know perfectly well, that the employment of capital in a nation like this, where every part of commerce is well understood, must be regulated by the advantages of the trade. If private capital would not of itself embark in the India trade, or ought not to engage in it, what is this but a confession that the trade of the East India Company has attracted capital from better application, and that the trade is a bad one? What is it, but to tell us, that the monopoly has withdrawn capital to a non-productive application from a productive? Every sixpence, therefore, which was employed in the Company's trade, while they were only traders, or which they now borrow to lay out in trade, is misemployed, and the nation suffers accordingly. It is true that individuals are not ruined, because the loss may be divided, but the nation loses upon the whole aggregate capital so employed, if that mass of capital do not produce the fair return which commercial capital, in its beneficial application, ought to afford. In as far as the capital employed in the East India trade produces less, it is wastefully and unprofitably employed*.

In their Reports upon the subject of the private trade, the Directors have given us their sentiments at large upon the subject. They tell us, that if the productive powers of India are to be cultivated, capital must be exported from Europe. The truth is, if the Company themselves are to carry on the trade, they must export capital, for there is not only no surplus revenue, but there is a perpetually growing debt in India, and it surely would be much better to borrow at English than India interest. But if private traders did export capital, what, upon commercial principles, is the evil of that, if it returns with an adequate profit? They say, too, that it must be withdrawn from other branches of trade nearer home. Is that at all necessary? If the trade of this country, indeed, were like that of the Company, a trade in which the capital is wasted, not increased, there certainly would be no capital to be employed in a new branch of trade. But, when so much commercial capital is beneficially employed, there must be a perpetually accumulating excess springing out of that beneficial

* Smith's Wealth of Nations.

employment, and applicable to new adventure. There is no necessity, therefore, for impoverishing any other profitable branch of trade by the investment of capital in that of India.

Lord Wellesley, upon this subject, is of an opinion directly contrary to that of the Directors *. He says, " If the capital of the merchants in India, and the remittance of the fortunes of individuals, should not afford funds sufficient for the conduct of the whole private export trade from India to Europe, no dangerous consequences would result from applying to this branch of commerce capital drawn directly from the British empire in Europe."

" Beneficial consequences, of the utmost importance, would certainly result to the British empire in India, from any considerable increase of its active capital, which is known not to bear a just proportion to the productive powers of the country."

Both for the authority, and the reasons of this opinion, it deserves a decided preference over that of the Directors. Mr. Dundas, now Lord Melville, however, has given an opinion in favour of the Directors on this point; and though in almost every thing else he is at variance with them, on the subject of the private trade, they quote this opinion with triumph. If it were even true, that, relatively to the Company's monopoly, it would be improper to encourage any employment of British capital in India, because such employment would create that competition in India against the Company, of which they so bitterly complain; this, however, would form no argument against such an application of our capital to support an open, free, and profitable commerce. But, in whatever light it is viewed, the argument is founded on the most pitiful principles of mercantile monopoly.

* Letter to the Court of Directors, 30th September, 1800.

If British capital were to be sent out to India, it would be sent out to increase the active capital which in that country is so much wanted. But perhaps there is none of the instruments of trade, which tends so much to fructify and improve both agriculture and manufactures, as adequate share of capital. Price is regulated by the combined circumstances of effective demand and effective supply. But nothing contributes so much to supply as capital, which by affording the materials of industry, by advancing to the manufacturer those materials, and that subsistence without which his abilities would languish, and by producing the most convenient distributions of labour, tends to bring to market every commodity at the cheapest rate to the consumer. But what must be the surprise of the enlightened manufacturers of this country, when they are informed by Lord Melville, " that the manufactures of the finer and more valuable fabrics of India have always been produced by advances from government, or individuals, for whose behoof those fabrics are manufactured; and if the dealing with those manufacturers was to be laid open to the uncontrolled competition of every individual, the consequence would be a boundless scene of confusion and fraud, and ultimately the ruin of the manufacture."

This statement is every way extraordinary. Is it then advantageous for the manufacturers of India, that the capital which supports their fabrics should be doled out, like an eleemosynary gift, at the pleasure of the government? Is it favourable to improvement in any fabric that the capital should be fluctuating and precarious, that the manufacture should depend upon such a beggarly system of occasional advances? Is this a state of things in which cheapness of supply is likely to take place? Was ever the picture of monopoly, grinding a country, depressing the industry of whole nations, exhibited in more striking colours?

The Company grudge their unhappy subjects the benefit of being encouraged by the competition of new purchasers. They would condemn Englishmen at home, to buy under the limited supply of their monopoly, and they condemn the people of India, as far as possible, to depend on their exclusive demand. This system, however, is not less short-sighted than it is detestable. The first effects of competition, doubtless, may be as Dr. Smith has well observed in a passage already quoted, to enhance the price, but the second and the certain effect is to lower it. By exciting emulation in the producers, and by teaching economy and judicious distribution in the different stages of the work, the consumer is better supplied, while the situation of the producer is likewise improved. It is thus that, throughout this prosperous empire, we see the interest of the consumer and the manufacturer conciliated. It is thus we see competition prevail, fabrics improve, the manufacturers grow rich, and the public cheaply supplied. Capital, which facilitates and suggests judicious division of labour, is, perhaps, one of the most active agents in effecting these happy results. The introduction of capital into India, to fructify industry and encourage produce, ought to be eagerly desired by the Company, both in their character of merchants and of sovereigns. The advances which they or others are obliged to make, clearly show that one of the most natural and necessary divisions of stock has not taken place in India. The Company is at once the merchant dealer in the commodity, and the manufacturer of it. They must therefore have two capitals; one for supporting the manufacture, the other for circulating it when produced. But every one in the least acquainted with the nature of commerce, knows that such an union of characters is not beneficial. It is very likely that the two capitals employed by those who act in this double capacity, will not be so well managed as if each belonged to a separate interest, and were managed under a separate direction. In all countries where manufactures and commerce have made considerable progress, such a separation has taken place. It surely therefore must be important to bring India to that state. The Company, as a merchant dealing in the produce of India, has an interest in that separation. They would be cheaper supplied, if there be truth in those great principles of trade, which Smith and others have proved to demonstration, and of which principles, as well as of all experience, the Company and their advocates must have fallen into the most perfect oblivion.

But it is only British capital which the Company are unwilling to see employed in the trade with India. They tell us in the Third Report, that the trade of foreigners with our dominions should be encouraged, because that trade, if *bona fide*, introduces specie, of which India stands much in need. This argument would prove more than the Company intend. It would prove that for India at least, the bona fide trade of foreigners is beneficial, but that the trade of the Company cannot be so; as the latter, were it not for the mal-administration which prevents a *surplus of tribute*, would trade only to carry away that tribute, and not in any manner to promote the prosperity of their territories. But if the merchants of this country, by means of vested capital, knowledge of the trade, and economy in its prosecution, could supply foreign nations with India commodities as cheap as those nations could supply themselves, it is evident that the bullion derived from the trade with foreigners, and imported by our own subjects, would be just as beneficial to India as if it were imported in Portugueze, Swedish or Danish ships. The question then comes to this—Could the merchants of this country supply other nations, and even partly those mentioned, as cheaply as they can themselves, or other nations; for part of their trade, and almost all that of the Americans, is for the supply of different parts of Europe? If the question be answered in the affirmative, it is manifest that British merchants would then fructify India with specie precisely in the manner the trade of those foreigners now does. There is no occasion then, that foreigners should be invited to trade, if, by the fair encouragement of our own subjects, the commerce of India can be brought into an English channel. Thus, by pouring in capital into Bengal, and carrying bullion, the produce of their successful trade with other nations, the industry of India would be encouraged, capital in that country would be increased, circulation, impeded by the enormous quantity of the Company's paper, would be revived, and trade, oppressed by the high rate of interest, would be improved and extended.

But, besides the fabrics of the finer kind, there are various other productions in India which, by due encouragement, might be improved and enlarged. The article of indigo alone, which is now imported to the value of more than a million sterling, is but of late cultivation in India, and the rapid success it has obtained may fairly be ascribed to its being left to private adventure. The raising of sugar, were it not the policy to discourage it in favour of West India produce, might be carried to any extent. This could be demonstrated beyond contradiction; but if the monopoly is to be reserved to the West India planters, whose interests, at the present moment, seem peculiarly deserving of consideration, it is not necessary to discuss in detail a question in itself undoubtedly very important.

The extension of the British dominions in the Bombay Presidency, has afforded additional facilities for the supply of cotton, an article now so necessary to our domestic manufactures. To suppose that so bulky an article can be conveyed to Europe in the princely vessels of the Company, at the enormous rate of freight which they pay, or on the scale of royal extravagance, which distinguishes every branch of their commerce, is to trifle with the subject. The thing is impossible. The Company know it full well; and as a proof of their liberality, they make the offer of letting the Lancashire manufacturers supply themselves. In the Third Report*, they say, "The Company however have abandoned the importation (of cotton) in consequence of the *loss which has been sustained, but they are ready to grant free permission to the manufacturers of Lancashire and elsewhere to send out ships, and to import for their own account on the usual regulations for private trade*, provided the ships to be employed are British built or India built."

* See Asiatic Annual Register for 1802; State Papers, page 68.

This, to be sure, is wonderful condescension. It seems to be of the same species of facetious liberality with that recorded by Lord Bacon, in his Apothegms, of the scholar, who could not spare his bellows out of his chamber, but was ready to permit his neighbour to come and blow there as much as he pleased. The invitation, at any rate, is given only because it cannot be accepted.

It may be very possible to get cotton from India, though it might not be wise in the manufacturers of Lancashire to divert their capital from its proper application, to that of merchant adventurers, in the importation of cotton. Their capital and their industry have occupation enough without this diversion. They have a right to expect that the India Company's monopoly shall not interfere with the fair supply of the market, in an article of the first necessity to their manufacture, particularly when the company formally announce, that " they have abandoned the importation."

The fact is, that, were it not for the jealousy of the Company, cotton might now be, and might for years have been, imported in very large quantities. But to imagine that cotton, or any other article which must come here to a competition with the same article from other parts with which the trade is free, can be brought while the Company's burdensome and oppressive system continues, is to be utterly ignorant of the nature of commerce. Were the whole trade of India open and free to be followed in all its branches, according to the demand of circumstances, and the dictates of enlightened acquaintance with markets at home and abroad, there cannot be a doubt that great quantities of cotton would be imported. But can it be expected that any set of merchants will accept the offer of the Directors for importing *cotton* solely? In so bulky a commodity, freight constitutes a most essential charge; but upon an assorted cargo, a bulky article, which of itself could hardly pay, might enter very usefully into the bill of lading. Do the Directors offer to let ships go to Surat or Bombay, to bring home cotton, or any other commodities the freighters chuse to ship; or do they propose to allow them to export what they please in their own way, and with an entire freedom from the burdensome formalities and restrictions of the Company's monopoly? Not at all.

But it is not necessary to rely on mere speculation as to what might be done, if the trade were open, or if it were allowed to be carried on in the manner which British merchants would now carry it on, if the Company would but wave a monopoly which, as to this article at least, is prohibitory to others, not exercised beneficially, or even at all for themselves. In the year 1799—1800, thirty-four thousand bales, each three hundred and ninety-two pounds weight, were imported into this country, in eleven thousand five hundred tons of shipping, belonging to the private traders; and if the facilities for importing at a cheap rate were afforded, not only the quantity in demand would regularly be supplied, but the quality would be adapted to the English market. The cotton in India, it is calculated, can be raised by the grower at about three halfpence a pound, whereas, cotton, raised by the labour of slaves, cannot be raised at less than a shilling*. The difference of freight, therefore, constitutes the difference of price. But if the Directors make the whole expence fall upon the homeward cargo, it is absurd to think that the article can pay. Sir Robert Peel, in a letter to the Court of Directors, dated November, 1797, accuses the Company of a positive breach of contract, in refusing themselves, and denying permission to others, to bring home cotton at a reasonable freight. He expressly states, that the discouragements to this great national object *had caused a rise in the price of cotton of* 100*l. per cent.* Such is the encouragement given by the Company to our domestic manufactures, by supplying them with raw materials! It is of the same kind with that mentioned by the merchants of Liverpool, in 1792, when they petitioned for laying open the trade. They assert, truly, that the Company did every thing in their power to

---

* See Henchman's Observations, page 23.

ruin our cotton manufactory, on its first establishment, because it was likely to interfere with some of the articles of their monopoly.

But the reason given by the Directors for discouraging the cotton trade, in the Second Report, is particularly deserving of attention. They say, " That the cotton of India cannot succeed; that the rate of freight is too high; that the cotton from the east is not the produce of British India, (since that time the cotton country has been annexed to the British dominions,) that enough is not raised in the Company's provinces for the employment of their manufacturers; that a large quantity is every year sent to China, as a means of providing the Company's investments of teas; that none has of late years been imported into Bengal by sea; that by vast importations into this country, part may again be exported, and minister to the support of foreign manufactures, which affect our own."

The abominable spirit of monopoly, which pervades this passage, ought not to escape without indignation and censure. It is the dread that some way or other their monopoly may be injured, which ever influences them; and that sentiment is in every instance as ignorant as it is odious. The fact is, that owing to circumstances, perfectly well known, Bengal now raises the supply itself, and it affords large quantities for exportation; such is the facility with which that happy soil lends itself to every sort of produce. But, perhaps, an exportation from Surat and Bombay would raise the price of cotton, to the prejudice of that part of the investment which goes in cotton to buy teas? Good God! and is the interest of India committed to such rulers? Is the interest of Englishmen dependant on such fellow-citizens? The Directors surely cannot be ignorant, that in an article, the cultivation of which is unlimited, the supply will meet the demand; and that the increase of demand, by a natural and invariable law of free commerce, tends to reduce the price. Yet, upon the malignant apprehension of a possible loss to themselves in their investment for teas, the cultivation of an article, raised by people entitled to British protection in India, is to be sacrificed to the Company's monopoly; and the manufacturers of this country are to be deprived of the raw material of a fabric of vast national importance. The Directors are wonderfully alarmed for the interest of our manufacturers! Their charity, to be sure, begins at home. They begin with fears about their own investments to China, but they afterwards feel for our manufacturers, and anticipate their ruin, should cotton be so cheap in the port of London that they will not buy it! It is not very probable, that the manufacturers of Lancashire will be very uneasy about what may become of the cotton, of which they get the first offer, and the very importation of which will secure them a cheap and constant supply of the commodity.

It is not my intention to go into a detailed consideration of the different articles with which India is capable of supplying us; but I cannot help taking notice of one which is extremely important to our home manufactures. I mean SILK; and as the cotton fabrics of India are discouraged, for the protection of our own, it is our duty to compensate India, by favouring the production of silk, in which the interests of both countries would coincide. At present, we are dependent chiefly upon France and Italy for the supply of this commodity, and the East India Company, with the means of affording the supply, have been at no pains to bring the article to that degree of perfection that would enable it to compete with the produce of Italy and France. On the contrary, the Company have neglected the business entirely: Bengal silk has for some years been growing worse; and the only improving part of it is that which comes in the private and privileged trade. But to do justice to this resource to which our silk manufacturer is entitled to look, skill, and probably capital too, must be suffered to go to India, and must be directed by the zeal and intelligence of private interest. Were the enterprise and skill of individuals suffered to engage freely in this supply, there is no doubt the object would be soon obtained. Silk of the best quality might be procured from our eastern dominions; but, in order to suit the demands of the home manufacturers at a reasonable price, the silk ought to be organzined in India. A greater degree of attention on the prepation of it *there* must be bestowed; and that cannot be expected from the Company and their agents. Were the silk organzined in India (that is imported here ready for the loom), we should be able to preserve a large share in that important manufacture, which now is very precarious, and gained as much, through the disorders which have prevailed in France for these last sixteen years, as from our own resources or superiority. But till individuals are permitted freely to engage in the supply of this article in every stage, the British manufacturer will be dependent on our enemies, to whom we may pay more than *two* millions annually, for silk alone. Yet, with the remedy in our power, this mass of national interest is sacrificed to the East India Company's monopoly!

The Directors have uniformly asserted, that the trade with India, neither as to import nor export, is capable of extension. They have claimed the praise of giving " full scope to the internal powers of their territory in agriculture and commerce." To state, however, that the sovereign of a country, of near fifty millions of people, wishes to have an exclusive monopoly in the commerce of that country, of itself announces a pretension not very compatible with " *giving full scope to the internal powers of a country.*" There is something absolutely shocking in the union of the character of sovereign and monopolist merchant. That the same persons should at once exact the revenues of the sovereign, and seek to monopolize the commerce of the merchant, is the condemnation of the system. This rapacity of power, and this meanness of monopoly, compose, indeed, a nauseous and disgusting mixture. Is it in the nature of things, that the internal powers of the territory should be encouraged and developed, under a government which unites characters so irreconcileable with those objects? In the mechanical routine of the Company's commercial operations, there is no room for the enterprise, the discernment, the invention, and the discovery which are the sure results of fair competition, and an active and enlightened emulous private interest. In the Company's trade, every thing is languid and formal. It is conducted by agents who, indeed, may perform their task with fidelity, but not with zeal. Every transaction drawls on the lifeless routine of office; without spirit, without energy. It is not consistent with the nature of man, that under such a system, the full development of any branch of commerce can be obtained.

When we consider the enormous number of men now subject to the British dominion in India, when we consider the immensely rich and populous empires which are included within the limits of the Company's Charter, it will be difficult to persuade us, that the full commercial resources of those regions, almost equal in population to half the globe, have been explored and ascertained. And when we reflect on these things, it is impossible to contain our astonishment, that a nation, boasting itself enlightened, and pursuing trade as one of its favourite objects, should have restrained its subjects from exploring these fertile regions of trade, and should have conferred the privilege upon a monopoly Company, which from its very nature must be disqualified either to draw the proper benefit from the branches we know, or to enlarge the sphere of intercourse by new discoveries.

Indeed, it is very obvious, that in every respect the Company, since the territorial acquisition, are much less enterprising in commerce than when they were merely merchants. Their voyages resemble the dull regularity of the Spanish galleons, or register ships. It is observed, that when the Company were only merchants, they had upwards of eighty factories at different parts, from the Persian Gulph to China. There are not above four or five of them remaining; and the Company, in the sluggishness of a monopoly, pronounce that these four or five are sufficient for the commerce of all India. It is very probable that they who really are not merchants, they who can do nothing tolerably but business of mere routine, would find any addition to their trade, addition to their loss. They do not wish for new branches of trade. They are contented with mismanaging what they choose to undertake, and excluding their fellow citizens from any competition with them.

In the year 1792, previous to the renewal of the Company's Charter, the spirited, intelligent, and enterprising merchants of Liverpool were of opinion that most extensive fields of trade might be formed beyond the Cape of Good Hope. They knew that the chief access to the populous empire of Persia is shut up by the Company's Charter; that the countries around the Red Sea; that the innumerable islands and the populous empires of the East, can furnish valuable objects of trade, and would, if cultivated, present profitable markets to the infinite variety of our manufactures.

It has been objected by the Company, that a trade with India never can be beneficial to the merchants of this country; because, from moral and religious causes, the consumption of British commodities in Hindostan must be greatly limited. They have even asserted that " the emergencies of Government, or a prudent sacrifice to popular prejudice, may at times have favoured the views of private adventurers; " *but they only bought at a high price, from the poverty of the state or the venality of its members,* permission to ruin themselves."

We have seen in a preceding part of this inquiry who were the real parties, who " *bought from the poverty of the state, or the venality of its members,*" permission to ruin themselves. We have seen in 1694, the Company paying 170,000*l.* in bribing ministers of state, and members of parliament. We have seen their Directors committed to the Tower, and the whole nation animated with a common sentiment of indignation against them. At a later period we have seen them carrying on a wholesale trade of corruption; bribing many boroughs, their practices detected, and their members expelled and imprisoned. It was the Directors of the Company who bought from the " *poverty of the state, or the venality of its members,*" a permission not to ruin themselves, (for they were sure of their own job) but permission to deceive their subscribers with hopes of profit never realised ; to mismanage the commerce of India, and to strip their fellow citizens of the natural and almost indefeasible right to exercise their talents, their industry, their capital for their own advantage ; and, by an inseparable connection, for the advantage also of their country.

But when we hear the Company, the sovereigns of India, constantly undervaluing the commerce of that country, and see them inexorably obstinate in excluding from it all their fellow citizens, it is easy to discern their apprehensions of losing the monopoly. Yet what kind of sovereigns must they be who thus labour to narrow and restrict the commerce of their subjects? How despicable, how odious, that character of sovereignty so jealous of a commercial intercourse which an enlightened Government would cherish and invite? Their character indeed is uniform : " By a strange absurdity," says Dr. Smith, " they regard the character of the sovereign as but an appendix to that of merchant; their mercantile habits lead them in this manner, almost necessarily, though perhaps insensibly, to prefer, upon all ordinary occasions, the little transitory profit of the monopolist to the great and permanent revenue of the sovereign."

But obstinate as the Directors are, in excluding their fellow citizens from all share in the India trade, even from that which they do not pretend to carry on themselves, they can persuade no man that their representations of that trade are just. It certainly is true that, in proportion to the extent of the population, and the wealth of the British dominions in India, they do not furnish a considerable market for the produce and manufactures of this country. But, allowing much for the religion, the habits, the immoveable customs, the permanent moral character of the Hindus, it still appears wonderful that the latter should have imbibed no taste, if not for the capricious fashions, at least for the solid improvements, which their masters might be capable of furnishing them, in almost every thing connected with mechanical contrivances. Mr. Orme informs us, that nothing can be more rude than the tools and implements with which the Hindus work. It is personal industry, and minute dexterity, that supplies among them that which among us is performed by well contrived tools and skilful machinery. Yet it is almost incredible, notwithstanding the adherence of those people to old customs, that they should not be capable of seeing the infinite superiority of European contrivances, for abridging or facilitating labour, and for executing every mechanical task. From the immense sums which India has furnished to the rapacity of its different conquerors, we know that great industry, great circulation, very considerable consumption, must exist among this people. They are, in a state of agriculture, of manufactures, and of refinement, very considerably advanced. The frequent devastation of war, the perpetual revolutions in government, and the long series of oppressive administration they have suffered, must have limited their productive powers, and deranged their industry. But under a steady protective government their powers of production, and their ability to consume, should be increased. It seems almost certain that they might furnish a demand for many articles of English produce and manufacture, which they do not now use. The infinite variety of our manufactures in iron and steel, in gold and silver, in jewellery, in elegant furniture, in glass; particular kinds of woollens, might very well be adapted to the taste and the demand of Eastern luxury and magnificence. The Company deny this. They discourage the attempt, because they are not merchants. That they have made so little progress in introducing any thing English into their territories, capable of so much consumption, will be considered by intelligent men more as a proof of their unfitness or indisposition for pushing such active enterprises of commerce, than to the impossibility of succeeding in the object. Besides, there are other classes of people in India, not inconsiderable in point of numbers, and very considerable in point of wealth, particularly the Mahomedans. Why should the Mahomedan be unwilling to adopt the elegance of European arts? Why should they be averse to those manufactures which contribute to the comforts of life and to the embellishment of high condition? Other objects have been in view with the East India Company than to advance these purposes. Nothing has been done to facilitate the introduction of our manufactures, but every thing has been done systematically to discourage it. It could not be done by the Company, nor by any body else under the cumbrous regulations and the expensive detail to which all their traffic is subject. Our manufactures have not had a trial. The interest of England, as a producing country, has never entered into the views of the Company at any time, far less since they became territorial sovereigns.

The trade with India, and with the countries eastward of the Cape, has hitherto been depressed and confined by the influence of the monopoly. No fair experiment has has been made, either what commodities those regions might add to the objects of commerce for European consumption, or what demand they are capable of affording for our own manufactures. It is believed, that many articles of the first necessity might be cultivated in our Indian territories. For instance, I am positively assured, and indeed partly know the fact, that hemp*, of an ex-

---

* The article alluded to is called *Sann*, and is to be found in the Malabar provinces. It slightly differs from European hemp, but can be applied with advantage to all the purposes for which hemp is used. Not long ago experiments were made in this country, to ascertain how far it could be employed to make ropes and canvass. The result was, that it was found capable of being wrought into both articles of a very superior quality. The Company and their servants, however, have given no facility to the proper cultivation of this article, and its introduction into this country. On the contrary, they have neglected or opposed this object; not to mention the impossibility of transporting such a commodity at their rate of freight.

cellent quality and to any extent, might be raised in India, and might be brought to Europe for the supply of our military and commercial navy, were sufficient facilities allowed for importing it. It is probable that it can only be brought over, however, in a mixed cargo, as its bulk might render the transport of it as a single article too expensive, and it can never be done therefore till the trade is laid open or the monopoly modified. Very little, however, has yet been attempted towards deriving such advantages from the territorial dominions, by encouraging their productive powers.

Should the attempts of the British government to obtain a footing in Spanish America be successful, they will furnish additional reasons for rescuing the navigations of those seas from the present tyranny of the East India and South Sea Companies, and for opening the trade to India, for which the possession of South America would afford additional encouragement.

It is no wonder that the manufactures of this country have seen with dissatisfaction the renewal of the Company's Charter. The principal trading towns have evinced the same disapprobation of so impolitic a measure. The liberty of employing their talents, their industry, their capital, is one of the great objects which men expect to secure in a state of society, and to take that liberty from the many, to vest an exclusive privilege in a few, may indeed be consistent with legislative competence, but is hardly reconcileable to the great ends of government. No government has a right to interfere with those objects, unless when the paramount interests of the community dictate a modification or a suspension of them in favour of a system more generally beneficial. Unless, however, the establishment of such a monopoly, as that enjoyed

---

There are some other productions similar to hemp and flax to be found in India, capable of being wrought up into manufactures equal to the finest cambric. But these and a thousand improvements are stifled and overlaid by the dead weight of the Company and their monopoly.

by the East India Company, be demonstrably advantageous to the nation at large, and not merely an expedient of administration, as it has almost always been, the regulation is not less unjust than impolitic, which restrains the natural course of industry, labour, and capital.

IV. The commercial situation of the company itself will next deserve our attention. We have already seen, from the view of the Company's institution and progress, how unfit and incapable it is for the management of commerce. The Directors, however, tell us that the phrenzy of sharing in the trade to India, will ensnare unwary persons, whose rage for adventure will be productive of their ruin before they are aware of their error.

This is indeed a terrible denunciation, and, if it came from a discreet, prudent, and successful merchant, it would have weight, but we shall see, by and by, what sort of merchants the Company is. In one of their reports (and in a letter of Mr. Dundas) we are told that the *public funds and the tribute* constitute the trading capital with which the Company's commerce is carried on*. In the Third Report, we find the Directors stating that this tribute, admitted in the First Report to be one part of their capital, was not applied to that object, because it did not exist. "It is true (say they) that in the year 1793, there was a surplus of tribute in India of 1,159,000*l.* per annum, to be brought home through the medium of commerce, but that sum has been exhausted, either in establishments under the authority of the board of commissioners, or in political expences, neither of which were incurred by, or belong to the commerce of the Company." From the source of tribute it is acknowledged, then, that the Company have no aid at all.

As to the fortunes of individuals, we find them complaining, as if a most grievous injury, that these funds are intercepted by the private

---

* First Report of Select Committee on the India Trade.

traders. If they be so intercepted, there must be some good reason for it. It is, however, the opinion of many, that these funds are in part vested in the Company's Indian paper. At present let us hear the complaint.

" Individuals have not complained of the want of means to remit their fortunes to Europe, since the year 1793. It is the Company who *complain*, that it is the *British merchants* residing in India who are competitor for those funds, and who intercept a considerable portion which would otherwise flow into their *treasury, to enable the Company to purchase their own investment.*"

This passage is worth notice for several reasons; but suffice it now to remark the light which it throws on the trading resources of the Company. First, we find a tribute which has not been realized, and, secondly, a remittance of fortunes which individuals are not well inclined to remit through the Company. Is it possible that any merchant can trade to advantage when his proper peculiar trading capital is thus fluctuating and precarious, beyond his own disposal and controul? How then does the Company procure its trading capital? By the sale of its outward cargoes almost always sold at a loss; and by borrowing money at very high interest; and in such cases their investment is sure to produce, not a mercantile profit, but a positive loss?

As to the complaint, that the fortunes of individuals are intercepted, the truth is, that, whether these funds are obtained by private British traders or not, they never will seek the Company's treasury. They seek either the employment of other European traders, or that of the Americans, whose India trade has been raised into its present magnitude, by the oppressive monopoly of the Company, against the interest of British subjects.

That the trade of India is not a gaining one for the Company, is ascertained by various facts, and by the opinions of the most competent judges. No trade can bear the extravagance of freight under which the Company import, and the heavy charges under which their cargoes must be collected in India, where nothing of the diligence and economy of private merchants is observed.

They are said indeed to gain in the China trade, in which their sole gain arises from their oppressive monopoly at the expence of their countrymen.

The trade of the Company from India has been called a remittance trade, but be the name what it may, the mercantile charges, and profits of the trade, must be considered before we can ascertain whether they gain or not. As a merchant, the Company cannot gain, unless the money brought into their treasury, in the shape of tribute, is so laid out in India, as to afford a fair profit on the *first cost, charges,* freight, insurance, &c. of the goods invested. If they do not realize the principal sum, with all the various charges, there is a mercantile loss. On the other hand, if the Company act as the banker remitter of the fortunes of individuals, unless the sum they receive in their treasury in India can be realized in Europe at the fair rate of exchange, they are losers on the principal sum brought into their treasury. They would diminish the amount of their own tribute in the one case; they would lose as bankers remitters in the other. But if it be manifest that the Company, as merchants and as bankers, lose on their transactions, why should they continue the trade? It is demonstrable that whatever they lose might be gained to the nation. The tendency to trade between this country and India is powerful, nay, irresistible; when individuals are chased out of one channel, they find another. Does not this point out to us what is the course to follow, and what we ought to do? That trade, which the company vainly and absurdly attempt to carry on, should be left to the enterprise of individuals. If there be any surplus tribute to be remitted, it will be realized in the speculations of individuals. The trade of the private merchant will bring it home cheaper in the shape of merchandize than the Company can do, and will bring into the coffers of the sovereigns in England, be it the Company, be it the government, every farthing of tribute which is to be received.

The tribute, therefore, will be realized safer and more commodiously through the channel of private commerce, while it will fructify a gainful trade, instead of being diminished, as now, in a losing one. There is no reason that the Company should be a merchant for the remittance of tribute. It can be remitted through the channels of trade, and the mutual intercourse of nations. If the Company's revenues were paid in kind, there might be an apology for remitting them to a market in kind. But when they are realized, if realized at all, in money, and afterwards converted into commodities by the *Company-Sovereign*, surely this process is the most unnatural and superfluous that can be conceived. We see that individuals of all nations endeavour to obtain this traffic: will not, then, the private merchants be very willing to pay the Company, in London, the amount of the sums which they receive from them in India? and such is the expensive system of the Company's trade, that no rate of change could diminish the amount so much as the loss upon their mercantile enterprises. There appears no reason, therefore, to admit with some, that the Company ought to be merchants, even to the extent of the tribute they might have to remit. That remittance through trade can be made better by private merchants, and if the Company be unfit for commerce in any other way, they are unfit for it in this way. Nothing but necessity could justify their remitting their tribute in kind or in commodities. There is no necessity for it, and they lose by the adventure.

As to the fortunes of individuals, of which they wish to be the remitters in goods, they lose on a capital which is not their own, but borrowed, because they give bills in India to be paid in England, and the funds, out of which alone they can be able fairly to pay, are the returns on the commodities invested with the money, for which they so give bills. But, if the trade is a losing one, the trade of remittance for others is, *a fortiori*, more losing than when they remit their own tribute. If, however, they borrow money at a very high rate of interest, (perhaps 12*l.* per cent.) in order to lay in an investment, on which it is notorious they do not, when the money is their own, gain a mercantile profit, it is clear that, in addition to all other loss, they lose this very high interest, which seems of itself to preclude profit, and they accumulate in India a debt, which preys not only upon them, but upon the commercial resources of that country. In England, our public debt is, in some measure, a facility for commerce; but in India, the necessities of the Company withdraw capital from beneficial employments, and make it active only for the purposes of stock-jobbing, and the gains of brokerage; as their debt is large beyond all proportion to the active commercial capital of their territories.

It will be proper to consider, a little more in detail, the advantages which the Company derive from their commercial operations. The rate of profit, indeed, or rather loss, at which the Company trade, is much disputed. In the year 1805, the accounts, containing the following statements, were laid before the House of Commons.

In ten years, up to 1804 inclusive, the whole costs and charges on the India trade, separate from the China, are stated at 27,112,195*l.* Sale amount 31,467,287*l.* Balance 4,354,792*l.* In the same paper we find the following statement of the China trade: Cost and charges 25,964,342*l.* Sale amount 33,066,301*l.* Balance 7,101,959*l.* The difference between the amount of profit on the China trade, in the same number of years, and upon a quantity of sale, less by two millions, is well worthy of attention. The cause of this difference has been repeatedly pointed out. The China trade is a close monopoly, for which the Company oblige the people of this country to pay, in proportion to their demands, which are great, and to the supply of the article, which is limited. The Company, therefore, gain more on the one branch, than they can on the other; and it surely requires little address to defraud a customer, who must buy, and has no choice of his market.

But, upon their profits for ten years, as stated by themselves, it is proper to make a few remarks.

The whole balance of profits, including the charge and duty on the private trade; the amount of annuity at the bank; and a pretended profit on exports, amounting to 678,486*l.*; is 13,779,577*l.* But, in fact, all these sums should be deducted, for as to profit on exports, no such thing exists; nor, indeed, any profit, if the account were dissected on mercantile principles. In the Reports, in 1792, it is admitted, that there was a loss on the India exports; and there is no reason to suppose there is a profit now. Take this account, however, as it is given: there are various payments, part of which are called political; but in the whole, including every charge, and comparing the payments and profits, (including in the latter the articles mentioned,) there is the following balance:—

Total profits	£13,779,507
Total payments	12,797,796
Total surplus in ten years. . . .	£981,781

In this account there are many articles which are not commercial profits. Such are the profits on private trade, amounting in ten years to 1,482,056*l.*; and the amount of annuity from government, in ten years, above 362,000*l.* Thus we have near two millions, which do not arise from trade; and were not this included, there would be an excess in the payments of more than a million, instead of a surplus of profit of 981,781*l.* It appears, likewise, by the papers laid before Parliament, that the profit on sales, in the year ending 1st March, 1805, was

	£1,172,779
Charges.................	1,591,319
Leaving a deficiency of....	£418,540

And though several articles of a political nature, such as the charges for St. Helena, other charges on account of the territory, be deducted, there still remains a deficiency of 25,000*l.* by the admission of Mr. Grant, the late chairman[*]. But, the fairness of such deductions may be questioned, because the charges here, called territorial, are particularly connected with commerce, and not with the power of the sovereign. This statement, clearly proving a deficiency, is moreover liable to the remark already made: that the Indian charges are not fully brought forward; and the interest, not at all. It is clear, however, that three years India interest, on every transaction, (for that is the time it fills up,) should be charged, and it is needless to point out to merchants how that would affect the result.

The Company set out, in 1793, with the childish expectation of a surplus tribute of a million from the territorial revenue, as a trading capital. This was a bubble, not so bad in immediate effect, but as delusive in principle, as Mr. Law's Mississippi scheme, which was founded on India trade too. There was no such capital to trade withal. It was a delusion, if not a deception. The Company were obliged, therefore, to trade on a borrowed capital, under whatever name that borrowing was disguised. It was substantially borrowing, if they gave bills to private individuals remitting their fortunes. It

---

[*] See Cobbett's Debates, vol. vii. page 1133.

was borrowing, more openly, if they created a floating debt in India, to furnish investments. The latter resource, in addition to the sale of exports, has been their only trading capital. One cannot help being astonished that any such scheme of setting a trading company afloat should have been listened to, but it did obtain approbation; government even got the first 500,000*l.* participation money, and got it for the first and last time.

How could it be expected that so great a trade as that with India and China could be carried on, without a real *bona fide* capital? The capital of the Company arising from the subscriptions was sunk and gone. They paid interest for it to their subscribers, but it was not active and productive in their affairs, as the borrowed capital of a private merchant, for which he pays interest, is. The project deserves no other name than that of a bubble. The intricacy of the accounts, indeed, the distance of the object, and various other circumstances, create a fog and mist, through which common people cannot see; but a bubble it is, with the loss on which the nation, the great patron of it, must finally be burdened.

The Company themselves say, that their wars in India have absorbed their means of investments. If there is any sense in this apology, it serves to show, that *government* and *commerce* form a bad association; and that government, like the lion, takes the lion's share, and leaves commerce to shift for itself. Every one knows that this is likely to happen always. It must be so; and unless commerce be placed on a different footing, it must be sacrificed to government. But the worst of the matter, even by the Company's own account, is, that the government, that is, the wars of India, have absorbed the *surplus revenue*, that *visionary* capital, on which the whole superstructive of the act of 1793 is built.

Let any man, however, take the trouble to look over the accounts annually submitted to Parliament under the name of the India Budget, and he will see good reason to dispute this plea; he will see that the revenues of India, up to 1802-3, for ten years, were—

$$£94,756,281$$
The Charges 83,253,417

$$£11,503,864$$
Being more than eleven millions above the actual charge.

It is, however, a thing not to be disputed, that, in the year 1798, the revenue of India was about £8,039,880
In the year 1806*.............. 15,600,000

Increase £7,560,120

The debts of India, in the year 1796, were.......£11,032,645
Debt in April, 1806, by computation............28,500,000

Increase.................................. £17,467,355

Mr. Grant calculates that, on the 30th April 1806, the India debt, deducting the amount of sinking fund, would be thirty millions, and consequently the increase of debt near nineteen millions.

This increase of debt would be nothing very formidable under good management, when compared with the increase of revenue. Even putting the whole increase of debt to the score of government and conquest, it is little more than two years purchase. Even that is injustice to the administration of India. But of the India debt, the

---

* Mr. Francis, in a speech in Parliament in 1805, says, the revenue is much under-rated at fifteen millions. Mr. Francis is a great authority for that fact.

Company claim, and will get, three or four millions*, for the conquest of Ceylon, for expeditions projected or executed to Batavia, the Moluccas, the capture of the Cape, Egypt, &c†.

To this there is to be added, that the funds with which the Company laid in their investments, over and above the proceeds of their exports, were to be procured by borrowing, and that at India interest, and therefore have swelled the mass of debt. The precise amount, in which the debt in India has been created by the demands of commerce, could not be ascertained without the examination of a vast number of accounts, to which very few have access, and also without a cautious settlement of the principles on which the computation is to be made. It is for want of settling this principle of computation that the superfluity of arithmetical statements, laid before the public, affords so little useful information or accurate inference.

Some persons, extremely intelligent in India affairs, have asserted, apparently on strong grounds, that a very large proportion of the India debt arises from money borrowed at Indian interest, to purchase investments. That this is the case, to a very considerable extent, is clear beyond contradiction. Lord Castlereagh, in the House of Commons, last July, admitted that, of the increased debt since 1793, 8,093,631*l.* was assignable to commerce; but there cannot be a doubt but much more belongs to that account. The investment, both for the China and for the India trade, for many years past, has been laid in with money borrowed in India, and the accumulating interest on the debt there composes a considerable proportion of the gross amount. Lord Wellesley, so early as June 1798, states the fact beyond dispute, that investment was laid in with borrowed money. In a minute of that date, he says:

---

* See the curious documents on this subject in the *As. An. Reg.* 1803.

† It is to be observed that the Company make government pay for all their acquisition, and even those on the peninsula.

"The investment, at once *the most powerful cause of our temporary distress,* the main spring of the industry and opulence of the people committed to our charge, and the active principle of the commercial interest of the Company, *is more likely to be increased than to be diminished in any future year, and consequently the embarrassment of our finances must be progressive, if some means be not devised for aiding the resources of this presidency,* which must now be considered as the general treasury and bank of our Eastern empire, furnishing supplies for all our other possessions in India, as well as a large *and increasing proportion of the capital employed in the trade to Europe and to China.*"

Here is a distinct warning given at the very commencement of Lord Wellesley's administration, of what was sure to happen, unless the Directors took some means to procure capital from other sources. There was no surplus tribute. The fortunes of individuals, of which they speak so much, were probably in a considerable degree absorbed in the Indian floating paper.

It was manifest, therefore, that either funds for investments were to be sent from Europe, or that they must be borrowed in India. The latter has been the case, for the Company have not sent funds from Europe to any considerable extent. It is undeniable, therefore, that all the difference annually between the produce of outward sales, and the amount of the investment to China and to Europe, has been borrowed at India interest, and must have formed a very great proportion of the Indian debt, because the very interest of Indian debt adds so rapidly to the amount of the principal. What is the precise amount of the share, it may not be easy for an individual to fix. The subject ought to be referred to a select committee of the House of Commons, to investigate and state the result clearly. The public is deeply interested in the question, for all this accumulation of debt by a ruinous commerce defrauds the nation of the benefits of the participation, stipulated in the Act of 1793.

The Company ought to be restrained from pursuing a traffick so mischievous to themselves and to the state.

Much has been said of the increase of the Company's assets, as a set-off to their debt; but many things are put into the stock by computation which cannot bear examination. The result upon the whole seems to be, that the Company have not means to pay their debts; and if the debts in India, payable in Europe next year, are actually demanded, there cannot be a doubt that the aid of government will be absolutely necessary. Such is the state of the Company's finances, that they were lately obliged to obtain from government a prolongation of the term for the payment of the tea duties now due; a thing that in a private merchant must have ruined his credit.

Indeed, by the Company's own statement in what is called the stock, by computation they assume a balance in their favour of 6,181,267*l*. but it is manifest that the sum due to the stockholders must be paid before they can state a balance in favour. That sum is not included; but taking what the Company's capital actually cost (which is not disputed) at 7,780,000*l*. the balance against them is 1,598,733*l*. on their own showing. To balance that, they state nine millions worth, and upwards, of fortifications, and other dead stock, which it is manifestly absurd to estimate at such an exchangeable value. Indeed, many of the items in that statement are perfectly ridiculous. Nearly two millions consist of household furniture, farming stock, pleasure boats, plate, and table-linen; such a list as might be expected to compose the stock of a concern in Duke's Place. If the articles included in the assets were to be fairly estimated, and allowance made for bad debts, &c. there would be found a deficiency of above five millions. This, added to the amount of capital, would give a balance of deficit, even admitting the nine millions for buildings*.

* See Cobbet's Debates, for July, 1806.

It has been stated that the debt in India, on the 30th April, 1806, was probably not less than thirty millions, at any rate above twenty-eight; the interest, payable on that part bearing interest, would be considerably above two millions. Such has been the accumulation of the debt, by means of the Company borrowing to carry on a trade, which is a losing trade *to them* in any circumstances, but when carried on with a capital borrowed at from eight to twelve per cent. absolutely ruinous.

The situation of the revenues in India, viewed as connected with government, may be considered flourishing, notwithstanding the debt; but what man is sanguine enough to think that the Company ever can regularly draw commercial capital out of those dominions? Neither ought it to be. The project of embarking the revenues of a government in traffick, which is the basis of the Act of 1793, is the most extraordinary imagination man ever indulged. Let the state take upon itself the whole responsibility and management of the civil government, and give its subjects the right of trading to India. The productive powers of that country will then be promoted; the trade will be supported by capital, independent of political events, and if there be surplus revenue, it will come to England through natural channels, instead of that clumsey, ill-contrived vehicle of remittance—the monopoly trade of a joint stock company.

It has sometimes been proposed, that the Indian debt should be transferred to Europe, and in some shape or other converted into stock here. This project, though undoubtedly calculated to alleviate the pressure, is liable to many very grave and serious objections. In a constitutional view it seems a matter of very doubtful policy to consolidate the existence of the Company still further, by giving it so formidable a mass of influence distinct from the government. The national debt is said to have owed its origin to a desire to identify the interest of multitudes with the new establishment at the Revolution. The further extension of any principle of influence or support, independent of the government, or, perhaps, different from that of the government, seems calculated to produce something of a similar effect, and to give the East India Company a more rooted and decisive hold of the community, founded upon an interest, which may be altogether separate from that of the nation at large. To create such a body of European debt, solely under the authority and responsibility of government, in the first instance, might be adviseable, as preparatory to the abolition of the Company; but if it is to be a Company's debt, and to create a new and more extensive body of adherents and dependents to it, without relation to the utility or inutility of the institution in other respects, it is a plan highly dangerous. The East India Company, as an *imperium in imperio*, are already too powerful, and perhaps too dangerous; but will any wise minister, or reflecting man, choose to allow them to inlist recruits or dependents, to the number of subscribers requisite to fund in Europe twenty or thirty millions sterling of India debt; or augment their democracy at the India House by such an accession of new citizens?

Perhaps, too, it is worth while to consider what might be the effect to public credit, of so large a fund, under the auspices, and fluctuating with the fortunes of an institution like that of the East India Company. The past management of that body gives no great security for better in future. It will be in vain to look to the Company's commerce for aid; let the authors of such a proposal, be who they may, count solely on the wisdom and economy of the Company's Indian administration. If there be any solid security, it is solely the Indian territories. Let sober-thinking men consider what may be the consequence to our funds at large, of the fluctuation that must inevitably arise in the Company's stock, if it is to vary with their commercial success, and their military enterprises. South Sea schemes and bubbles ought to have cured us of the insanity of granting privileges and power to any Company, capable of shaking the pillars of national credit. No man, who loves the constitution, and who respects the prerogative of the crown, will concur in a measure, so dangerous to the purity of the one, and the lawful authority of the other.

If it be necessary to save the India Company from ruin, by transferring the debt to Europe, the government ought to resume its rights; because, such a state of the Company, of itself, forfeits their Charter, and defeats the ends of their institution. The guarantee of government would, at all events, be necessary; but, in undertaking the ultimate risk, let us have a real security on the estate which is to pay the debt, and let us trust nothing to the bankrupt tenant, who has mortgaged our property, which he held only upon lease, and who has forfeited his rights, by the breach of every covenant into which he had entered. It is in vain to think, that the Company can retrieve their affairs in India, or afford any security for the permanent interest which the public has in that estate.

V. Having now taken a general view of the Company's commerce, and the enormous debt they have contracted, in order to carry it on at a loss, it is necessary to call the attention of the public to the private trade; because, till something better is done, the encouragement of that trade seems the only expedient for securing to the country the commerce of India. The encouragement of that trade is perfectly consistent with the Company's rights, and therefore it appears preferable to do so, rather than excite any clamour, by proposing to resume, before the expiry of the Charter, the privileges which the Company have used so little to the public advantage.

It is not the purpose of this tract to advocate the claims of the private traders, or even to discuss them, except in so far as they serve to illustrate the larger principles on which I contend for the general rights of the subjects of this country to a share in that trade, from which their capital, their talents, their industry, their enterprise, are excluded by the Company's monopoly. The private traders have gone no further than propose compromises and temperaments, founded upon the entire recognition of the Company's monopoly. Perhaps, indeed, the private traders may not wish the trade of India to be laid open; and the folly of the Company, in irritating and oppressing a class, who would probably have joined with them in supporting the monopoly, is fortunate for the country. Private traders may have their particular narrow views, their false conceptions of advantage in a secondary and subordinate monopoly. In the present circumstances, however, they contend for nothing but that which it is the interest of the State and of the Company to grant. Nay, what they ask ought to be granted speedily, unless the trade of India is to be diverted into foreign channels, from which it may be impossible to recal it.

At the time the Company's Charter was last renewed, a good deal of discussion took place, on the subject of laying open the trade, and, as before stated, several petitions were presented praying for that measure. The proposal unhappily was overruled. It was thought necessary, however, to do something in favour of the public, and to adopt some modification of the monopoly.

It seemed particularly to be felt on all sides as absolutely necessary to secure some channel, by which private individuals in India might, to a certain extent, be allowed to trade with this country*. A disease existed in the body politic, arising from obstructions, caused by the Company's monopoly; but the state doctors, though they perceived the mischief, either had not discovered the cause, or would not apply the proper remedy. Indeed, all the foolish and violent methods taken to force trade into particular channels, and exclude them from the

* See Historical View of Plans for the Government and Commerce of India, &c. page 582.

natural vessels of circulation, inevitably cause similar disorders. Men who possess the means of carrying on a trade, which the unreasonable will of the government attempts to force into one course, cannot be prevented from following the bent of their interest and the nature of things. It is in vain to complain of this. Whether called illicit trade, or smuggling, or interloping, it will continue as long as the temptation remains.

What was called an illicit trade, existed in India long before the Act of 1793. The British settlers there found out that they could trade to Europe, with great advantage, in foreign bottoms, and they were assisted in these speculations by the funds, which individuals were remitting home, and for which the Company would not furnish bills but on the most disadvantageous terms.

After a good deal of negociation, it was at last settled and provided, by the Act of 1793, that 3000 tons of shipping in the Company's ships should be set apart for the private export and import trade, according to certain regulations specified. The restrictions of the law against the Company's servants, or others acting as factors for foreigners, or lending money to foreign Companies, or on bottomry of their ships, or assisting them with remittances by bills, was repealed*.

This repeal is a sufficient censure of such prohibitions. The object of this recognition of the private trade was to render it unnecessary for British individuals to embark their capital in a trade carried on by foreigners, and to afford them the means to bring that trade to their own country.

We cannot, however, praise much in the arrangement, except the intention it professed. The provisions for realizing it were not well

* 33 Geo. III. cap. 52.

contrived. It is universally admitted that they have failed, and Lord Melville, the author of the act, has candidly acknowledged it.

Indeed, the failure can excite no surprise. It was perfectly impossible that private traders, who carry on commerce for a mercantile profit, and who therefore must carry it on with economy, and in that course which seasons and markets require, could carry it on under the same disadvantages as the Company, who do nothing upon the principles of ordinary trade. To tie them to the Company's system, and prescribe the same circle of operations to both, was like chaining a living body to a dead carcase.

Every man, in the slightest degree acquainted with commerce, knows, that nothing is more essential to it than that it should be entirely under the command of him who engages in it, to carry it on in the way he deems most advantageous. A merchant must have an opportunity to ascertain the state of markets, and to adapt the cargo he exports to the demands of the distant market; and to calculate, on the other hand, what in return will be most suited to his home market. But to prevent, as much as possible, the uncertainty of such calculations (always uncertain) it is important that the time in which the whole operation is to be completed should be as short as possible.

If, however, he is compelled to ship his goods on board of vessels which are not under his own direction, as to the time and course of the voyage, it is perfectly manifest that he ought to be wholly independent of mercantile profit, or he must be ruined. Indeed, nothing but a very strict monopoly can support that mode of doing business. It was the mode pursued in Spain, and under which, subject to the controul of the *Casa de Contraccione*, individuals were allowed to ship goods for South America in the privileged ports[*]. These ships at that time used to

---

[*] Brougham, vol. i. 415.

sail once *in three years*. Our Company do not interpose quite so long an interval; but, it is undeniable that their voyages last much longer than the voyages of private ships would do; not to speak of the interruptions and deviations to which their ships are subject from the political character of the Company.

It must be evident to every man, that nothing but a close monopoly could render a trade so carried on profitable; and even if it were a gainful trade to the Company, it would be for the interest of the nation to abolish such a monopoly, because in proportion to the trade being gainful must the nation itself be taxed in the price of the commodities consumed at home: or lose, inasmuch as the monopoly, by causing high price, prevents re-exportation for the foreign supply.

But individuals trading for profit cannot support these multiplied inconveniences. Their whole operation is rendered uncertain, by the time consumed in it; and also the quantity of capital, necessarily employed in it, is increased, from being so long tied up in one transaction. The capital is not replaced, and the profits realized, probably in less than three years. It is manifest, therefore, that a greater quantity of capital is occupied in circulating a smaller number of goods than need be employed; the quantity of business done is lessened; and the profits of the merchant are smaller, more distant, and uncertain.

This will be evident from a few considerations. The extra ships, which sailed from Portsmouth on the 10th of August, 1805, are stated to have arrived at St. Helena, on their return to this country, about the middle of January, 1807; probably they are now arrived, being expected about the middle of April. Their cargoes will be sold in August or September; so that, allowing nine months for the prompt or payment, the proceeds will not be realized by the merchant till November or December, 1807.

Thus very nearly three years are necessary from the commencement of the transaction to its final close. It is evident to every practical merchant, that three capitals, at the least, are requisite to carry on the business;—one in India, to provide the goods; one to pay the bills drawn against them before they arrive (always the case); and another, supposing it a British capital, to remit to India for the succeeding year's investment, before the preceding ones are realized.

This is the train of the Company's trade, and fully justifies the assertion that it requires three capitals: some indeed assert it is nearer four.

The waste and expence of this system will appear at once, by comparing it with the course of the American trade to India. It is perfectly well ascertained, that the Americans perform their voyage from the ports of their own country, and back again, in nine or ten months. They come to Calcutta, take in their cargo, and sail again, sometimes in five and twenty days; this is a fact well known.

It is clear, however, that with the same capital necessary to carry on the Company's single voyage (or that of the private trader under the oppression of the Company's system) to the same extent, the American can perform two operations at least. Suppose that he gets credit at Calcutta, by giving a bill upon an opulent merchant in London, perhaps Baring and Company, payable in six months. He returns to America and realizes his profit there, or perhaps at Hamburgh or Amsterdam, in cash or good bills; and this fully enables him to meet the bill on London, for which he got his cargo at Calcutta. He is ready immediately to proceed on another voyage. Probably the second time he goes to Bombay direct; to which he carries Madeira wine, or any other articles that suit the market: he then takes in a cargo of cotton, and proceeds to China to take in tea, if he thinks that operation more advantageous than going to Calcutta, and renewing the first transaction on which he has made a large profit. All this he shall do before the Company can once realize a single outward and homeward voyage to their own territories.

The Americans, it is true, have the advantage of peace insurance, and other circumstances which press upon us in time of war; but is it not evident that the very system of the Company's trade secures them a much superior and more certain advantage over us, in the quantity of capital employed, the quickness of the return, the economy on the whole transaction, the expence of which is so much lessened by the shortness of the voyage and all the concomitant circumstances?

It is absurd, therefore, to expect that the Company can contend with the Americans; but how then stands the private trader, who ships on board the Company's vessels; has he any chance of trading to advantage?

In the first place, he is obliged to apply for the tonnage he thinks he may require, long before it is really wanted. After repeated applications, he is left quite uncertain on board of what vessel his goods may be shipped, or when she will sail. Before the voyage begin, his risk commences as to almost every thing that constitutes the real adventure of a merchant. He ships to a country, as to the state of the markets, of which he cannot even make a conjecture at the time his cargo may arrive; because the vessel may be detained, or may be obliged to deviate, or may be converted into a ship of war. In a word, the vessel, in her voyage, is subject to none of those essential conditions which every merchant who ships goods would insert in his charter party.

Let any merchant look back at the quickness and certainty of the Americans, in all their Indian transactions, and then let him pronounce whether a trade, carried on in such a manner as ours, can thrive, unless it is supported by the advantage of a very close monopoly.

The reservation of 3000 tons in the Company ships, for the benefit of the private trade, is one of the most extraordinary measures that ever was gravely proposed to a legislative assembly*. It carries its own condemnation with it. How it could even have been thought of is truly amazing. The Directors† triumphantly inform us, that it never has been used by the private traders, and that the Company have lost 70 or 80,000*l.* by providing the tonnage. This is not surprising. It would indeed have been wonderful if sensible practical merchants had condescended to trade on such terms.

Had the Company been carriers, going backward and forward, between London and Calcutta, with a power to charge what freight they pleased, this reservation on the part of others, to have a certain quantity of goods carried at a moderate rate, might have been prudent and proper, if the things carried had no reference to commerce, and if the provision had been merely a security against the overcharge for the carriage of a certain quantity of luggage. The owner of the goods in this case, like the passenger in a stage coach, would have paid the price, submitted to the inconvenience, and considered the matter no more. But a merchant, whose object is to bring his goods to market as cheap as he can, regularly, systematically, and in fifty successive instances, is compelled to look to the means he has of carrying his produce, as much as to the means of raising it. Indeed, it is just as important that he should have the means of sending the goods to

---

* It is quite amusing to see in what flattering terms this project is opened in the *Historical View* already quoted. See page 580, et seq.

† See their Three Reports.

market, as the means of providing them in the first instance. Then, what sort of a conveyance is that which this stipulation secures him?

The law says, that the rate of freight is to be *moderate*. Very well. Granting it is moderate, how small a matter is that, compared with the other disadvantages! It is not said, that the freight in the extra ships is of itself extravagant; and the fact is, the Company, against their will, and to remove one complaint, provided these ships, at a great loss to themselves, charging much less to the shippers than they pay to the owner. But is the freight all? Suppose that a merchant pays 20*l*. 30*l*. or 40*l*. per ton, on a four-months voyage: if, on paying that tonnage, his goods are immediately brought to the market for which they are destined, is it not evident, that he may be more a gainer on the adventure, than if they were carried much cheaper, but did not reach the market till six or twelve months after he has them shipped, or ready for shipping? The *freight* is but one, though an important article. The interest of money, the uncertainty and inconvenience of every sort, when added to the account, may render a particular mode of conveyance an absolute prohibition of the trade, independently of mere freight.

What good roads are to the internal communications of a country, quick intercourse by sea is to the inhabitant of different countries. It is no matter however that the road is good, if the journey is not performed with dispatch. The East India Company is an obstacle to our rapid intercourse with India, as bad as the most boisterous ocean, or the most impervious desert.

Every man, acquainted with human affairs, must be sensible how much commercial intercourse is promoted by an easy, regular, and speedy communication. To take a familiar illustration. It will be remembered by many, that the trade between London and Leith, and indeed most parts of Scotland, formerly resembled the phlegmatic dulness of the Company's voyages to India. They were rare, and took up six weeks or two months each time. Within a few years past, a system has been introduced, by which the ships perform the voyage with the quickness and regularity of a mail coach, not only to Leith, but every other sea port, and the beneficial effects to both parts of the island have been astonishing. This single improvement has annihilated the distance that divides the two countries, and has made the advantages of each common to both. The principle is the same when applied to larger transactions. Rapid intercourse abridges expence; augments capital, by facilitating the business it can perform; and renders commodities cheap, by promoting their circulation.

The regulation, proposed in 1793 in favour of the private trade, must have proved nugatory, because it furnished the merchant with a channel of conveyance which it was impossible for him to employ. Such a conveyance never could be used for a trade to be regularly carried on, paying its expences on commercial principles. It was soon found, therefore, that the plan of providing tonnage on board the Company's ships, for the private trade, could not answer the end proposed. Indeed, Lord Melville, the author of the arrangement, frankly owns that it has failed. "Although," says he, "I proposed the measure, I should be uncandid if I did not fairly acknowledge, that experience has proved it to be inadequate to the purposes for which it was intended*."

The Directors, in the First Report, say, "Nevertheless, after making these proper distinctions, your Committee are *ready to allow, that much uncertainty, in the times of arrivals and departures of ships, and in respect to procuring freight on them, with long deten-*

* Letter to the Chairman, April 2, 1800.

tion and circuitous routes, may naturally and justly be a ground of objection with individuals, who are required to depend on them for freight*."

But the admission, in the preceding Reports, that a remedy was necessary, appears abandoned in the THIRD Report. The whole private trade is there reprobated as mischievous, and treated as an invasion of the Company's monopoly. There is not a single passage which allows it to be deserving of any encouragement. Indeed, the persons employed in it are treated with a licentiousness of invective, which could hardly have been expected in a document signed by eight Directors of the East India Company. The Directors, and particularly the authors of this libellous Report, consider it as the most intolerable presumption in any British subjects to desire to have the opportunity of employing their industry and their capital in the India trade; in which, be it remembered, all foreigners in amity with us are freely permitted to engage. The private traders are represented as guilty of something little short of rebellion and treason, because they presume to solicit permission to do that which the Company cannot and will not do. In this Report, indeed, such decisive and universal hostility to the private trade and private traders is avowed, that nothing could be looked for, but that the latter should in every way be thwarted and opposed.

The Directors say, " they have too much reason to fear, that the *exclusive trade, as regulated by the Act of 1793, is not only necessary, but indispensable*, as a resource to save the *Company from destruction*."

From what has been already stated however, on the evidence of

* First Report on Private Trade.

their own accounts, it is demonstrated, that the more the Company trade on their present system, the more rapidly will their Indian debt accumulate, the faster will their ruin advance*.

It cannot be denied, that the Act of 1793 was intended as a facility to private trade; and the spirit of that Act requires, that the facility should be provided, though the letter of the law has been found not to accomplish its intention. The Act of 1793 appears to limit the amount of the Company's investments to one million, for such is the appropriation of a supposed surplus of tribute directed to be so applied: For want of such surplus, however, the Company is obliged to borrow; hence, as we have seen, their large India debt.

Now, then, it is manifest, that there is a quantity of Indian produce, which the Company's capital, on this scale, would not have embraced. The Directors say, in the Third Report, that it is better that such surplus produce should be taken up by foreigners, by the Americans, than be brought to the port of London. One of their reasons for this avowedly is, that the private traders intercept the funds of British individuals in India, which otherwise would come into their treasury, and supply the means of their investments.

The Report says, that " the British merchants residing in India are competitors for those funds, which would otherwise flow into their treasuries, to enable the Company to purchase their own investment." In a very few paragraphs after, it is stated, that " *the private trade already exceeds the extent of the Indian capital,*" and that a very considerable " British capital enters into the trade."

It has already been shown, that there can no inconvenience arise

* See antea.

from the employment of British capital in the trade. If such British capital were employed, must it not answer all those good purposes which the Directors think would flow from the encouragement of the *bona fide* trade of foreigners with British India?

It is proper now to take notice of the complaint of the Directors, that the private traders intercept their funds, and reduce them to the necessity of borrowing money with which to lay in their investments.

'It is indisputable that, ever since the year 1802, the Company have acted on the principles of the Third Report, throwing every obstacle in the way of the private trade. Have they by this conduct obtained any facilities for laying in their investments? or, by suppressing the private trade, have they increased their own?

The fact, on the contrary, is, that the foreign trade with India, particularly that of the Americans, has continued to increase rapidly. If there be any funds arising from private fortunes, to be invested in any shape, they either go into the Company's Indian paper, or they are tempted into the American service. But, be this as it may, the very effects which the Company complained of, from the competition of the private traders, meet them in the trade of foreigners. By the encouragement of the latter, the trade is carried to foreign channels.— This is all the difference.

It is perfectly well known, that at all times a considerable portion of illicit trade was carried on, with the funds of British individuals, in foreign bottoms. That trade is no longer illicit. The act of 1793 completely legalizes it. The Americans and other foreigners, therefore, have derived all the benefit from that Act. The British residents in India may lawfully be the agents of foreigners. The consequence, under the present system, is obvious. Those British residents would prefer English connections. They would prefer sending their goods to the British market: *but that* is rendered impossible by the Company. They naturally, therefore, must be driven into the connection of the Americans, who can carry on the trade much more advantageously. The sole effect, therefore, of the repeal of the prohibitory regulations against illicit trade, enacted in so many laws*, has been to shut the trade against Great Britain, and to open it to foreigners. Is it to be endured, however, that foreigners should have the advantage of a free, open, lucrative commerce with British territories, in which native British merchants dare not engage, in order to bring it to the ports of their native country?

When the Americans first entered into this trade, they were supported by British capital or credit; and the houses in London that gave them the credit, and which now give it to them, are perfectly well known. The Americans, indeed, have now raised a large capital out of their profits. They take out silver for part of their investments; but a very large share of the commerce they carry on is supported by bills on London; which, after getting their cargoes upon them, from the quickness of their operations, they are able to discharge from the proceeds before the bills fall due.

Indeed, the share which the Americans have obtained in the trade, is an evil which is growing daily, and it has risen through the impolicy of the government, and the Company cherishing this foreigner at the expence of Englishmen. But they will one day repent this unnatural turn of their affections. Mad Tom would teach us better:—

> The hedge-sparrow fed the cuckoo so long,
> That she had her head bit off by her young.

* See antea.

Our present system of India trade has nourished a rival which threatens to destroy it.

The number of American ships which entered the port of Calcutta alone, in the year 1800-1, was twenty-six; in 1802-3, thirty-two; in 1803-4, twenty-seven; in 1804-5, twenty-nine; together with ten Portugueze, two Danish, and one Swede. The number in 1805-6 shows an increase, and it is to be observed, that the American ships, which at first were small, have now become much larger; and that the increase of tonnage is much greater than the number of ships. This is evident from the increased tonnage entered in the port of Calcutta, which in the year 1801-2, was 493 vessels, and 104,870 tons; and in the year 1804-5, it was 581 vessels, and 147,176 tons. During these years the trade of the Company has declined according to the unquestionable evidence of their sales. It is clear, therefore, that the foreign trade with British India has increased, while our own has fallen off.

Is it possible, then, to conceive any thing more deliberately foolish and absurd, than for a nation to undertake the government and defence of a distant Empire; the commerce of which (and that is the only thing those territories have *yet* afforded) it thus gives, not merely by negligence, but by absolute choice, to other nations? Among the follies of states, fighting for commerce has been one; but this is the first instance of a government absolutely restraining its own subjects from that commerce which it freely indulges to others!

The people of this country, we suspect, however, will entertain different notions of the policy of encouraging foreigners in a trade which it is in our power to bring to the ports of England.

Is it proposed, then, to exclude foreigners from all share in the commerce of India? By no means. All that, with respect to this, and for the present, is required, is that the subjects of this country should be enabled to carry on that trade which the Company do not carry on, and which their capital cannot embrace.

The loss already sustained by the Company is very great. In the following years the amount of their India and China sales stands thus :—

    1799............£8,345,673
    1800............ 7,359,676
    1801............ 7,595,181
    1802............ 6,626,347
    1803............ 6,042,526
    1804............ 5,866,075
    1805............ 5,267,578

Thus it appears, that the sales of 1805 fall more than three millions below those of 1799-1800.

The following account of the sales of the Company's piece goods, for the years mentioned in it, will prove, that not merely the amount, but the profit has declined.

85

AN ACCOUNT of the PRIME COST and SALE PRODUCE of the following Descriptions of COMPANY'S GOODS, sold at their Sales, from 1800 to 1806, with the Rate per Cent. of such Sale Produce upon the Prime Cost.

March and Sept. Sales.	BENGAL PIECE GOODS.			COAST PIECE GOODS.			SURAT PIECE GOODS.			SUGAR.		
	Prime Cost.	Sale Produce.	Rate per Cent. of Sale Produce on Prime Cost.	Prime Cost.	Sale Produce.	Rate per Cent. of Sale Produce on Prime Cost.	Prime Cost.	Sale Produce.	Rate per Cent. of Sale Produce on Prime Cost.	Prime Cost.	Sale Produce.	Rate per Cent. of Sale Produce on Prime Cost.
	£	£	£ s. d.	£	£	£ s. d.	£	£	£ s. d.	£	£	£ s. d.
1800	729,770	1,406,879	192 15 8	303,040	963,706	191 11 6	153,713	205,283	133 10 11	120,456	246,569	204 13 11
1801	596,390	1,179,417	197 15 3	367,396	751,722	204 12 2	13,940	11,751	84 5 11	60,824	147,191	241 19 11
1802	348,110	660,019	189 8 8	217,408	516,041	186 0 5	143,662	184,436	128 7 8	54,508	102,151	186 14 4
1803	340,160	672,031	152 13 7	222,326	419,901	188 17 5	100,760	91,219	90 10 7	40,274	56,879	141 4 7
1804	290,370	438,961	151 3 6	299,172	449,731	150 6 6	20,535	14,679	71 9 8	98,014	208,059	212 5 5
1805	424,920	620,454	145 0 3	390,256	529,315	135 12 6	66,350	84,617	127 10 7	137,416	294,704	214 9 3
1806	373,850	499,714	133 13 4	165,000	184,693	111 18 8	87,537	92,735	105 18 9	82,842	144,506	174 8 8

The following will give us a view of the private trade:—

SALE AMOUNT of PRIVATE GOODS of the following Descriptions, in the Years 1800 to 1806, both inclusive.

	PIECE GOODS.		INDIGO.	COTTON WOOL.	SUGAR.	COFFEE.	DRUGS.
	Bengal.	Coast.					
March and September Sales 1800	£ 234,157	£ 51,616	£ 772,357	£ 103,025	£ 239,450	£ 3,343	£ 258,348
1801	374,795	56,993	805,174	142,480	43,383	153,632	224,739
1802	957,673	112,569	878,575	187,350	42,251	36,189	336,808
1803	901,831	163,421	771,137	67,073	45,195	12,950	206,302
1804	568,081	285,823	1,081,140	117,572	65,391	9,071	56,625
1805	467,838	304,679	1,392,858	23,045		6,020	220,997
1806	150,761	47,714	774,388	141,446		4,730	94,195

Total of Bengal Piece Goods. 3,655,149
———— Coast ditto. 1,022,815
———— Indigo. 6,475,629
———— Cotton Wool. 1,081,991
———— Sugar. 435,970
———— Coffee. 225,935
———— Drugs. 1,398,014

—————Grand Total £14,295,533

These documents are important in another view: they show, that in proportion as the private trade has been restricted, that of the Company has suffered, and it is not therefore the success of the British private trade that hurts the Company, but the undue share the Americans have obtained in the India trade, by which the latter now supply our West India colonies with coarse piece goods, and the greatest part of Europe with the different products of India.

In the year 1799—1800, the amount of the Company's sale was 7,359,676*l*. The amount of private trade that year was, 2,336,980*l*. In the year 1801-2 the Company's was 6,626,347*l*. The private trade 2,304,725*l*. In the year 1803* there was a falling off in the Company's sale, below the amount of the preceding year, by 170,000*l*. and in the amount of private trade of 970119*l*. In the year 1804-5, the Company's sales were less by 609,991*l*.; the private trade, however, was more than the preceding year by 229,115*l*.

We see here that the private trade, after having, by the discouragement of the Company's regulations, expressed so clearly in their manifesto of 1802 sunk from 2,304,728*l*. which it was in the year 1801-2, down to somewhat more than 1,300,000*l*. got up again by 200,000*l*. or more; but it has since declined still further, as the preceding accounts show.

Let any man, however, look over these statements, or the more extended papers to which the reader is referred, and he must then see how much the trade of the Company, particularly in respect to India, has fallen off since 1801-2. It is above three millions value a year; and at the same time that of the private trade has declined a million. In all

---

* See the Budget in the Asiatic Annual Register for 1804. In the statements of the Accounts of the Company, and in the India Budget, there are trifling differences in the figures, probably errors of the press, or transcribers.

four millions of trade is lost to Great Britain. Government loses the duties, individuals the profit, and industry the encouragement, afforded by transactions to so large an amount. The reason is quite simple and obvious.

While encouragement was given towards bringing the trade of India to the market of England, the states on the continent used to trust for their supply to England. The merchants of Germany used to visit this country at the time of the India sales, as they still do their own great established fairs of Frankfort, Leipsic, &c. Such fairs are not now known in England; but on the continent they were, and still, in part are, the great marts of exchange for all commodities. But, on coming to buy India goods, they bought many of our own manufactures. They acquired a taste for our produce, and discovered its fitness to supply their own wants. All this we have forfeited. The Americans, with their usual assiduity and good fortune, getting into the channel, have been labouring hard to secure the market of the continent. By degrees their efforts have succeeded.

It is said, however, that the war has shut the markets of the continent. This may be true to some extent, but it is not the cause of the falling off of the Company's trade; and, be it observed, that the falling off is solely in articles of the India trade; for the China trade has its consumption chiefly in the British dominions, and is not so greatly affected by the war. But, during the year of the greatest sales of the Company, the years of 1799, 1800, we were at war, and with Bonaparte; and the interruption to our commerce, particularly in the subsequent year, existed in the north of Europe to their full extent. What, then, has caused the vast falling off? Evidently the supply of the Americans, who have got into the trade, certainly not for their own consumption, but as the carriers and suppliers of Europe. By this supply the British market for India articles is anticipated, and all the commercial advantages we now might have from our Indian empire are sacrificed.

The exclusive supply of ourselves with tea, indeed, remains to the Company, and with this, were they allowed, the Americans would supply us much cheaper; and they will supply us in time of peace, whether they are allowed or not.

It is easy to see, therefore, the loss the nation sustains by the competition we have enabled the Americans to make against us in the foreign market. Indeed, we must completely sacrifice the commerce of India, distinct from that of China, if the present system is allowed to continue. The Company, as their own accounts show, lose by it, and they must lose; but individuals would gain if they had fair play.

In November, 1801, Sir William Pulteney, a person as free from party spirit, from fanciful theory, from the delusions of false representations, as any man ever was, made a motion in the House of Commons respecting the private trade.

It is not unimportant to advert to the character of the mover, because it is a pledge for the sobriety of the motion. To those who knew the man, his character must in a matter of this sort carry great authority. Sir William Pulteney was a person of a mind turned to political disquisition, and fitted to comprehend the most abstruse theories; which, however, he had the patience to verify by the most minute practical investigation. Capable, therefore, of estimating the value of theories, he was peculiarly qualified to sift them, and to separate the plausible from the real. His judgment was never misled by his passions, nor did his opinion ever precede inquiry. To find such a man make a motion in parliament in favour of the private trade, is of itself a proof that there was nothing factious, nothing showy and unsubstantial, nothing delusive, in the proposition.

The question he wished to have examined was not decided; for it was the fashion of that day to decide nothing, and a vain and nominal promise was offered. There was no security for the execution of the compact, had it been favourable to the oppressed party, which it was not. But, in consequence of the complaints against the Company, something was to be done, and the ministry stepped forward to give redress. No effectual security, however, was provided for the execution of the arrangement, and the private traders got nothing by their complaint but the renewal of their ill usage, and the abusive scurrility of the THIRD REPORT.

What the private traders have chiefly contended for, is the liberty of sending home their goods in India built ships.

Their application for that object was entirely approved by Mr. Dundas, by Lord Wellesley, nay by all the governors who have presided over the Company's affairs in India; and Lord Wellesley has more than once been compelled to allow ships to be taken up in India, to answer the pressing exigencies of commerce.

The Court of Directors, however, have shown a most decided hostility to this measure, although they have been obliged, on some occasions, to suffer India built ships to be taken up for bringing home cargoes. The want of a proper mode of conveyance for the trade being notorious, (for that it cannot be carried on in the Company's ships, on the same system with *their* trade, is demonstrated) it is matter of astonishment that the Directors did not perceive, that it was for the interest of their own monopoly to allow that mode to be pursued. It retained the private merchants in the most complete dependence on the Company, and gave them an additional interest in its continuance.

The Directors contended, however, that to admit such ships would be to injure the rights of British built vessels; and that, if a new class of ships was to be introduced into the trade, British ships should be preferred.

With me, this dispute about India built ships or British built ships is of no importance, except in as far as the trade may be carried on cheaper in the one way than the other. Facility and cheapness of conveyance are circumstances the most essential to commerce; but the thing carried must always be the principal object; the vehicle is only the second. The carriage in every view is a charge upon the commodity. It ought, therefore, to be as cheap as possible, unless the end is to be sacrificed to the means. The merchant, who sends goods between Manchester and London by the waggon, can consider nothing but the expence; and if there is a cheaper conveyance than the waggon, he will avail himself of it. The carriage enhances the price of his goods; and if he is compelled, in deference either to the proprietors of a waggon or a canal, to use the vehicle of the one which is dearest, he is taxed, or rather the public is taxed, for the advantage of such waggon or canal proprietor. In general, water carriage is for cheapness preferred to land carriage; and the cheaper water carriage is preferred to the dearer. The protection of the carrying trade, if by such protection is meant that commodities, by a particular mode of carriage, are to be raised in price, is, in effect, laying a tax on one class of the community, to the benefit of the other. It discourages the manufacture or production of the thing carried; and it condemns the consumer to pay, in the price of the article, for the unnecessary expence of its carriage. The shipping trade of this country has, by the Act of Navigation, a monopoly, to the manifest prejudice of the labour and industry of Great Britain. Probably that law is politic and wise; but unless British ships carry cheaper than other ships, the law imposes a real tax on the grower and consumer of all commodities liable to be so carried.

It was for the purpose of exciting jealousies in the minds of a most jealous and irritable class of men, the British ship owners, that the Directors threw in this hint about British built vessels.

But whether the ship owners of this country would have any right to complain of East India built ships being introduced into the India, or any other trade, may very well be doubted. East India ships, built by British merchants, are in no sense foreign ships. Where is the law that deprives them of the privileges which ships built in all British settlements and colonies possess? Nothing but the omission of a clause in Lord Hawkesbury's Act, with respect to certificate of registery, can have raised any doubt on the subject. The dominions in India belong to the crown of Great Britain. British merchants, there, never cease to be the King's subjects; and upon what pretence, therefore, India should be excluded from a benefit which all other colonies and settlements possess, is perfectly incomprehensible.

When the North American colonies belonged to this country, it is well known that the building of ships for sale was a considerable branch of industry in that country. The ships were brought to England and sold. In fact, it appears, from Mr. Chalmer's *Political Estimate*, that, in the year 1775, the quantity of American built ships and tonnage in the trade of this country was 1,334 ships, and 225,489 tons. It was never considered prejudicial to our interests, that we were enabled, by cheapness of ships, to carry our produce cheaper. On the contrary, nothing more contributes to encourage the industry, and to increase the wealth, of a country.

It might perhaps be maintained, beyond contradiction, that it would be for the interest of this country to encourage the building of ships in India, if by that means we could be enabled, through the cheapness of the vehicle, to diminish the price of the articles carried. In carrying more under the British flag, we should extend the nursery for British seamen, which the monopoly of British built ships at a dear rate evidently tends to destroy. In regard to saving our native oak, (with respect to a scarcity of which much apprehension has been entertained) perhaps the measure would be wise, particularly since the loss of supply in American built ships has compelled us to consume our oak so much the more largely. This is a question not absolutely necessary to be discussed here; but it is of great importance. It is worthy of remark, however, that, in 1772, such was the alarm respecting the consumption of timber, (though the resources of American built ships then existed) that the Company was by law* prohibited from building more ships in England, though they were permitted to *build* in *India* or the colonies, or to hire ships built there. It is very strange, then, to hear them exclaim against the employment of East India built ships, as a dangerous *innovation*.

Certain it is, that the introduction of East India built ships would cause no loss whatever to the ship-builders of this country, because for this particular trade not a single ton would be built the more *here*, by continuing to drive the trade of India into American and other foreign channels. On the contrary, every Indian ship that comes here furnishes employment to our shipwrights, which they would not have had. In one of the years, in which the East India built ships brought cargoes to London, the outlay in repairs, &c. was above 200,000*l*. the profit on which was all so much gain to that class of men.

If then the East India built ships can be employed cheaply, there is no reason whatever why they should not be employed. The Directors contend they neither can be built nor employed so cheap as British built ships. The merchants say they can; and, in a matter which concerns their own immediate interest, the latter will probably be considered the best judges.

It is to be remembered, too, that there may be a considerable recommendation to the employment of India built ships, from the very na-

* 12 Geo. III. cap. 54.

ture of the trade. India is admitted to be the great exporting country, and the quantities of the commodities it is capable of sending must depend upon circumstances which the merchant resident in India must best understand. If he find that he can lay in a cargo of cotton at Bombay, or a mixed cargo at Madras or Calcutta, advantageously, he will do it. The inconvenience of sending to Great Britain for a vehicle on which to export the commodity, must be perceived by every person; nor is it easy to see what pretence there can be for depressing, by such discouragements, the industry and produce of our own territories in the East, and the enterprise of British subjects who are there settled.

The objection to sending out ships taken up here to India is obvious, and has been satisfactorily proved by the agents, in their observations on the Eleven Propositions of the Directors*, in the beginning of 1802. They show clearly that the tonnage sent out may either be redundant or insufficient: they show that, in order to prosper, the private traders must be permitted to send out their ships at any time they judge convenient, and that they ought not to be confined to the fixed and determined seasons, to which the Company confine themselves. A proposal more reasonable cannot be conceived. The idea of the Company condemning others to the absurd system they pursue is monstrous. No fair and legitimate trade can live under such a system.

The merchants complain, too, that the Company endeavour to restrict and limit them as to the assortment of their own cargoes in India—a regulation which, on the face of it, shows that it can be made with no other view than to harass. What merchant is unacquainted with the importance of arranging and laying in his cargo? Surely, of all things on earth, a merchant may be safely indulged with this liberty, especially if he and his friends undertake to load the whole ship

---

* See the printed Papers.

on which their goods are to be carried. But it was the Company's purpose every way to embarrass and to create delay. Nothing can be better calculated to defeat the best concerted commercial plans, than uncertainty as to the ship on which goods are sent, the time of sailing, the making insurance incident to that system, which indeed was presented by the Directors as a boon and as an indulgence.

The same principles of objection apply to all the proposals of the Directors, either for building British ships, or hiring for eight voyages India built ships, on an inferior scale of equipment. The Directors persist in exposing the merchants using those ships to all the inconveniencies of protracted voyages, of deviations, of irregularity and uncertainty in arrivals and departure, and indeed of every thing necessary to enable a merchant to trade, or authorize him to decide whether, in all the circumstances of the case, he ought to trade at all[*].

In a word, the whole efforts of the Company are employed to manacle and fetter the private merchant, and to compel him to trade under all the inconveniencies to which their mode of business is subject.

It is not true that the private traders particularly preferred the East India built, provided that, in the extra ships supplied by the Company, they were to have the same command over the vessel and her operations which every merchant secures by his *charter party* with the owner of a ship, and that direction, as to the whole assortment of cargo, which is of the very essence of trade.

But in fact the Directors never have complied with the terms of their own conciliatory proposition of 1801, as it was called. Their second proposition is—

" That the shipping to be thus annually employed shall be wholly

[*] See the Proposals.

applied to the use of the private traders, and *shall neither be destined or detained for any political or warlike services in India, but sail from thence directly for the port of London, at fixed periods, within the fair-weather season.*"

It has been proved how inadequate this system is at the best, and how contrary to the true principles of mercantile adventure. But the merchants of India take issue with the Directors on this point, and deny that this proposal, such as it is, has been faithfully executed.

They now complain that ships provided for the private trade have neither sailed in the proper season, nor arrived at Calcutta at the time when it was possible that they could be dispatched home again in the fair-weather season. In the season of 1806, only two arrived in time; and in the year 1805, it was impossible to dispatch the ships from Calcutta till the month of June and July, by which they were dispersed over the bay, and exposed to every sort of danger. In fact, they had only to choose between the voyage at the bad season, with all its risks, or the immense loss of interest on the cost of goods provided, by postponing the voyage. It is a fact, that several of the extra ships, loaded at Calcutta in May 1806, did not sail from Bengal till September following. The inconveniences of such a system need only be stated: they cannot be exaggerated.

This hostility of the Directors to the private trade, and their encouragement of foreigners, can be ascribed to nothing but the worst spirit of commercial jealousy or malignity, for it is easy to demonstrate that the private trade is a source of great revenue to the Company.

It is well known that the private trade pays a duty of three per cent. on the sale amount. In fact, this is perhaps the only clear source of revenue the Company have, though undoubtedly the whole three per cent. is not gain, nor is the charge considered as exorbitant.

By the accounts laid before Parliament for ten years, up to 1804 inclusive, it appears the Company had received, for charges and profit on private trade, 1,482,056*l.* being nearly 150,000*l.* per annum. But it appears, by the same authority, that, including all the payments out of these commercial sources, the clear surplus in ten years is only 984,781*l.* So that, had it not been for this resource of the private trade (included in the receipt), there would have been a large deficiency instead of a surplus.

So considerable a source of clear gain from the private trade ought to induce the Company to encourage, instead of persecuting it; and when it is known that the merchants only trade in such articles as the Company do not choose to deal in, and particularly when they only trade in piece goods and saltpetre by licence, the hostility is the more extraordinary. The goods brought home by the private trader do not anticipate the Company's market. They are exposed at the Company's sales, and do not interfere with the monopoly of the Company, as to their sales of goods; for the Company's goods anticipate those of the private trade. It has been shown, too, that the years in which both the sales of the Company and of the private trade were the greatest, the trade was most beneficial to both. Since the quantity of the private trade has been greatly diminished, the Company's have fallen off in amount, and still more in profit. In fact, both the Company and the private traders are driven out of the foreign market by the Americans, and the Company, in burdening the private trade with such discouragement, cause a loss to the country of all the customs, and to themselves of a proportion of the three per cent. on all the sales of the private trade. In the year 1805, they lost the whole charges and profit on a million's sale of private goods. Their loss then, whether as warehousemen, or as government imposing a tax or toll, is very considerable.

Such however are the inconveniences arising from the present system, that, provided the Company would allow the private merchants to ship, load, &c. in their own way, as all other merchants do, they would pay *four*, or even *five* per cent. to the Company, on the amount of their sales. If the Company would give up trade altogether, and content themselves with such a duty, paid to them as sovereigns, besides the duties to the state, their affairs would be in a better situation. Had they done so sooner, they would not have loaded themselves with a debt in India of thirty millions, at ruinous interest, contracted in great part to carry on a losing trade.

An objection has been urged to the employing of Lascars in India built ships. But it is notorious that Lascars would only be employed when British sailors could not be obtained. Besides, does not every body know that, in time of war, Danes, Swedes, Germans of every tribe, navigate our ships. What objection, then, can there be to employ Lascars? The Company employ natives of India to fight their battles; can they object to let them be employed to navigate our ships? But, in truth, the objection is too despicable for notice.

The question, however, is so urgent, that it deserves the immediate attention of government. It is different from the great question of laying open the trade at the expiry of the Charter, and ought not to be a moment deferred. In time of peace, the evil will be more dangerous, for the trade, being fixed in the foreign channel, will not only supply foreigners independently of us, but will dispute with us our own supply.

VI. I now proceed, therefore, to consider the share which foreigners now possess, or will acquire, in the trade, restricted to the Company's monopoly, and the consequences of their competition, should that exclusive Company be continued.

The situation in which we stand with regard to our Indian possession, even since the territorial acquisition, renders it extremely necessary to consider what may be the effect of the competition of other nations. We have conquered India by the valour and with the blood of our fellow citizens. It is maintained by the same sacrifices against continual danger; and surely we are entitled to every advantage which, without injury to others, we can derive from it.

The relation, in which Great Britain stands with her possessions in the East Indies, is not that of a mother country with her colonies. The circumstances which led to our territorial acquisitions in Hindustan, the tenure on which some important parts of them were obtained and have been held, oblige us to consider that branch of our empire in a different light. If then the impolicy of our government shall determine to cramp the exertions, and to restrain the enterprise, of its own subjects in favour of a privileged Company, it cannot establish the same exclusion against other nations who have possessed, or have been struggling to obtain, a share in the commerce of the East. Our monopoly, therefore, is wholly against our fellow citizens at home; only in part against our native Indian subjects abroad. Even, since Great Britain and the Company have become real sovereigns, they have not ventured to exclude the other nations of Europe from a participation in the commerce of India. The Directors, in the reports on the subject of the private trade, admit the right of other nations in amity with us to trade to India as unquestionable. Nay, not many years ago, when the trade was laid open to all the subjects of France, a French merchant at Calcutta refused to pay a duty of 4 per cent. demanded in that port, saying, that $2\frac{1}{4}$ was the sum paid under the Nabob of Bengal. The demand was not enforced. The Americans, though unable to plead any use or prescription, have, by Mr. Jay's treaty, been admitted to trade with the British settlements in India. The share then which foreigners can have in the trade of India is, whatever their capital can embrace, and the markets to which they have access require. If they can furnish other nations cheaper than we can, they may engross the supply and the carrying trade for those nations. It is only against British subjects that the monopoly of the Company is established; it is established, therefore, *in favour* of other nations, for it affords them the incalculable advantage of entering into competition, not with the capital, the skill, the enterprise, of British merchants, but with the negligence and prodigality of a joint stock company.

This is a consideration of the greatest importance. There have been times in which the expensive and extravagant absurdity of joint stock companies for carrying on trade might perhaps have been indulged, if not with less injustice, at least with less mischief to the community. They might have been endured, when we had to sustain the competition of joint stock companies as prodigal, as wasteful, as ill qualified for the management of trade, as our own. The circulating stock of folly was so equally distributed, that sometimes the balance was in favour of England, of France, of Holland. The only formidable competition, that of a free trade, and of individual merchants being out of the question, the companies, at home and abroad, might perhaps have been left to rival each other in misconduct. But the case is now very different: America has started in the career, and will carry off the palm from all the competitors for the trade of India, who do not qualify themselves to run the race with her on equal terms. The Americans are not oppressed by the delays, the uncertainty, the extravagance, disorder, and incapacity of a joint stock company. Nourished and supported in the outset by the British capital, which the impolicy of our government and the blindness of the Company forced into their hands, or which the temptation of a lucrative traffick led them to borrow on any terms, they have now created, from their immense profits, a capital adequate to carry on their increasing share of the trade. By the rapidity of their voyages, their skilful observance of times and seasons and markets, in the wise spirit of mercantile economy, they far surpass all their competitors. The East India Company cannot support their rivalship. In time of war, which is represented as favourable to us*, it has been shown that the amount of sales has already sunk below that of 1799—1800, to the extent of four millions sterling. Still further reduction must we expect under the present system. The Americans are driving this country from the supply of the rest of Europe. In time of peace, more certainly they will supply all the markets of the continent with India commodities, unless other nations choose to avail themselves of the same liberty of trade which the Americans enjoy; and unless we avail ourselves of the cheapest mode of carrying on the trade, in order to sustain the competition. Nay, the Americans, or other traders under the protection of foreign flags, will, by means of smuggling from the free ports on the continent, which are already projected, interfere with the supply of our home markets.

The China trade is that on which the Company are supposed to be enabled to support the loss occasioned by their India trade, and the profit of which recompences them for part of their other losses. But it is very important to consider that this branch of their trade is, of all others, the most precarious. It rests upon a close monopoly. The duties levied on their grand staple, teas, are perhaps, during a time of war, necessary and proper, but no government, which the people of this country can endure, will be able, when peace arrives, to protect the Company's monopoly, and the high duties—those two mighty causes of high price. Whole navies would be necessary to collect them, and the duties would be spent in the charges of levying them.

The necessities of the state, and the possibility of levying duties, fre-

---

* In the Third Report, the Directors say, " And as the *Indian* trade to the River Thames must be considerably diminished in the event of peace, whether that reduction falls on the Company or on private individuals, it must operate to lessen the means of employing those British ships that are already in the service."

quently form the only circumstances which regulate their amount. But the possibility of levying them imposes a limit much short perhaps of that at which financial avarice or legislative competence would stop. We may save ourselves the trouble of railing at the obstinate perverseness of mankind, but they will buy cheap, if they can, the articles they want, and they will sell their articles, if they can make a profit on them. Wherever, therefore, duties are so high as to tempt smuggling, smuggling will be carried on. Every one knows the history of the Commutation Act, and its happy effects both to the East India Company and to the revenue. But we are fast approaching to the state in which we shall require commutation acts for almost every commodity sold at the India House, as well as teas.

A free port at Ostend or Flushing would baffle all our custom-house regulations, and put an end to our revenue. Our enemies and our rivals would set up the China and India trade against us, and will do it, as in all *former times*, with British capital. The monopoly of the Company and high duties cannot *both* be maintained; perhaps both must be mitigated and modified. In as far as the monopoly of the Company tends, as it most unquestionably does tend, to render the supply of a commodity dearer than the price at which the article can be furnished by a free trade, in so much the danger of rivalship is increased; and to preserve that monopoly, the government must sacrifice its share of the profit, viz. the duty, in order to give it to a useless, prodigal, and mischievous Company. If a certain duty is to be levied, the cheaper the commodity can be supplied, the greater is the duty government may touch. That cheap supply never can be afforded by the Company.

That the different nations of the continent will endeavour to obtain a share of the India trade, when peace enables them to resume commercial pursuits, cannot be doubted; and, instructed by the example and success of the Americans, they will not embarrass themselves with the expensive incumbrance of joint stock companies. All they have to do is to declare the trade free to their subjects, and to make one or two of their most convenient havens free ports. Suppose Antwerp, or Flushing, or Dunkirk, were declared free ports for India produce, could the East India Company maintain a competition with the spirit, the adventure of a free trade, or could they prevent British capital engaging in such undertakings?

The following remarks upon this subject, from an official publication in 1793, entitled, " Historical View of Plans, &c." already alluded to, are very deserving of attention.

" It is suggested that the 9th Geo. I. which established certain penalties against those concerned in the Ostend East India Company, shall be explained and amended. Though this Company was abolished by a treaty subsequent to that period, the trade has, *of late years, assumed a new and formidable aspect*. It has been a practice with private adventurers in London to purchase old India ships: after giving them a thorough repair, these ships are sent to Ostend, and loaded with goods from Holland, the Austrian Netherlands, and France, with a small quantity of British produce, such as the Company send out, but chiefly with military stores, to be disposed of to the country powers. On a British capital, in this manner, and with a British supra-cargo, though with a nominal foreign captain, and under a foreign flag, the vessels employed in this trade have resorted to India and to China. Such part of their exports as are Dutch, French, or German, as spirits, wines, &c. give advantages in the Indian markets to foreign nations, and check the Company in their sales of the same articles. Did their exports of British produce consist of British woollens, hardware, &c. only, there might be reason for encouraging them; but as they chiefly consist of military and naval stores, to be disposed of among the native powers, allowing these articles to be furnished by Britain, the trade is only calculated to injure the British provinces in the ports in which these nominal foreigners, but really

British subjects, find protection*. Upon the return of the vessel from India or from China, under pretext of touching at Britain, one part of the import cargo is smuggled, and another part has been carried to Ostend, either to be disposed of in Flanders, Germany, and the north of France, or *to be kept in warehouses, to be smuggled; as part of a contraband cargo of European goods, into Britain or Ireland, or to be sent to our American and West India dependencies*†."

Agreeably to these views the Act of 1793 was framed. But has it removed the danger likely to arise from the causes above enumerated? On the contrary, the pernicious system of the Company only affords a bounty to all such adventurers, by giving new advantages to the competition they will set up. What passed between 1714 and 1730, while the Ostend Company existed‡, ought to instruct us what we are to expect in future.

The relation in which the country stands with regard to its eastern possessions, therefore, is of the utmost importance in the present discussion. It deserves the most serious consideration, whether this country can retain the trade at all, if it is still to be committed to the care and to the management of a joint stock monopoly company. It is to be considered, too, that it is not merely the share of the trade of India necessary for our domestic consumption which we have to guard. Some time ago we possessed a very large share of the supply which the rest of Europe requires. That share indeed is daily growing less, thanks to the encouragement given to the Americans, and the discouragement thrown in the way of private traders. But it is well known, and is proved by the custom-house books, that at least three-fourths of the India

---

* " It has of late been a practice with the owners of these ships, to purchase French woollens at Abbeville, and French imitations of the British hardware, for this trade, at a lower price, and of an inferior quality, than they can find them in Britain."

† HISTORICAL VIEW, &c. p. 586.—Since the above was written, the Americans themselves have seized on the last branch of the supply.   ‡ See antea.

imports (exclusive of tea) imported, were re-exported to different parts of the continent. If, then, the mode in which we carry on the trade through the Company is so expensive and so inadequate, we not only endanger the interference of an illicit trade with our home consumption, but we absolutely abandon every foreign market to our competitors. Let any man consider the quantities, not only of piece goods, but indigo and other articles, we used to export, and he will see how great a stake the nation has in the preservation of the trade, both in the mercantile profit and the sources of revenue which it affords. We have long been taught to look at India as a source of vast wealth; we know, at least, that it has been maintained and defended with the national blood and treasure, as a national object. It is fit we should know whether it be a national object or not.

From the view already given of the present state of the trade, and of the private trade, this branch of the subject has been incidentally treated, and requires no further illustration. It is sufficient to have pointed out the circumstances of foreign competition, by which the trade in our hands must be influenced. It is not merely a matter of policy, therefore, but of necessity, to improve our system of India commerce, and to place it on the best footing.

Such, then, is the situation in which the vast stake this nation possesses in the commerce of India is placed, through the misconduct of the Company. It is proved indisputably, that the Company have created an immense debt in India—a debt, the amount of which our ancestors would have been confounded, even as the accumulation of long expensive national wars; but in this instance, contracted for the purpose of a single branch of commerce.

Is this, then, a state of things in which we ought to feel much gratitude for the commercial services of the East India Company? Does the experience of the past, or the prospect of the future, authorize us to renew the Charter, and shut the commerce of India against all other British subjects?

On what pretence, then, could this be done? This leads me to the second branch of this tract, viz. A consideration of the objections against a free and open trade.

The objections against laying open the trade, are both commercial and political. I shall touch upon such as appear to have been most relied upon, though the answer to some may have been already involved in the argument upon other branches of the subject.

I. The commercial objections seem to be; 1st, the connection between the trade and the revenue, and the differences of remitting the tribute: 2ndly, the inability of individuals, for want of capital to carry on the trade with regularity, and the danger therefore of losing the trade altogether: 3dly, the connection of the India and the China trade, and the unfitness of individuals for the latter branch.

II. The political objections seem to be; 1st, the advantage now arising from the union of trade and political power; the danger of an influx of strangers into British India, and consequently of colonization if the trade were laid open; an objection indeed which has been urged also against granting any facilities to the private trade.

III. The objections as to the system of government for India, if the Company were abolished.

I. It is necessary, however, first of all to remark that the present system, that of 1793, was adopted after a variety of plans of administration for India had been proposed and considered. I have already had frequent occasion to quote the official review of these plans, introductory and explanatory of the act of 1793, which professed to be no longer an *experiment*, but a *system* of government and commerce for India. In perusing that work, published for the very purpose of recommending the scheme of 1793, I have, from the facts and reasonings it contains, been led to doubt the policy on which that scheme was founded. I therefore have no hesitation to recommend the book to every intelligent man, as supplying the strongest arguments in favour of the principles I have ventured to urge.

Indeed we have the advantage of comparing the principle and the hopes held out in 1793, with the system and with its effects. Surely then, after what we have seen of the state of the Company's trade, their debt, their government, few will be so bold as maintain that the system, such as it stands, is sufficient to answer all the purposes for which it was intended. If any change be proposed, it cannot be pretended that things are well as they are, and that no change is necessary.

We have seen that, though the plan of 1793 stipulated for the public a participation in the revenues to the amount of 500,000*l.* a year, there has been but one payment (that of the first year) received. We have seen that, instead of a surplus tribute to carry on the trade, the trade has, to a very great extent, been carried on with money borrowed at India interest; and we have seen that foreigners have now obtained that large share of the commerce of India which the Company and private merchants have lost. The whole system has completely failed.

1st, It has been urged that the revenue and the trade are so interwoven, that they ought not to be separated.

If this were true, I should not hesitate to assert, that every effort ought be made to separate them; because it is contrary to the very nature of things that commerce, so blended with public revenue, can be carried on with any regularity, economy, or prudence. The very idea of such an union is contrary to the character of trade on the one hand, and with the objects of political government on the other.

We have seen, however, that in point of fact, the Company's trade has for many years been carried on without any surplus revenue. The example of the past forbids us to believe that things for the future will be very differently managed. A commerce dependent for capital on the revenues of the sovereign, who is also the merchant, cannot thrive as commerce.

Nothing but absolute necessity, then, could justify such a system of trade; and, indeed, its friends disclaim the ordinary character of trade, and plead necessity. It is stated with considerable force, in many parts of the book already alluded to*, that the Company gain nothing by their India trade, and only, if at all, as connected with the China trade; though in neither would the undertaking, on mere mercantile principles, be considered as a profitable employment of capital.

If that view be correct, the Company, then, is considered, not as a merchant, but as an instrument for bringing home a surplus tribute, of which whatever is brought home is gain; though were that tribute a capital employed on mercantile principles, the trade would be a most ruinous one. If there be no surplus tribute, all this argument goes for nothing. When there shall be a surplus tribute in India, who will venture to predict, far more to assure us? The trade of India, therefore, ought not to be calculated on such a baseless fabric. It is a good trade, however, independent of the revenue, and it ought to be cultivated as a *trade*. Government and trade will thus, as they always ought, be kept distinct.

But, supposing there were a surplus revenue to be remitted, what is to hinder its being remitted through the hands of individual merchants? What are the objections?

---

* See page 230, et seq.

The official author, so often quoted, says, "If the surplus tribute had been entrusted to the credit of the private merchant, what security could government have obtained, that the amount would be realized in the treasury of Great Britain ; or what security could individuals have given that they would bring the goods to England, pay the duties to government, or that they would not have carried them to foreign markets, to evade the payment of these duties ? Had the surplus of the revenue been entrusted to such merchants, they would have had it in their power to make their own terms, and might have reduced the value to the public, either by offering a depreciated rate of exchange, or by demanding an unreasonable length of credit*."

Such are the objections on this ground against a free and open trade. I am glad to find them put so clearly, for they admit of the easiest answer.

If the trade of India were free and open, presenting to the merchants of Great Britain a vast field for the employment of their capital and industry, would it be difficult to find men of credit, whose bills upon their correspondents or houses in England it would be so very *unsafe to take?* Is such the character and credit of British merchants? Would there be any difficulty or danger on that head? It will hardly be maintained that there would.

But the merchants (whom this official writer seems to consider capable of every fraud) might take the goods to other markets. Was ever any thing so extravagant as this? What security is there that a West Indiaman shall not carry her cargo to Hamburgh direct, instead of coming to London? Does our custom-house possess no means to prevent such frauds, and to ascertain the delivery of the cargo at the destined port, according to documents given at that where a vessel is loaded?

* Page 241.

Nor would there be any danger of government being cheated as to the rate of exchange. On the supposition of an open trade, the merchants would be numerous, and they would be competitors for the government funds or surplus tribute in India, for which they gave bills. It would be easy for government, therefore, to fix the rate of exchange on terms as advantageous as they ought to be.

Perhaps, however, my readers may think that objections, founded upon the *probability* of a large *surplus tribute* to be remitted to England, need not have been so anxiously refuted!

2ndly, That there is an intimate connection between the Indian trade and the China trade, no one denies, though there is no *necessary* connection between them. The China trade is carried on either with bullion wholly, or with certain kinds of woollens called camlets, and various other British commodities; or with a cargo partly consisting of cotton from Bombay or Calcutta. It is now understood that much less bullion is required; the *Chinese* finding it as advantageous to take commodities, for which their country furnishes a demand. It is considered adviseable to procure as considerable a vent of our home manufactures as possible, and to carry out as little bullion.

If the trade were open, there appears no difficulty in a private merchant performing the business, whether the operation be direct or roundabout, just as well as the Company. It is stated by the Company*, however, in order to deter individuals from engaging in the trade, and to afford a popular argument in their own favour that they (patriotic souls!) export woollens, and merely for the advantage of the *Yorkshire* and *Wiltshire* manufacturers; and that it is more lucrative to carry on the trade with bullion.

* See the Reports in 1792, and the " Historical View, page 530.

There is something very suspicious, if not deceitful, in this kind of appeal to the woollen manufacturers. It is liable, however, to different observations.

Granting that the Company lose on that part of their outward cargo, it does not follow that individuals would lose. The Americans, who deal very largely in the China trade, find it advantageous to carry out camlets and other British manufactures.

In the next place, granting that it is a national object to force the exportation of British manufactures to China, individuals might be obliged to do it in that manner to a certain extent, as well as the Company; and probably they would be indemnified on the rest of the outward or on the home cargo for that loss. If the Company are not so indemnified, the trade is a losing one.

If they are indemnified by putting a higher price on the home cargo for the loss in exporting British manufactures, to what conclusion do we arrive at last, but that in order to sell a particular article in China, every man in England who drinks tea pays so much the higher price for it? That is, in plain words, the nation lays on itself a tax to the amount of a supposed loss, in driving the sale of an article, and then we think ourselves very wise in manufacturing or selling on such terms. We repute the whole sale of the article so forced as clear gain! Such are the absurdities to which the *mercantile* system always leads!

Merchants, however, ought always to be allowed to carry on their trade in the cheapest way they can, and in doing so they will carry it on most benificially for the country. And as to this particular case, we may be assured that private merchants are always anxious to have a profit on the whole of their cargo and the whole of a voyage, instead of trusting to one part of the cargo or voyage only. They will, therefore, be disposed to sell commodities if they can, which the Company undoubtedly feels less *interest* to do. The Company's assertion is either a vain glorious pretension to patriotism, for which there is no ground, or a paltry appeal to vulgar prejudices.

It is further objected that, if individuals were to be allowed to go to China, they would, by their ignorance of the customs of that country, and the mode of carrying on the trade, expose themselves to ruin, and all *those* who speak their language to be driven out of it.

There, doubtless, may be a certain degree of caution and delicacy necessary in the China trade, on account of the singular character of that government, and a very few simple regulations would gain the end. Would there be any difficulty in keeping up a factory at Canton for the trade, under the authority of government, as now under that of the Company, the persons composing it to be paid by a tax *ad valorem* on those who engage in the trade? At present, as has already been stated, the Americans embark to a vast extent in the China trade. They have no factory at Canton, but their business is chiefly transacted by the English Company's agents. Has any inconvenience arisen from the Americans going to China, as individuals wholly unconnected with each other? Could not a British factory then transact the business of British individuals, and the latter carry on that commerce upon the footing of an open trade, as the Americans now do? By this means, Englishmen would have their favourite beverage cheaper, government could levy as high or higher duties, and large commercial profits would be gained by the private merchants.

There is an objection urged by the Company and their advocates on this head so curious, that it is impossible to pass it over unnoticed. In fact, it is a summary of the whole argument in favour of the monopoly, whether of the India or of the China trade.

They repeat, whenever they have an opportunity, the old " *doleful tale*," about the mischiefs of open competition in matters of commerce. Terrified at the idea of a free trade, they assailed the Privy Council, or Board of Trade, in 1792, with the following lamentable story, which appears to have had its weight with the right honourable and intelligent persons who compose that body.

They tell us*, that " when the Company sent each ship under separate management, European goods fell, and those of China rose." In proof of this they add, " The Americans now carry *ginseng* in such quantities that the Chinese allege it has *no virtue*, and refuse to give any price for it."

This illustration is, indeed, worthy of the argument. These grave doctors of the school of commerce are not a bit more scrupulous in administering provocatives than the grave physician that Chaucer and Pope celebrate†: but it is to be suspected, that the argument of these practitioners is not more infallible than their medicine. They surely do not mean seriously to tell us, that because the effete sensuality of their patients has discovered the vanity of provocatives, and found that the quality of ginseng is not aided by its quantity, the eternal laws of commerce are overthrown? Surely it might have occurred to these sage doctors, that ginseng may fail, and the principles of commerce hold true. Nay, on the basis of their own illustration, their conclusion is false.

It is extremely probable that, when a trade is just begun, when the demand for any commodity, therefore, somewhat exceeds the supply; when the channels of supply are not sufficiently replenished by the at-

---

* See the Reports, and Historical View, page 548.

† But first thought fit th' assistance to receive
Which grave physicians scruple not to give, &c. &c.
January and May.

traction and the expectation of regular demand, a very small additional demand will cause a considerable augmentation of price.

This, in the instance of the ships alluded to, was the effect, not of competition, but the want of competition; not of demand, but the want of demand; as is proved by the different result which took place when the full effect of the Company's demand was anticipated, and provision was made for it. The enormous demand for tea has not raised the price at Canton, since the time when a single chest would have supplied all Europe, in proportion to the vast consumption that has arisen. Is not this, even allowing all the absurdities of the Chinese system of managing foreign trade, a most decisive proof that demand, while it procures supply, lessens the price?

The Directors of the East India Company ought to know this. They ought to know, too, that those improvements in the state of the China trade, which they fondly ascribe to their wisdom and good management, are only the natural consequences of that tendency which exists in human affairs, and particularly in mercantile concerns, to come to a level when wants are mutual, and when reciprocal exchanges are beneficial. The worthy Directors in Leadenhall-street take vast credit for making the Chinese buy four or five hundred thousand pounds worth of woollens; and we may believe that the Chinese *mandarins* claim no less merit, for having, by their vast wisdom and boundless dexterity, made the English nation consume, to the value of a million a year (prime cost), of a paltry weed called tea! Such is the nature of man! He ascribes every effect to his own foresight and exertion! " It was prettily devised of Æsop," says Lord Bacon*, " the fly sat upon the axle-tree of the chariot-wheel, and said, ' What a dust do I raise !' " So are there some vain persons, that whatsoever *goeth alone*, or *moveth upon greater*

* Works, vol. i. page 518.

means, *if they have ever so little hand in it, they think it is they that carry it!"*

The China trade has always been the object of competition among all the commercial powers of Europe, and the question is how shall we, as a nation, be best able to maintain our interest in it against that competition. The Swedes had a large share in the China trade, but it was destroyed by the commutation act. Since that time the Americans have been extending their intercourse with China; nor has it ever been found that they suffer any inconvenience from the want of a joint stock company to "*give them lights.*" They can manage their own concerns perfectly well without those establishments, which distinguish the magnificent and aristocratic commerce of our Company. The trade of China must be subject, like all other trades, to fluctuations, and it may experience inconveniences from the jealousy of the Chinese government; but if it is lucrative to a Company, it must be lucrative to individuals, and the freedom of the trade would enable the people of this country to consume at a reasonable price, instead of being wholly at the mercy of a monopoly for their supply; a monopoly which makes them pay, in the price of a favourite article, for so much of the extravagance, waste, and unskilful management of the joint stock company.

3. It is objected also, that individuals do not possess sufficient capital to carry on the trade of India (they include the China trade) with regularity and success; and that, if they failed, the country would lose the trade, and government the duties.

How justly we can expect to retain the trade, if the present system is continued, has already been considered. As to the capital requisite for carrying on the trade, it would be just as reasonable to include the surplus tribute as part of the capital, were the trade open, as if it were to remain in the hands of the Company. But it is not very creditable to build a system on such an assumption.

There exists, however, in this country, capital fully adequate to carry on the trade of India upon the most extended scale. Indeed, it was hardly to be expected that this objection would be urged at this time of day. Such is the facility with which capital can be found for any promising undertaking, that it should be our policy to afford every facility for its employment. The very exuberance of capital is an argument for laying open the trade to India. Are we to be seriously told, as we are so frequently in the official work alluded to, and in the Company's reports, that the merchants of Great Britain, who trade to every part of the globe, who engage in every branch of commerce, are unable, for want of capital or skill, to carry on this?

After having emancipated commerce in every other quarter, and in every other direction, from the pupillage of government, and the restraints of companies and monopolies; must we submit in this alone to those tutors and preceptors who, in every other have proved, not only useless, but mischievous? Are the merchants of Great Britain less rich, less discreet, less capable of procuring credit, or inspiring confidence, than the Americans who now trade so largely and successfully both to India and to China? It is impossible to hear such an objection urged, without feeling a sort of national reflection cast on us by the Company, who declare that our merchants would ruin themselves, that they cannot carry on the trade of India, that the aid of " *their lights,*" their experience, their talents, are necessary to preserve for the nation those branches of trade, the monopoly of which they usurp.

The capital of this country is now so large, the enterprise of its merchants so great, their skill in every branch of commerce so extensive and so complete, that it is universally acknowledged they far excel the individuals of every other country, in their capacities of successful commercial adventure. All the former objections against an open trade, that in the hands of individuals it would be unsteady and irregular and uncertain, are arguments that deserve no attention, for they are contrary to the experience furnished by every other branch of trade. The same arguments might be applied to any branch of trade. They were used in favour of the Plymouth Company, and the London Merchant Adventurers Company, in regard to the trade of the North American colonies. They were employed in favour of the Royal African Company, till it was ruined. They were used in favour of the South Sea Company, which has not sent a ship to sea these fifty years*.

They would even prove too much. What reason is there to suppose that a successful trade will not be prosecuted by individual speculation, when we see capital and industry so promptly seeking new channels? If the trade is lucrative for a company it must be more lucrative for individuals. If it cannot be lucrative for individuals, it should not be followed. If it is lucrative only in a certain medium, that medium will soon be found. All branches of trade have so found their level. They have discovered, without the least assistance and interference of government, the quantity of capital and industry they can support; and no other criterion can be applied.

What is to hinder the British merchant, like the American, to go to India and lay in his investments which he will find provided by his correspondent? Nay, must he not trade with superior advantages in a territory where the resident merchants and agents are his countrymen;

---

* It is impossible not to notice the disgraceful situation in which the government of this country was lately placed, when the South Sea Company started up to complain of an encroachment on their Charter. It seems that, when Buenos Ayres was taken, people forgot it was within the South Sea Company's limits, though I believe the South Sea Whalers have licences from the South Sea House. The consequence was, that all insurances on ships for the Rio Plata were legally void. It might be contended, perhaps, that by *non user* the South Sea Company's Charter was forfeited; but if there can be a doubt on the case, an Act of Parliament should be passed, declaring the South Sea Company's exclusive privilege terminated. Those who have not traded for fifty years, forsooth, to assume the right to hinder their fellow citizens! To be obliged to take a licence from them, is a shameful badge of servitude.

where his credit is known, his correspondences fixed, and every facility of trade pre-arranged? What is to prevent him from taking to Bombay, Madras, and Bengal, his outward cargo; there lay in his investment of cotton, or whatever else is requisite, in addition to his bullion, his camlets, &c. to obtain a cargo of tea at Canton? All the objections against the fitness of individuals to carry on either the India or China trade are visionary and unfounded.

As to the objections of mere detail, such as the difficulty of collecting the duties, if the trade is spread over different ports, though they have been gravely stated, they are too trifling to be anxiously refuted, and they have been in substance anticipated. It certainly has been the policy of some countries, to force their colony trade to one port, for the facility of collection of the duties, or for purposes less intelligible. Such an arrangement is perfectly unjustifiable in any view. It is not extraordinary that it was once adopted by Spain, the country of Europe which has been the most illiberal and unwise in its commercial policy* towards its colonies, and which therefore has derived the least benefit from them. But even Spain has now departed from this absurd regulation. In Holland, while the Company existed, the trade was divided between the ports of Amsterdam, Middleburgh, Delft, Rotterdam, Enkhusen, and Hoorn. Indeed there can no better reason be assigned for giving one part of the country an exclusive privilege, than for giving one set of men an exclusive privilege. The trade should be left to the skill and enterprise of those who choose to engage in it; and, with all deference to London and its celebrated merchants, they ought not to claim so unfair an advantage over those of Liverpool or Bristol, Cork or Glasgow.

As to the collection of duties, the objection is below any government. The same argument might be used for bringing all the trade to one or two ports, as was the case formerly. But surely the vast success of our

---

* Brougham, vol. i. 414.

commerce, so widely diffused in extent, and so happily shared in its enjoyment, ought to secure us against the influence of these narrow views.

It frequently has been urged too, that all the persons the Company employ, would be reduced to beggary, if the channel of trade were changed. But surely, if there is the least truth in the foregoing arguments, all kinds of industry would be promoted by the change; more people would be employed, more duties paid, more wealth accumulated. It is pitiful argument *ad misericordiam*, therefore, to tell us of ruining and beggaring the unfortunate dependents of the Company. The nation will gain greatly; every source of industry, every division of labour, will be invigorated; very few, if any, individuals will suffer; and, in winding up the affairs of the Company, fair and liberal indemnification would be granted to those who had any claim, and, undoubtedly, every engagement of the Company, in provision for past services, &c. would be strictly and punctually fulfilled. This kind of appeal, however, (and it is seriously urged) might be made in favour of those, who thrive by public abuses, who lose by every improvement in the collection of the revenue, who complain of the abridgment of labour, and the economy of retrenchment. If they were to prevail, no improvement could be introduced, because there are some men interested in the abuses, or in the imperfections, which are established.

II. The political objections which have been urged against laying open the trade, demand a diligent and careful examination. It is upon these, after all, that the advocates of the Company are compelled to rest. To defend the Company, as an establishment useful to commerce, is a desperate task. It has been attempted, indeed, whenever the question has been argued on commercial grounds. But at last the friends of the monopoly have taken refuge in a political fitness or necessity.

In the preceding part of this inquiry, it seemed necessary to consider the importance of the trade very much at length, for, in reality, commerce, and not direct revenue, has been the only thing hitherto gained. Great Britain has realized no tribute; and if the commerce of India has not been the advantage derived from our eastern territories, we have gained nothing, except the fortunes which political and military adventurers may have brought home. Commerce, therefore, is a consideration of the utmost importance; for the territory has hitherto only been accessary to the commerce; and a commercial system ought to be established upon a different basis than that of territorial revenue.

Finding, however, that the present system of Indian commerce will not bear a scrutiny on commercial principles, it is alleged, that trade and government are so blended that they cannot be separated, and that the defects of the commercial system must be endured for the sake of the political objects.

It is often alleged that, upon the present footing, the Company's commercial navy is of a kind which, though ruinously expensive for trade, is capable of affording assistance, in case of emergency, to our fleets in the eastern seas, and of being a bulwark to the territories *.

It would not be difficult to show, however, that this scheme of strengthening our defence in India is repugnant to every principle of economy. It would be far cheaper to keep a constant naval force for the defence of the vulnerable points, than to make the commercial navy serve for both. Whenever it happens that the Company's ships are diverted from their commercial purposes, the loss upon cargoes and commercial operations, thus suspended and rendered uncertain, is enor-

* It has been proposed, plausibly enough, to render the Lascars useful in the naval defence of our Indian territories. There can be no objection to teach them our naval tactics, if we venture to teach the Sepoys the European discipline.

mous. In this way commerce is said to be subsidiary to power; but, in realty, commerce is sacrificed, and political power is consulted, by a very expensive and very inefficient expedient.

Suppose, however, that if the trade were open, the ships employed by individuals were to be of inferior equipment, and not so convertible into men of war as the Company's large ships, would not the encouragement given to our commerce and navigation furnish a nursery of seamen that would indemnify the government for keeping up a more regular and powerful naval force for the defence of India? Would not the number of sailors, who could be obtained upon an emergency either at home or abroad, be a resource that would afford government the means of giving the most effectual protection to our commerce and territories in the East? It is ridiculous to argue that any ships meant for commerce ought to be convertible into men of war. Merchant ships should be adapted to their purpose, and to afford the cheapest mode of carriage. It is then that navigation flourishes, that seamen are formed, and thence military navies derive their strength and support.

To build merchant ships therefore, on the speculation that they may be wanted as ships of war, is really to sacrifice the means by which a military navy is created. It is to ruin commerce, without promoting the objects of war. Whenever navigation thrives (and it can only thrive by carrying cheaply), government will easily be able to afford convoys, and to defend foreign settlements. Every thing else is an incongruous mixture of things incompatible.

To increase and improve the commerce of India is, then, to add to our navigation, and to create new means of defending every part of the empire. Petty local considerations ought to give way to large and extended views.

2. It has been urged also, that our ascendency in India, which

depends so much upon the *opinion* of the natives, would be endangered by the influx of adventurers, who would find their way to that country, and by the colonization which would ensue, were the trade laid open. This was not only urged in 1792 by the Company, but it has been repeated in the different reports on the private trade, as an argument against granting individuals any increased facilities for carrying on that trade, particularly in India built ships.

As to the danger of adventurers flocking to India, and endangering the safety of our dominions there, either by embroiling us with the native powers, or in any other way, it is well known that while there existed upon the peninsula sovereign princes, who could boast of any thing like independence, it was considered desirable that English military adventurers should be preferred to those of any other nation, and a considerable number of these has been at different times in the service of Scindia and other powers. In the present circumstances, however, the system is utterly to prohibit any such adventurers being entertained by the native princes.

It does not appear then, that laying open the trade would in any degree facilitate the introduction of such persons into India; for, however introduced, they would not be suffered to engage in any military service but our own. When they did so engage, it is admitted by Lord Wellesley that they had been encouraged to do it*.

But if it were necessary to prevent such a supposed mischief, it might be done by preventing our own traders taking passengers, a thing that would be very easy. Were our own ships, and no others, to visit the ports of India, it would be easy to prevent any persons going there without a licence. While foreign nations have so large a share of the trade it is impossible. At present, any man may get

* Papers respecting war with Mahrattas, *As. An. Reg.* for 1802.

to India on board a Dane or an American: the only check then, at present, exists in India. Laying open the trade would make no difference.

Whether the government in India were exercised through a Governor General, appointed by the Company or by the Crown, any danger on this head might easily be prevented. Whatever useful and necessary powers are vested in the Company's governor and servants, to prevent such a danger, would surely remain vested in the King's government and administration.

If, then, any adventurers were to go out, and attempt to embroil us, either with the native powers, or with our own subjects, they would instantly be amenable to a controul, which they surely would respect and fear fully as much as that of the Company. Were our Indian dominions placed under the power of the crown, and the controuling supremacy of parliament, agreeably to fixed principles applicable to the peculiar state of India, a thousand anomalies would be avoided, which the present incongruous system produces. Numberless inconveniencies, which weaken lawful government, and require a distempered and unnatural violence, would cease. The relation in which the country would stand to the native powers would be more clear and simple. If British adventurers chose now to go to India, and engage in the service of Holkar or Scindia, there is no law of England by which the governor of India can recall them. Lord Wellesley indeed did recall them, but he, as the Company's governor, had no right by law to do it; though the propriety of the invitation to quit the service of those powers no one can doubt. But it is most improper, and of very pernicious example, to delegate this, or any thing which belongs to the regalia of the sovereign, to a Company of merchants and their nominees; and such dangerous absurdities can only be prevented by lodging the authority directly in the crown and its responsible servants. If then any British adventurers chose to enter the service of native powers, they might be recalled by the King's prerogative, which it does not appear that they *legally* can be by any the highest of the Company's servants.

3. But a still greater apprehension of danger is expressed from colonization within the bounds of our own territories, should the trade be laid open, or a greater facility of communication be allowed.

At present it is well known that the Company are bound, by the ninety-sixth clause of the Act of 1793, to licence agents in India, and if they do not the Board of India Commissioners may compel them. It is supposed, however, that if the trade were laid open, an additional number of resident merchants in India would be the consequence, which it is supposed would lead to *colonization*. This point has been so earnestly insisted upon by the Company, in their different Reports, that I am compelled to examine it at some length.

By colonization, the Directors no doubt mean that British subjects will be tempted to go to India as their permanent residence, and adopt it as their country. But if this be their meaning, they seem to apply the term colorization in a manner calculated to mislead. The relation which subsists between Great Britain and India, bears no resemblance whatever, and never can have any, to that of colonies and the mother country, either in ancient or modern times.

The Greek colonies in Asia Minor, Italy, &c. appear to have been migrations, rendered necessary by an overflowing population at home, or sudden occasional sallies of adventurers in pursuit of fortune and conquest. The Roman colonies were settlements of confiscated lands, formed by numerous bands of adventures to ease the excessive population of the city; or they were founded on the spoliation of the peaceable proprietors, whose lands were assigned as the reward of the veteran troops of the republic. They were intended, in the later times of the empire, as a barrier to the state, upon its exposed frontiers.

The colonies of modern times are of a different kind, and owe their origin to different circumstances. They have been the fruits of commercial enterprise, of domestic discontent, of religious fanaticism, or that rage for distant adventure which so eminently distinguished the century that succeeded the discoveries of Columbus. The colonies of every European state on the continent of America, or in the West Indies, were strictly *plantations*, as they are properly termed in our old English, nay, indeed, in the technical language of acts of parliament, and in our official style. They were settlements in waste lands, or in thinly inhabited districts. They were formed, and they have flourished, upon the basis of agriculture; and the colonists became inseparably attached to a new country, not merely by moral habitudes, but by interests which could not be transferred, and establishments which could not be abandoned.

But is there any similitude between these cases and the colonization of India, of which we have heard so much? What is the situation of India? Is it inhabited by tribes of fishers, of hunters, or of shepherds? Is it possessed by savages, who are willing to cede the banks of their rivers for a present of rum, and to sell their forests for beads and toys? Is there any room in India for those agricultural occupations in which the emigrants to America were forced to engage? If such an employment of industry rewards the undertaker with the plenty, the comfort, and independence of rural life, surely it presents little to tempt the impatient avarice of transitory adventurers? Is the establishment of manufactures in Hindustan a pursuit in which the emigrants from Britain are likely to embark?

The apprehension of great numbers of Englishmen fixing their abode in India, so as to approach to the nature of a colony, is visionary and chimerical. India is more likely to resemble the form of a Roman province than a Roman or English colony.

The class of men who quit Britain for India are very different indeed from the settlers of New England or Virginia. They leave their country in general through "that necessity of owing a better fortune to their own exertions," which is the parent of so much useful enterprise. They are not the lowest members of the community. They have generally enjoyed the advantages of education, or at least they have lived in that society in which they have tasted the sweets of opulence or elegance, and to acquire the means of emulating that splendour they have witnessed is their motive in submitting to temporary exile. The desire of making a fortune, to be enjoyed in their own country, is most particularly the object of all our Indian adventurers, military, civil, and commercial. Great indeed must be the change of circumstances, and of opinion, before our youth, the enterprising cadets of respectable or wealthy families, can be induced to forego the prospect of revisiting their native land. Ill success may dissipate their projects of ambition and their dreams of future greatness; but the same ill success would equally defeat their projects of permanent establishment in a new country. A solitary instance indeed may occur, of an adventurer attaining importance which he is unwilling to exchange, or of a merchant who outlives the memory of his early connections; but from such instances (if there be such) can any one deduce the inference, that Hindustan would become the spot where the natives of Great Britain would fix themselves to perpetuate a name, an influence, and an authority? Not only the political or commercial situation of India, but every moral cause, combines to dispel the strange apprehension of colonization.

The state of agriculture, the advanced progress of manufactures, the abounding population of India, leave little or nothing for *plantation* in any sense of the word; but the religion of the natives, their moral character, renders a mixture of the races, beyond what arises from licentious indulgence, highly improbable. A community of sentiment and feeling cannot be expected to unite people of such opposite prejudices, manners, and character, as the natives of England and of Hindustan. No object of ambition or pleasure can present itself to the mind of an Englishman in India equal to those enjoyments he has left behind him, and to which he longs to return. The dull state and insipid magnificence of Calcutta can weigh little, in his estimate of happiness, against the active independence and the real importance of an English gentleman. Little probable is it that even the enervating influence of an Asiatic climate, the blandishments of Eastern luxury, or the easy and inelegant sensuality of Eastern manners, will attract to India, or retain in it, those men who have been taught to value other enjoyments, who have a relish for a higher society in the one sex, and more dignified intercourses with the other, than can be found in the country where they take up a temporary residence. Notwithstanding all the faults, and even crimes, with which Englishmen in India have been charged, their hearts have always been fixed on home. They have never met with that celebrated herb, whose taste made the companions of Ulysses forget their country*.

But from the class of which I am now speaking no colonization ever can take place. Wherever colonies, whether Greek, Roman, or English, have been formed, the common people have been necessarily by far the most numerous class of adventurers. The emigrants to America from Great Britain were of a class the most different which can be imagined from those who subject themselves to a temporary absence in India in pursuit of fortune. The ends, the occupation, the character, the nature of the pursuit, are totally dissimilar. Of the class which Lord Bacon enumerates as proper to found a plantation, there is hardly one that is in the least degree requisite in India,

---

* Των δ' όστις λωτοιο φαγοι μελιηδέα καρπον
Ουκ ετ' απαγγειλαι παλιν ηθελει, ουδε νεεσθαι.

Od. ix. v. 93.

Ulysses was obliged to have recourse to violent measures to prevent these gentlemen from colonization among the Lotophagi. He drove them to their ships much against their will, " κλαιοντας, αναγκη." The Governor General of India claims and exercises the same power to send back to Europe the British *Lotophagi* who wish to settle in that country.

or who is by any accident carried thither. The English who go to the East Indies, carry with them few of the inferior ranks but domestic servants, and comparatively few of these. Sailors are not a race of men likely to establish themselves on the coasts of the peninsula. How then is the colonization to take place? The very idea is repugnant to all experience, and to the fixed order in which the human species is diffused. The European population in India must be transient and fluctuating. It cannot multiply by the ordinary process by which increase is produced. The habits of the individuals, the circumstances of their situation, the restraints and obstacles which their ambitious and money-making views impose upon them, must ever render the increase of European population in India very slow. The same restraints on marriage exist there as in *old countries*, and in the most refined communities. The facilities to population which *new countries* present are not to be found in India. The British population, therefore, must be kept up by new adventurers from home, in a degree, perhaps, beyond what could be wished, for the solidity and permanent defence of our Eastern empire.

As a proof of the extravagant opinions broached upon this subject, it is sufficient to refer to the three Reports on the private trade, performances that afford the most decisive evidence of the narrow views of the Directors, and their unfitness to govern an empire. There is to be found however, in a speech delivered in the House of Commons last July by a Director, so whimsical a statement of the perils of colonization that I cannot help quoting it. Speaking of the danger likely to arise from encouraging the *private trade*, this enlightened gentleman observes as follows:

" The system would substitute in the Indian trade ships built in India for ships built in England; teak ships for oak; the Lascar, or Indian sailor, for the British tar; and the Ganges for the Thames. The home of his (the Indian agent's) trade, is India; and it would soon make India the house of thousands of artificers, agents, and adventurers of all descriptions. At every outpost and subordinate factory, there would be an European public, and in the space of sixty or seventy years the number of Europeans in India would exceed *the number of British Americans in North America, when that country declared its independence.*"

This is a specimen of what may be called *John Bull* logic, which rivals any thing ever produced of the same kind. The worthy Director (Mr. Hudleston) seems very little acquainted indeed with the principles and the progress of population. It is well known, that in the places he has mentioned, the population is kept up and increased by emigrants from other quarters, and not so much from their independent resources. It is in the agricultural districts of new countries where population rapidly increases. Dr. Franklin, a very profound and cautious observer, estimates, in his Thoughts on Population, afterwards incorporated in the Quebec pamphlet, that not above 80,000 persons, up to that time (1751), had emigrated to the American states from Great Britain. Allowing that the statement errs on the side of diminution, still it is an approximation to the truth. The population of the American provinces grew out of their own resources, stimulated by the demand for hands occasioned by their agricultural advantages. Every thing in that *new country* contributed to the utmost vigour and developement of the principle of population.

But in Hindustan every thing is hostile to it, at least to Europeans. All the facilities to British settlers in India, which the nature of things could afford, probably would not produce 70,000 in the seventy years, which are to give us *three millions*. The line of employment, the low rate of wages, must discourage labourers from Europe, even could they find their way and pay their passage. Besides, artificers are not a class on whom population most depends: the number of *agents, brokers, clerks,* &c. must be limited by the employment for them, and never can multiply to a very great extent. Indeed, such persons would go to Calcutta, as an Englishman goes to Bourdeaux, Leghorn, or Cadiz, with a view of returning as soon as he could; and in such a population, transient or fixed, what could there be dangerous?

The dread of colonization, therefore, is wholly chimerical, supposing it were a thing to be dreaded. There is no room in India for that species of adventure to which the colonies of North America owed their origin. Hindustan presents even less temptation to a permanent residence than the West Indies, because the capital in the former is never likely to be of so fixed and so immoveable a kind as that of the West India planter. In any circumstances therefore, even of the most unbounded freedom of intercourse, there can be no danger that Englishmen will ever become the willing permanent inhabitants of our Indian possessions. The spirit of speculation in trade, as well as the hopes of military or civil preferment, will always draw a certain number. But the military and civil adventurers must, under every system of administration, be subject to the inspection and controul of the government; and there seems little danger indeed that, whether they seek other services or our own, they ever can amount to that number, or maintain that connection, which could inspire dread or cause danger to the feeblest government. The extent of mercantile adventure must be limited by its object and its means. If the business should be over-stocked, the rage for emigration will soon cease; and men, who are led by necessity to seek new scenes for the exertion of their industry and talents, are much more likely to prefer other countries to the rich, but full peopled, territories of the East. At any rate, the numerous class, those in whom, if I may so speak, the great force of the principle of population resides, never can direct their views towards India. The expence of the voyage, as well as the little demand for *their* industry and talents, must discourage them from looking to India, as the place where their fortune can be pushed. If the spirit of emigration exist among that class, America is likely, at least for a long time, to be the favourite resort.

Having said so much to show the improbability of the British population in India ever becoming very numerous, it will not be necessary to say a great deal of the dangers which are anticipated from colonization. These seem to be of a very opposite and contradictory nature. Either the European population is to become dangerous to the state, by producing a separation; or our ascendency, which rests upon the *opinion* of the natives, will be brought into question by the vices and degradation of our countrymen.

It is hardly possible that both these events should be realized, and it would be extraordinary if either were to happen. The one seems to be the phantom of a sickly imagination, and presents something in its aspect alarming, did we not know that it is but a phantom. The other might be supposed to be the argument of a schoolboy, illustrating in his theme the effects of climate or of moral causes on the human character.

By those who have studied the history of the world and the principles of human nature, it would not, perhaps, be considered too dogmatic an assertion, that no revolution can ever take place in British India, at all resembling, either in its causes or its principles, the separation of the American provinces from Great Britain. The elements of the two societies are in every respect different. The separation of the American states from this country sprang from a strong and characteristic similarity of temper and feeling between the child and the parent. In both, an invincible hatred to every species of arbitrary power, a love of independence, a detestation of foreign subjection or dependence, have been conspicuous. Admirable features these! But the native spirit of the offspring tended to the family schism which ensued. An authority to tax the colonies was naturally claimed, and as naturally resisted. The *forasfamiliated*, emancipated progeny, disputed the *patria potestas*. The distance of the colonies, and their local interests, made it impossible to govern them as England was governed. They required a separate code; and that was the fiscal code, which, of all species of legislation, touches men most sensibly, and excites the greatest irritation. When that code began to be applied (and it threatened a principle more formidable than the actual application) the source of separation became visible and tangible. The spirit of liberty was deeply laid in all the American provinces, and strongly animated their republican forms. The people felt their own strength. They availed themselves of a series of colonial measures, devised without policy and prosecuted without vigour. The separation ensued, but it was an event which judicious and profound observers had long predicted; and though it might have been postponed, yet it may well be doubted whether it would have been possible long to maintain the ascendency of Great Britain over a country of vast extent, covered by an immense population of men, educated in the principles of liberty, under republican forms of government; men too, whose commercial interests were daily growing into rivalship, if not with the true interest, yet with the inveterate commercial prejudices of the metropolitan state.

But the circumstances which rendered America difficult to govern do not exist in Hindustan. The circumstances which prepared the separation of America are totally inapplicable to the situation of British India. In the latter there is no spirit of republican freedom, impatient of controul or of dependence. The natives are passive so long as their prejudices of mere opinion are not violated. Mere oppression and mal-administration they will endure. The sovereign princes may be impatient of our controul, but that touches upon a question of external rather than internal policy. It is not among the people *governed* then, according to this view, that we have to apprehend a rebellion, but rather among the agents of government that we have to fear a mutiny.

But is this really a terror that can fall upon the mind of a firm and rational man? Perhaps it may be said, that the army itself, the great instrument of government, may mutiny. That dissatisfaction, to an alarming extent, has prevailed among the Company's officers is unquestionable, and the very existence of such a mischief reflects full as much discredit on the sovereign of that army, *the Company*, as upon the persons concerned. In that body, as composing a branch of the British army at large, no such sentiment ever could have existed; for either the cause would not have been furnished, or the prevalence of a common feeling with the army at large, of which they formed a part, or reverence for the authority of a sovereign whom they could not despise, and the sense of danger in the attempt, must have rendered such an occurrence impossible. Perhaps, however, the danger from the instance alluded to was much less than was apprehended. Certain it is, that if the officers, whose notorious correspondences were, as to the form at least, so inconsistent with military discipline and subordination, had proceeded to extremities, they must have perished themselves in the ruin they would have occasioned.

But this incident, though it tends little to exalt our ideas of the respect in which the Company is held as a sovereign, or even of their liberality to their servants, cannot in any degree support the argument, that danger is to be apprehended from colonization. The arrangements it produced have given the Indian officers additional motives to fix their views upon home. They never showed any tendency to fix themselves in India, nor is such a sentiment ever likely to influence them. Grievances, real or supposed, may lead them to complain or cabal, but their manners, their habits, are all averse from permanent settlement in India. Nothing can be more unlikely than that they should be seized with such rebellious views as to attempt an independent empire in Hindustan, nor could their views, if so desperate, be carried into execution, while the King's troops form so large a part of the effective force in our Eastern dominions.

But if such scandalous views could ever be imputed by the Company themselves to the able and meritorious officers of their own army, what probability is there of such an influx of Europeans, or such an increase by population, as to produce either an inclination or an ability to dissolve the connection between England and India? To the British subjects, unless indeed under the controul of the monopoly government, what ground of dissatisfaction could ever be given? If the trade with their native country was free, would the merchants complain? It is now that this class are discontented, and with justice. Would the army be discontented? Would the civil servants of the government be discontented? What elements of discontent or separation could exist? Would the English population increasing, and as natives of that climate degenerating, become hostile to the mother country, and ambitious of the frantic importance of establishing an English empire over Hindustan, independent of Great Britain, under all the dangers both of resistance from the natives and of attack from other European powers? A speculation so purely theoretical, so contrary to any example or tendency of human affairs, never was broached. Countries have been conquered and subjected; India has been overrun by the Mahometans, who, after a successful invasion, established themselves in the conquered territories, like the swarms from the Northern hive in different parts of Europe; conquerors have at various times melted into the mass of the people they have subdued; but the annals of the world present no example of a state of civil government, like that of British India, which by slow advances and gradual usurpation became rebellious as a state towards the parent protecting power, and yet remained perfectly distinct from the people over whom it set up an independent sovereignty. No moral or political causes are likely to produce such a disposition; no increase in the amount of English population is likely to afford either the temptation or the means to such extravagant pretensions; and reduced, indeed, must be the power of Britain, if she could not soon punish the pride and presumption of a few rebellious citizens that should attempt so desperate a design.

A very few words will suffice, with regard to the degradation of the British inhabitants in India, through their increase and their permanent establishment, and the consequent overthrow of that *opinion* on which our power is founded. It has been shown that, though the trade were thrown open, and the most unbounded licence of emigration were allowed, the emigration of the numerous class never could tend to India. It has been shown, that the civil, the military, the commercial adventurers, would continue to have the same disposition, as now, to return home. It is possible indeed that, with the increased facility of commercial speculation, a greater number of individuals would find employment in India, but from the very nature of that employment they would not fix themselves there. The supposition, that idle useless adventurers would go to India, is contrary to all experience. The nature of that country is too well known, to make it probable that any great influx of mere adventurers would take place. In proportion as the means of fair commercial enterprise were afforded, would the respectable part of the English population be more numerous. Mixing among the natives in the pursuit of their commercial objects, what danger could there be that they would expose their inferiority, or dissolve that charm of mysterious awe on which our empire rests?

Perhaps it might be desired that the English population in India were more numerous than it is. Certainly the chain of authority in that country is slender enough. Never was so immense an empire maintained by so small a number of those, by whose agency, and for whose interest, near fifty millions of men are governed. If then the British population, particularly in certain commanding situations, could be increased, it would tend to secure our power against the danger of sudden combinations and unexpected rebellion. In the present circumstances, however, it really appears more difficult to procure than to prevent a considerable and efficient English population being established. Nor, if sufficient provision and encouragement could be given in India for British settlers, would there be any danger (as some apprehend) that it would weaken the mother country by the drain of its population. A proper vent for population, that is, facility of obtaining provision and establishment for children, is the greatest promoter both of a numerous and of a comfortable population, because one of the greatest restraints to marriage which exists in cultivated society is thereby removed.

I am almost ashamed of having wasted so much time upon a point apparently so clear; and the only apology I can offer is, the inveteracy of the prejudices with regard to it which must be encountered. In all the Reports of the Court of Directors, the subject of colonization is treated as the strongest objection, not only to the laying open the connection with India generally, but to the indulgence of allowing the private trade to be carried on in India built ships. If this be indeed the greatest objection, there can be no doubt of the verdict of every impartial man. Never, indeed, was so weak an argument employed on so grave and important a subject.

III. I come now to consider the question of government, and how the laying open the trade would affect the system by which our Indian territories are now administered. It must be agreed by every one that a government for British India must be suited to the character, manners, and prejudices of the natives. That is, whatever shape the political presiding power may assume, no alteration ought to be made in the municipal institutions, no violence offered to the peculiar customs, no change attempted in the religious opinions or establishments of Hindustan. It was thus that the Romans left to the people they conquered the undisturbed enjoyment of their laws and their religion. The executive power was changed, the political relations of the state as a body were altered, but in the institutions, which distinguish different nations, no forcible innovation was attempted. The exterior aspect, not the interior constitution, was changed. If in the progress of time the conquered people came more and more to resemble their conquerors, it was the result of imitation, not of force.

It is thus that in India the British government ought to be modelled. It should leave every thing in the peculiar structure and frame of society as it is. The political character and direction of the state, as a body, or confederation of separate bodies, are to be changed, but nothing more. The Hindu, in private life, in his relations with his neighbours, in the management of his property, in the exercise of religion, should feel no difference but that which results from a more paternal government and a more enlightened administration.

Indeed, in the settlement of the present system these objects have been carefully considered. The judiciary and financial departments have been modelled upon the peculiar customs of the inhabitants. To introduce the laws of this country, or the forms of our free government, is impossible. The only part of the British constitution, from which the people of Hindustan can derive benefit, is the spirit of it, which considers the good of the subject as the end of government; and that responsibility of all authority, which is the security against abuse.

These general principles are so universally admitted, that they require no argument to support them. It never, however, can be wholly superfluous to impress the necessity of adhering to them as essential maxims in the government of India, and to keep in mind that a departure from them, in any instance, ought to be considered as an offence against the state, of the most dangerous nature.

But keeping these objects in view, and enforcing them as far as possible by positive law and precise instructions, there appears no reason to conclude that India would, in any respect, be worse governed if the

Company, as an instrument employed by England for that service, were abolished. It does not appear that any violent change would take place in the government of India, though the Company, or the Directors, as the board at home for directing that government, were to be deprived of all political authority.

The East India Company, viewed in all its relations and all its parts, is certainly one of the most extraordinary institutions that ever existed in any age or nation. We have frequently seen companies possessed of considerable weight and property, but destitute of any direct political authority, far less any sovereign power. The COLLEGIA and *Corpora* of the Roman law are known to our own. They are the models on which modern corporate bodies have been formed. A monopoly of different branches of trade has been often granted by the ignorance or the venality of governments; but like the East India Company nothing was ever seen in human contrivance or politic institution. They have obtained from the King and Parliament of England, not only the monopoly of an immense commerce, but imperial and sovereign powers of the most unbounded extent. Crowns have been bought and sold; but what can be compared with the majestic enterprise of a British Company farming out on leasehold the functions of empire over a territory as large as all Europe, and purchasing a right to dispose of the lives and happiness, the property and industry, of fifty millions of men? A right of government, thus purchased, thus held by a company of merchants in the city of London, far surpasses the wildest vagaries of political speculation.

Nothing surely, in the history of mankind, was ever more extraordinary than the relation in which an empire, at the distance of so many thousand miles from our shores, stands to the superior government, which hires it out for money like a tax or a toll. We are astonished at a band of adventurers daring to farm out from their sovereign the right of exercising the functions of government over fifty millions of their fellow creatures, as a mere speculation of commerce ; managing, and working, and tasking their wretched subjects through all the chain of their graduated servitude, in order to obtain the funds for paying an annuity or dividend to five or six thousand English gentlemen and ladies ! To form an association for such purposes, and divide the gains, as if it were the proceeds of a coal-mine, or a fishery, or a canal, is truly a singular phenomenon. It is either imperial commerce indeed, or it is a perversion of the purposes; a systematic, regulated abuse of the sacred trust and duty of government, beyond the guilt of the most capricious tyranny.

The folly and iniquity of this *locatio-conductio* of empire must strike the mind of every man who possesses either feeling or understanding. It undoubtedly is something for doing which, if there be a legal competence, it implies a moral wrong so to exercise it. The government of our fellow creatures is a trust sacred beyond the most solemn conventions of man. It cannot devolve upon us, or be acquired, without bringing with it a relative obligation and an awful responsibility. We have no right to make a compromise with it, or to neglect the duties attached to the rank of sovereign, either for interest, ambition, or indolence.

If it be true, as many have asserted, that there is no blacker page in the history of England than that of India, our national guilt, perhaps, arises as much from permission as participation. But that is no apology. He who intrusts another with the power to do evil, far more he who sells that privilege, incurs a heavy load of blame, and ought to be answerable for the abuse of the trust he delegates.

Attempts have been made at different times to remedy the evils which India has suffered, from being sold as a job to a company of speculators. Almost from the first acquisition of the territories, the attention of Parliament has been directed to this object; and, after infinite contention, the Regulating Acts of 1784 and 1786, new-cast and amended in the Act of 1793, have made some advances towards a correction of the system. But the mischief is, that the evil is deeply inherent in the nature of the thing. The legislative remedy is practically inefficient. We may acquit the British government of a wish to encourage the misconduct incident to the administration of India. Be it so. But is there any thing in the arrangement, as it now exists, that fulfils either the obligation of duty or the object of humanity?

The system of government for India ought to have two leading objects in view; the protection and happiness of the people governed, and the prosperity and power of the paramount government at home. The system, therefore, should be so framed as to secure both the subjects and the allies of this country in India from the arbitrary exercise of the authority with which the British resident government is invested. It should be so constituted as to secure the direct dependence and the perfect responsibility of India rulers in relation to the supreme controul of the British government.

Perhaps never was a system more incongruous than the present. We have a delegated trust without an adequate security against the abuse. We have established in the East India Company a direct authority to administer, and we have established in a government board a direct power to controul. We have set up jarring authorities which are irreconcileable but through the usurpation of ministeral power, or the corruption of ministerial influence. We enable the Court of Directors to appoint the chief governors of India, and the government retains the power to recall, or, in effect, to annul the appointment. The Directors propose measures, and the Government has the power to alter and to amend. We, therefore, subject the governors of India to two masters; serving only one, perhaps obeying neither. We make the Company the nominal sovereign. We give them authority to instruct and command their servants, but their servants are aware that they have other masters to please, or to obey. By this complicated system, either the Company is nothing, or the Government is nothing, and often both. The persons in authority, at the distance of so many thousand miles, are thus under no controul.

They cannot respect the Court of Directors as masters. How can it be? Can noblemen of high rank, politicians and statesmen, receive, without a feeling of repugnance, commands from men in rank much below them, whose abilities they do not esteem, whose power to censure or punish they cannot dread? What is the consequence? An arbitrary system in India naturally ensues; neither that of the Company which claims the right, nor of the governor who exerts the power, nor of the government that possesses the controul.

The result is, that there is no system whatever dependent either on the constituent or on the lord paramount, or on the established superintending controul, to be found in the history, even the most recent, of our Indian empire. We find wars begun and ended without the least knowledge, concurrence, approbation, or censure of Parliament. This is a monstrous anomaly in our constitution, and may lead to the destruction of its very principles. It may not always be possible to consult Parliament in the wars of India; but it is a most serious consideration that British subjects have, for now these fifty years, undertaken and prosecuted wars without the leave of that controuling body, to which our hereditary sovereign and his most powerful and most popular ministers are subject. We do not know the *fact* of the war; we do not know the cause; we do not know the consequence; we do not know what British blood, what British wealth or honour, are engaged in the quarrel, till it is too late to recede or to remedy.

The late extraordinary transactions in the Carnatic, in Oude, and in other places, have never been investigated. Perhaps the conduct of the British government of India was perfectly justifiable in these instances; but the government at home has never fully, or even formally, examined and passed judgment upon acts apparently very questionable both as to justice and policy. The policy or necessity of the wars with the Mahratta states have never yet been submitted to the decision of parliament. The conduct of the administration of India may have been right; but what I complain of is, that it has been a conduct of mere discretion, subject to no efficient controul or real responsibility. It may have been highly unjustifiable, but whether right or wrong is matter of mere opinion, and no way settled by the judgment of that authority to whose decisions the people of this country are accustomed to submit.

As matters now stand, transactions, national as to their extent and as to their consequences, wars in which the King's troops have been cut off by thousands, and the reputation of the British government has been loudly traduced throughout Europe, and compared to the licentious despotism of Buonaparte, have as yet received neither censure nor confirmation. Whether this be a system which can last, or ought to last, may be submitted to the plain sense and unsophisticated judgment of the people of England.

But it may be said, that the necessity of such political revolutions, and of such revolutionary wars, that to act without or against orders are circumstances incident to the distance of our Indian dominion, and to its situation. This may be questioned. It results from conflicting authority, or from none. Were the governors of India directly commissioned by the government, and responsible to it, they would be compelled to act right at their peril. At present, they act under no superior; they get orders from the Directors which they despise; they know that, between the Board of Controul and the Directors, all unity of power is destroyed. They are not the servants of the King, whom they would not dare to disobey, but of the Company, whom they are ashamed to obey. In the mean time, between the India House and the Board of Controul, it is impossible to decide whether a man acts by the direction of one or the other, or according to the views of the one or the other. The whole system, therefore, is of a complexity which banishes unity of principle and consistency of object. No one knows what is obeyed or disobeyed, where opposite and different masters exist. Obedience is not enforced, when the one master is afraid of giving to the rival master a right of interference, should he insist on his particular mandate. No controul therefore exists, when the executive authority is thus stripped of its power to direct. No responsibility exists for disobedience, when there is no regular command. There is no remedy for abuse of trust, where the administrative superiors are afraid of giving each other an advantage by preferring accusations, and when they are content to murmur but have not courage to correct*. The consequence is, that, without imputing blame to individuals, the system itself leads to disorder, and at last we see charges of malversation made, which only excite contention, without promising amendment; and justice is pursued through channels so impracticable, that thinking men must prefer the impunity of guilt to retribution so obtained.

Indeed, the attempt to correct the evils of a bad system by criminal severity, instead of preventing abuse by a wise regulation, ought to be resisted in every state. It is the worst species of tyranny, and it is of a kind that more than any other tends to injustice; because they who must be conscious that, by their neglect of preventive means, they are accomplices in the mischief that springs from the facility of transgression, are too apt to think that they exculpate themselves by severity of punishment, however irregular, inflicted on those who are accused of malversation.

If such are the pernicious consequences of the present system of

---

* It is very disgusting to see Directors, in the House of Commons, conniving at charges, without the courage to state boldly their complaints or accusations.

governing India, can there be danger in any change? Can any change be for the worse? The only good part in the present system is, that there is an approximation towards putting India under the protection of the British government, and the direct responsibility of its administration and its parliament. But we are as yet far from the unity and simplicity of the executive system. At present there is no sufficient responsibility in law or in opinion for the government of India. It is in every and in the worst sense arbitrary. I do not say that the Directors are not well-meaning respectable individuals, but that they should be honoured as a supreme government is totally impossible. They are not a potent republican assembly to which men must bend: they are not a majestic wise aristocracy that inspires reverence: they are not a monarchy invested with the prejudices and the authority of a long prescription: they cannot be, as to personal qualification and talents, the fit governors of an empire. By reverting then to the simple, direct dependence of the government in India, or the government at home, we destroy those pernicious anomalies that lead to the perversion of the principles of the constitution. We attain that unity which is the perfection of executive power, and that responsibility which is the check of delegated authority. We establish that direct controuling power of parliament which is congenial to the spirit of the British constitution.

It would be easy to illustrate the necessity of a change by striking facts and examples. But it is enough to have hinted at them. Sure it is that every thing would be better conducted in India, for the advantage of those whom Providence has made it our duty to cherish and protect, than under the present anarchical and contradictory code. These things, however, may become the subject of a separate discussion, should the people of this country begin to perceive how their interests and their duties concur in the establishment of the just and wise administration of India.

The machinery for the government of India which the Company employs, and which, it is not denied, is in many respects well contrived and well worked, may, with very little difficulty, be transferred to the government. The inconvenience arising from the transfer would be very inconsiderable, and there would be no derangement or convulsion at all. The civil system of the Company would easily fall under the regular authority of a Governor General, appointed by the Crown, amenable directly to the King's government; and the details of administration would be continued on the same footing as at present, unless some improvements were found to be necessary.

Some difficulty may be supposed likely to arise from transferring the whole military force of the Company to the entire direction of government. But no change of *system*, at least, seems necessary in this branch, more than in the civil and financial departments. The military system of the Company is well contrived, and upon the whole well conducted. The Company have an army, and a good one. It is good, because their officers study their profession; and because it is their profession. No offence to their countrymen in the British army—from these causes, perhaps, the officers of the Indian army are fully as good as any other description of British officers. Continuing the present system of officering and disciplining the Indian army, great advantage would arise from putting the whole under one direction, and opening to the officers of that army the prospect of chief command which, as the servants of the Company, they are now precluded from enjoying. The affairs of the nation would profit by presenting this object of ambition to those who are, as to all personal qualifications, entitled to aspire to it.

It is not to be denied, however, that unless some virtue and some sagacity be exercised, in the appointments, both civil and military, danger might arise from ignorant and improper persons being sent to govern or to command men with whose feelings and character they are totally unacquainted. The late unfortunate event at Vellore ought to be a lesson how command, civil or military, is intrusted to persons who, for objects the most trivial and contemptible, are capable of outraging he most sacred and invincible prejudices of nations. That affair, for the sake of example, demands the most rigorous inquiry. If those engaged in it, do not merit punishment, at least the act should not pass without the most pointed and public reprobation. It is against similar misconduct that we have most to guard; for in India mere folly may prove as mischievous as the most enormous crimes.

Careful provision, therefore, ought to be made (whether indeed the Company be continued or not) to secure a certain period for gaining experience in every department, to persons intrusted with power. This would be some security against the influence of favour, and the choice of unqualified persons.

In the military branch, the existing system, with regard to the native troops, should be maintained; the officers ought to be introduced into the service on the same footing as now; and the most anxious provisions enacted, to prevent the native battalions being officered through improper influence. It has often been thought that a distinct colonial force is desirable for this nation. At present we have an Indian army excellently disciplined and appointed. It must be kept quite distinct from the detail of the other services, or it must fall to pieces as an army, and perhaps with it the empire of India will perish.

This branch, however, appears to be capable of very simple and efficient checks to guard against abuse. I am perfectly sensible of the danger of making India a mere job for patronage, but that is more or less an evil incident to every system. The government may exercise its patronage sometimes indiscreetly, and so, no doubt, may the Directors now. But the abuse must be very vigilantly checked, and powerful preventive remedies enacted, to limit the abuse, and to guard against its greatest dangers. . If it be contended that the government is more prone to abuse in this particular than the Directors, the argument proves too much. It would prove, that even the bad republic of Leadenhall Street is more capable of wisdom, purity, and uprightness, than the British government. No man, therefore, can maintain the Company better qualified to rule India than the government, without passing a most severe condemnation of that constitution which is the boast of this country.

The objection of patronage is often stated in another view, viz. as to its dangerous effects upon the constitution.

Did we consider this objection as well founded, we would say, Perish every thing—let the constitution live! Not that India should be committed to bad government, but that it should be given up and abandoned. If we cannot reconcile our interests and our duties, we must make the proper sacrifice.

The objection, however, of the augmentation of patronage, which the government would acquire if the Company's Charter were suffered to expire, is made by a class of men who, in general, display so little jealousy of the influence of the Crown, that their fears upon this occasion appear somewhat suspicious. Every war, every conquest, must, to a certain degree, augment the patronage of the Crown; but it does not follow that wars must not be undertaken when necessary, or conquests made when they are advantageous. If the government of India would create an influence dangerous to the freedom of the constitution, we ought either to erect some new bulwarks against that danger, or we ought altogether to renounce the benefit that would be purchased at too high a price.

But we apprehend, that it is not in the detail of Indian patronage that the influence of the Crown or of a minister would acquire its principal aggrandizement. The constitution of the East India Company, as it now stands, gives the Crown and the minister an influence, in the gross, much more formidable. The power of conferring favours in the detail, would, to a certain degree, augment the patronage of government, and, consequently, the influence of ministers. But at present, that government must manage very ill indeed which does not obtain some share of India patronage. Examples are needless. I speak of what is notorious and undeniable.

But there is a much more dangerous influence, because, when it exists, it is in the nature of a conspiracy against the public. The East India Company, indeed, receives its *lease* from time to time from the legislature; but the independence which it derives from the certainty of the period is not perfect and entire. The Company are to exercise every part of their power under the legal superintendance and controul of the government. Thus, with a lease for a term of years, they are in a considerable degree tenants at will, and subject to the interference of the landlord. The right of the Company, and the controul of the government, sometimes clash; the parties quarrel, however, like *Peacham* and *Locket* in the Beggars' Opera, but they never come to a rupture, for the same reasons that induced those honest worthy gentlemen to bear with each others humours.

Influence in a more formidable shape than this, and more incompatible in its nature with the principles of a free government, cannot well be conceived. The influence acquired by conferring favours is scattered and dispersed. It probably might not gain many votes in Parliament, and decide very few elections. At any rate, if government had the patronage, the influence it would produce would be over individuals unconnected, in whom the favour or the expectation would cause no permanent indissoluble tie of dependence. But the East India Company are a regular organized body of agency and power, which the ministers may almost always guide, and which hardly dare rebel against them. A corrupt minister, the enemy of his country and its liberties, could desire nothing more useful than such an instrument, as a bad minister would find the greatest facility in employing it. Look at the parliamentary history of the Company, and the conduct of their servants for many years. Do we find the Directors in the House of Commons in the ranks of opposition, or thwarting a minister? On the contrary, do we not hear it laid down as a general principle, that the Company *must not quarrel with Government?* Indeed, this is so clear and obvious, that it requires no particular illustration. The mutual advantage of their good understanding, upon the whole, leads the Company and the Government to *conspire* together, the former for fear of losing their Charter; the latter, in order to secure a powerful body of adherents. A very strong mass of influence in the state is thrown into the ministerial scale, ready to support all measures, good or bad, of those who have power for the day. There is no *delectus personæ* in this prostitution. It is of the most grovelling kind, and in no way does it associate with itself any public spirit, or tend to any national interest. The virtuous minister perhaps has it for his hour; but the most corrupt or the most feeble minister is supported by it to-morrow; and, by his weakness or his crimes, enabled to waste or endanger the commonwealth.

This view of the thing is so evident, to those who are acquainted with the interior history of public affairs, and even to those who may have observed what has passed openly, that they can be at no loss to perceive which is to a minister the most effectual influence; and there is little doubt whatever that this has been the chief cause why the Company has been maintained on its present footing, notwithstanding its gross mismanagement of commercial affairs, and its unfitness for exercising political power.

Besides the danger to the constitution, from so servile an instrument of influence as the Company has shown itself to be, perhaps there might be no inconsiderable danger if it were to become a power in the state hostile to administration. The means which it possesses are very great. It circulates in its commercial operations a great deal of money, and employs a great number of people. It has contracts and jobs to bestow. The whole of this mass is under one direction. Were the trade open, it would be dispersed; and though as to commerce, larger in extent, it would not have the force of concentration. If the Company then were really independent of administration, and were to be animated by a spirit of faction, it would be an *imperium in imperio*, utterly incompatible with all good government. Nothing can prevent this direction of abuse, but the dependence of the Company and their precarious tenure. But suffer the present system to continue, and to acquire an establishment, which it would be very inconvenient or difficult to abolish, merely because it had long existed, and the East India Company would constitute a mass of organized power in the state, perfectly anomalous, and in the highest degree dangerous. Suppose that those, who have large armies in their pay abroad, who have establishments at home, almost as considerable as those of many ancient and powerful monarchies, and consequently could bring their influence to act with united effect, were to turn it against a minister, or perhaps against a king, labouring under a temporary unpopularity; suppose that such a Company were led by fanatics in religion, or in politics, and chose to take a side in questions of state, unconnected with the object of their institution, what danger, what confusion might not arise? Blind must the man be, who does not see the danger; heedless must that government be, which does not provide against it. Some striking illustrations of this might be given, but it is not necessary for the present purpose. It is enough to have laid down such principles, and stated such reasons, as must show, that even the dependence of the Company on the Government is a less evil than their independence. So long as the Company has a precarious dependence upon Government, either for the right under which they enjoy their power, or by the mode in which the Government controuls the exercise of it, so long they must compromise, by being subservient to their masters. They will continue to perform homage, and render service, for the fief which they possess. An able and vigorous government will partly by law, partly by address, retain them in that subjection; but, like the feudal vassals of former times, they may become refractory or rebellious. Unless they were constantly kept in a subordinate state, they would naturally seek to enlarge their authority, and to throw off dependence. They would seek to render their *feud* perpetual. They would endeavour to evade the superiority of the liege lord. They would be seized with that love of independent power, so natural to man, the moment they had secured rights which the government could not withdraw, or which it had not ability or spirit to controul. They would, from a servile tool, become an organized faction. Such a body as the East India Company will either be a tyrant or a slave. What they now are we know. With such constitutional dangers around us, flowing either from the independence or the subjection of the Company, are we to be frightened with the clamours of danger to freedom, if the Company were deprived of their rights, when they will expire at the end of their Charter? We ought to know the men who raise the objection better. They do not speak from affection for our liberties, but from a dread of being stripped of their own usurpations.

Without being deceived by such unfounded clamours, we are called upon to consider, what is the best mode of governing our Indian empire, and drawing from it all the advantages, commercial and political, it is calculated to afford. Whatever men may think of the means by which our dominions in India were obtained, all must agree, that it is now the duty of the British nation to govern that extensive country with justice, with wisdom, with a constant and zealous attention to its interests and prosperity. In an enlarged sense, all government is of divine institution, for the good of mankind; and the abuse or neglect of the power Providence has conferred upon us over any part of the human race, must be exercised under an awful responsibility. We have no right whatever to rule India solely for our own benefit, and neglect that of the men we rule. We have no right to abdicate the sacred trust; far less to let it out for hire to those who are altogether incapable of the high function they undertake. Of those who put the business of government to auction, and those who purchase the lot, it is not difficult to determine which are the most criminal.

If the official administration of this country, under the superintendence and controul of parliament, is not equal to conduct the affairs of India, the world has long been accustomed to pay a compliment to the British constitution which it does not deserve. The organ and intermediary of a monopoly company, it will be admitted, is at least a very singular contrivance to supply either wisdom or integrity. Surely the composition of such an institution promises nothing very superior. The East India Directors, no one denies, are most respectable men; but what qualifications do they possess for the station to which they aspire?

As an intermediate institution between the people governed and the supreme authority which controuls, we see nothing to praise in this contrivance of such a body as the Court of Directors, however modified. By passing through such a medium, authority is weakened and impaired, not moderated and improved. If the Company be an inferior board, to prepare things for the superior power, it is not placed sufficiently in the subordination of an agent. If it is a government acting under controul, it has no independent authority at all. There is no intelligence to originate, nor wisdom to correct, nor vigour to conduct; and in no modification have we any authority fairly responsible. We have neither active independent power, nor timely check, nor adequate punishment.

Every man who remembers past occurrences, or who has travelled through the labyrinth of Indian details, must be acquainted with the constant clamours and complaints of the Company against their servants, who did not obey their orders. The wonder is not that their orders were not obeyed. The wonder would have been, if they had found servants devoted and obedient. Since the bills of 1784, 1786, and 1793, every judicious observer must have perceived farther proofs of the impossibility of a Company in London governing India, and controuling those who by a fiction are called their servants. On the other hand, the Company's interference, while it never has prevented the errors or faults of which they complained, has prevented many excellent measures. Their governors have been too much above them; and the governors they would choose would be infinitely too much below the situation and its functions.

But though the Company, as a government, is not obeyed, and never can be duly obeyed by the governors of India, the case would be very different were a viceroy to act, under the immediate order of the Crown, in direct responsibility to it, and under the consequent controul or censure of parliament, without any concurrent authority, to furnish excuse or pretence for evasion. The King's government is never disobeyed by any of his officers, civil or military. If the system is good, and the choice of the men tolerable, the administration of India will be regular and consistent; but the orders which emanate from the Company, however wise and proper, will never be executed with that deference or that fidelity necessary to ensure success. All weak governments find their servants disposed, as Tacitus observes, rather *interpretari quam exsequi*.

It may be asked, what is to become of the Company and its proprietors, should their lease be terminated at the expiry of their present Charter; are they to be stripped of their property; or, are the proprietors of stock to be robbed of their dividends? This subject has often been discussed, and seems attended with no difficulty. It does not appear at all necessary to say much of the supposed rights of the Company to certain stations and districts in India, even were their Charter abolished. I do not believe they have any such right as they have claimed, nor could such a right be supported by any fiction or analogy of law. The Company, it seems, may exist, and may retain not only the possessions alluded to, but carry on trade on their joint stock, though the trade were laid open. That they might try to carry on the trade, even at a vast loss, merely to ruin private traders, I have no doubt, and in this view only their hostility is to be deprecated. Their fair competition is not to be feared. But that they have any right to retain, and exclusively to enjoy the particular establishments, originally gained under Charters notoriously illegal; that they have a right to shut out their fellow subjects from Calcutta or Madras, as a private gentleman can shut up his private road against the public, very few, I believe, will admit. Such possessions held in India by the Company, are in no degree to be compared to a private estate, either in their nature or tenure *.

But the rights claimed by the Company, it seems now generally admitted, are entirely subject to the wisdom and regulating controul of parliament. At any rate, if, as there can be no doubt will be the case, the Company on winding up their affairs shall be found bankrupt, their possessions must be taken into the hands of Government, which will make a settlement with all those interested, upon the most liberal footing. There will then be no dispute about the rights of the Company, either as to particular districts, or to trade on a joint stock.

The East India Company, as has been already observed, can with no propriety be considered an association of merchants following traffick. In fact, their stock is now entirely a public fund, in which, from habit, people buy without the least consideration, far less knowledge, of the nature of the security for the principal or interest. The proprietors

* See Historical View, p. 284.

are either persons who put their money in this fund, to enjoy the interest quietly, or they are persons who wish to facilitate their particular object of ambition, by having a vote at the India House. All who are candidates at the India House, or who wish to have influence there; all who deal in shipping, or in fitting out of ships, are holders of stock; there are besides some annuitants, and the widows and children in succession of many of the above description of men.

But the India stock has been considered as a fund yielding a certain revenue, nearly in proportion to other public funds. The private views of a considerable number, such as we have mentioned, have perhaps made the price a little better than it would have been, because to them this stock furnishes a collateral advantage, independent of the interest of money. With all this, however, India stock sells lower, or yields a greater interest to the purchaser, than government funds. But, upon the whole, it is pretty nearly on the footing of a public fund. Very few think of commercial gains as the source of the dividends they receive. They have seen the Government tamper so much with the East India Company's concerns, that they look to its responsibility; nor is this contrary to sound sense, and even to law. They have seen Government sharing the gains, or stipulating to share the gains of this Company, propping up its credit, and giving that sort of security for its contracts, which led every man to give it credit, independent of the knowledge or opinion he had of its separate solvency.

People then have considered the India stock a public fund, liable to little other fluctuation than that of the other public stock. When a share in the India stock was considered a share in a profitable adventure of commerce, the variations in the price were enormous; and, in those times, the very existence of a stock, that excited such a passion for gambling speculation, was a nuisance. Every one knows the infinite mischief caused throughout this country by the nefarious arts of joint stock companies holding out this temptation of jobbing to the ignorant and unwary. The fluctuations of India stock partook of those of the South Sea; but at different periods since, India stock has risen and fallen without any adequate reason, merely in consequence of the intrigues and arts of Directors. Fortunately people now consider nothing in this stock but an annuity, which very little participates in the success of mercantile undertakings. If it did so participate, it would cause infinite mischief. It would cause great derangement in general mercantile operations; and would create absurd and senseless speculations, in hopes of a large or small dividend. At present, as no body looks to any thing so chimerical as a great rise in the Company's profits on their trade, or their India warlike adventures, so as to raise the dividends, no mischief ensues. Their fund is a steady stock, and is only harmless while it is so. No proprietor could sustain loss, or suffer injustice in having his stock consolidated with the national funds, and equally secured. Government therefore must necessarily place itself in the situation of the Company, and fulfil its engagements. It may make an allowance for whatever can be called the Company's private property, private establishments, &c. I by no means admit the claims of the Company to some of these things. For instance, I do not admit that they can hold any dominion whatsoever in India, distinct from that which accrues to the Crown by unquestionable prerogative.

In doing this, the Government would only be doing that which its folly in making a partnership with the Company has imposed. The longer that partnership is continued, the larger will be the ultimate loss, and the Government is bound in justice and law to take the responsibility of the Company's engagements. The sooner it is done the better: the nation at large would be a great gainer by the freedom of the trade, and the Government would speedily be reimbursed for any direct engagements on the Company's account by the general prosperity of the country, and the augmentation of the revenue.

On the other hand, Government would then have a direct and immediate interest in the surplus revenues of India, if there be any. The hope of a real beneficial partnership in that fund has been long held out to us. In vain we have looked for it, and from day to day we are amused with the prospect; hitherto it has been " the triumph of hope over experience." The Company never *is*, but always *to be* rich.

Indeed the last act in favour of the Company is very entertaining, from the gravity, one would think ironical, with which these hopes are displayed. The application of the vast profits expected, is provided for by a distribution, which bespeaks a most lively and vigorous imagination. The immense surplus revenues, and accumulating profits of the Company, are to be laid out, first, to reduce the debt in India to two millions; then to pay £500,000 a year to Government; then in reducing the bond debt at home to £1,500,000; then after these operations *one-sixth* of the ultimate surplus is to increase the dividends; the other *five-sixths* to form a guarantee fund for the Company's stock, till it accumulates to *twelve millions*, after which the said five-sixths go to Government.* What a pity that all these wise and provident regulations have never been necessary, and that instead of being reduced to two millions, the India debt has risen to thirty!

Perhaps the reader may have perused the story of Alnaschar, the Persian glassman, as it is pleasantly related in No. 535, of the *Spectator*. Alnaschar was a very idle fellow; but having bought a basket of glass, he made so excellent an *appropriation* of his future profits, in an act of imagination he passed on the subject, that having through enormous wealth, arrived at the honour of being son-in-law to the grand vizier, he most unfortunately was so elated, that in the midst of his reverie, giving the basket a kick, he broke the glass into a thousand pieces, and totally dissipated his fortune, and the splendid vision in which it existed. Government and the East India Company have not been much wiser in their dreams

---

* See the act itself.

of wealth than Alnaschar, the Persian glassman. They have so managed matters, that not one of their fine projects is realized. The public have obtained none of that profit they had stipulated to receive. Their visionary riches have perished, like the brittle fortune of Alnaschar. The act of 1793 remains a monument of the vanity of political calculations; yet this act was the work of men, who deride theorists, and call themselves *practical* politicians.

After so many experiments, by which we have in vain attempted to render India an efficient aid to the government, from which it receives protection and defence; it is time that we should have some substantial indemnification. Hitherto the trade of India has been oppressed, the government has been ill administered, and Great Britain has never enjoyed the benefits stipulated for the sale of an invaluable privilege, and the cession of an immense empire.

There are those indeed, who may think that the trade to India can be laid open, and the government continue lodged in the Company, nearly as at present. That opinion may deserve discussion, if it does not merit an experiment. It is not my business at present to enter into that subject. Perhaps though the reflections I have ventured to make upon the political branch of our Indian system, are brief; they may be thought too tedious for the purpose of this inquiry. My chief object has been to point out the defects and the impolicy of the commercial system. The removal of those restraints under which the trade now labours, seems absolutely necessary to preserve to the state the benefits which it was the original object of our political acquisitions in India to secure.

A considerable period, however, has yet to run, during which the Company will claim the right to misманage the estate committed to them. It might perhaps be maintained, that having by their misconduct defeated the success of every stipulation in favour of the public, they have forfeited their Charter. Sure I am, at least, that they have done much more to justify a resumption of it than the old Company, who in 1698 were declared to have forfeited theirs, by failing in the payment of certain duties. Upon this, however, I do not insist. I do not believe that any minister has virtue and courage enough to take a step so beneficial to the country. If, at the same time, measures be not adopted speedily, to counteract the pernicious effects of the monopoly, the trade of India will be irrevocably lost to Great Britain.

This nation has incurred a vast expence in the conquest and in the defence of its Indian territories and commerce; a large proportion of the British army is employed in India; and in Indian wars British blood has been profusely shed. Hitherto the promised benefits have not been realized; and if the same system is to be maintained, India, instead of being a source of strength, will continue to produce a diversion of the public force. Instead of being a source of revenue, it will be an object of expence, and a cause of national decay.

If then, our Indian empire is capable of yielding those advantages, which have been so often promised, we should postpone as little as possible the golden æra of their enjoyment. We are now in a situation, in which the public spirit and the public strength cannot be supported by empty or distant hopes. We ought to bring into action all our disposable resources; and surely none can be more eligible or less burdensome to the people, than the wealth which springs from a judicious employment of our natural advantages, and the strength which arises from the encouragement of our industry, our commerce, and our navigation.

F I N I S.

C. Mercier and Co. Printers,
King's Head Court, St. Paul's Church-yard.

www.ingramcontent.com/pod-product-compliance
Lightning Source LLC
Chambersburg PA
CBHW031954230426
43672CB00010B/2149